Boris Karloff

By the same author
The Cinema of Fritz Lang

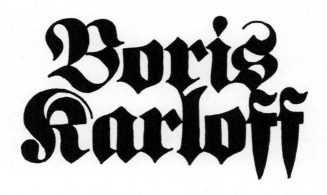

Boris Karloff

AND HIS FILMS

by Paul M. Jensen

South Brunswick and New York: A. S. Barnes and Company
London: The Tantivy Press

© 1974 by Paul M. Jensen

A. S. Barnes & Co., Inc.
Cranbury,
New Jersey 08512

The Tantivy Press
108 New Bond Street,
London W1Y OQX
England

Library of Congress Cataloging in Publication Data

Jensen, Paul M

    Boris Karloff and his films.
    Bibliography: p.
    1. Karloff, Boris, 1887–1969. I. Title.
PN2287.K25J4   791.43'028'0924 [B]   72-9940
ISBN 0-498-01324-3

Jacket design by Stefan Dreja

SBN 0-904208-35-4 (U.K.)

Printed in the United States of America

Contents

Karloff in his famous Frankenstein Monster make-up

Acknowledgements

This work has been in actual preparation since 1965, although its nature and format have changed several times since then. I want to thank all those who during that lengthy gestation period have informally listened to the author's monologues, read his many drafts, and provided general encouragement. These include William K. Everson, who generously made available various Karloff items from his collection, and the staffs of the British Film Institute, the Museum of Modern Art Film Study Center and Stills Archive, and particularly the New York Public Library Theatre Collection at Lincoln Center. I would also like to acknowledge the kindness shown me by various individuals at Uppingham School, Uppingham, and King's College, London, during my visits there. And I especially wish to thank Arthur Lennig for providing information from his files, and for functioning as an exceptionally sharp-eyed, demanding editor of both style and content. Acknowledgement for the use of stills is made to Universal-International, RKO, Warner Brothers, Metro-Goldwyn-Mayer, 20th Century-Fox, Columbia, Paramount, American-International, The Museum of Modern Art Stills Archive, and Mr. William K. Everson.

A modified version of my discussion of *The Mummy* appeared in "The Film Journal" (vol. 2, no. 2), and slightly varied versions of the *Frankenstein* chapter were previously published in "The Sound Film" (Troy, 1969) and "Film Comment" (Autumn, 1970). I am grateful for the editors' permission to reprint.

The superior numbers used in the text refer to the Bibliography in the back of the book.

1. The Early Years: Decisions and Development (1887-1931)

The success of *Frankenstein* started Boris Karloff on a career that flourished for thirty-eight years, and made him famous across several continents. Perpetually associated with horror, he became the model for countless caricatures and imitations. He inspires rubber masks and plastic model kits, and his name on books, comics, record albums, and even films activates an immediate conditioned response. He is a Titan of Terror, and King of the Monsters.

Unfortunately, simplification is the price paid for becoming a household name, and the "image" created by Karloff grew into his own Frankenstein Monster: it turned on him by failing to do justice to the man and his talent. Karloff's characterisations were never limited to the moronic, brutal, and inhuman creatures with which he is popularly associated. In fact, he rarely resorted to this *cliché,* and created instead a varied gallery of roles. As an actor of considerable intuitive skill, he infused trite material with life and improved worthwhile writing by his presence. He often gave his characters facets beyond the range of the co-stars and supporting players.

Karloff himself always appeared quite content with his position, for it had turned an obscure, forty-year-old character actor into a respected and profitable institution. Having learned his trade with touring stock companies, Karloff was used to depending on the approval of an unsophisticated crowd, and so he liked horror movies "because obviously this is the type of film that an audience prefers to see me in; that's my business, that's my job, isn't it? And I'm grateful for it."[92] After twenty years of occupational uncertainty, the security of type-casting was very much to Karloff's taste. Besides, it served as "a very good safeguard. You don't go getting fancy ideas as to what you think you can do."[17]

Though opposed to "fancy ideas," Karloff did manage to produce a surprisingly varied set of performances within the fairly narrow field of menace. Certainly he had a flair for the tortured and exotic, but his talent extended beyond a single *genre.* When horror films were not in vogue, he was generally resilient enough to adjust his style. Nonetheless, it was during the horror boom of the Thirties that

9

Karloff found his filmic niche; never before or later was he involved in a more impressive series of works. His rough, harsh features, plus the physical presence and dexterity of a stage veteran, resulted in solidly realistic performances. Even the monsters that he portrayed had very human feelings and needs: fully alive, though perhaps slightly warped, they inhabit a world that is akin to our own, and therefore believable. His more numerous "mad doctors" are practical, kindly men until their experiments encounter some malfunction; Bela Lugosi's scientists, in contrast, create evil for its own sake and live solely for destruction. Karloff's menace is more concrete and down-to-earth than that of his aristocratic rival.

Besides a sense of reality, Karloff projects a quiet malevolence that is often revealed through sarcastic politeness. Since his voice, personality, and appearance can automatically inspire fear, he need not be shown "in action" and so can understate his acting. Of course, suggestion and psychological mood have a less immediate and violent impact on audiences than do raving and bloodshed, but the former remain beneath the surface of the feelings, nagging at the viewer, for a much longer time. And this controlled approach allows for an emphasis on characterisation that more sensational horror films lack.

Karloff's characters were often based on the idea that "hearts of gold" beat beneath primitive or ugly surfaces. A classic literary example is Quasimodo, Victor Hugo's hunchbacked bell-ringer, who is shunned by "normal" people as a deformed monster, though he is tender and human within. Mary Shelley, by having a "monster" narrate part of her novel *Frankenstein,* allows us to contrast his thoughts and feelings with his horrible appearance. Gaston Leroux offers a similar situation in *The Phantom of the Opera,* with the title character's sensitivity masked by a repulsive exterior. Happily, this quality was generally retained when such works were adapted to the screen; from the films of Lon Chaney on, monsters have had a sympathetic streak and tend to be misunderstood. To portray such romanticised creatures successfully, an actor must convey both external menace and some sort of inner subtlety. This Karloff accomplished in many of his Thirties roles. Not inherently evil, characters like the Frankenstein Monster are driven to murder by the taunts and attacks of average citizens, who cannot tolerate anything that appears unusual or unpleasant. They are emotional innocents doomed by physical qualities over which they have no control.

Besides the strange and crass appearance that hides a sensitive soul, there exists also the "beautiful," or at least noble and normal, appearance that masks unknown styles and depths of evil. Aristocratic, cool, and self-controlled, this person has no need for outbursts or threats of violence—a semi-hypnotic intensity gives him easy power over others. Women, sensing the mystery, turmoil, and danger beneath the surface, find him fascinating. Lugosi epitomised this type of character, but Karloff too could create it, as in *The Mummy*. Both types of roles contain contrasting layers of personality, and demand an actor of considerable ability. Karloff's prior experience had been great, with half his life already spent developing his talent in various, often villainous, roles. In fact, his identity as a monster was almost an afterthought to an already long career on stage and screen. He had appeared in just over thirty movies before gaining fame in *Frankenstein,* and to this should be added a prior decade "in the sticks," getting a basic acting education in repertory companies.

The life of an actor was not the one first planned for Karloff, who was born William Henry Pratt (not "Charles Edward Pratt") on November 23, 1887 to a family living in the London suburb of Dulwich. His father was with the British Indian Civil Service and he planned the same kind of career for each of his eight sons. William, the youngest and still a baby when the elder Pratt died, was raised by his seven brothers and sisters. "One after the other they went into the consular, and one after the other they would come back on leave and get after me. I would no sooner be rid of one than another would come along and speak to me sternly about my negligence in preparing for the consular."[22]

Karloff, who later described his only living brother as "a gentleman of the tweedy country sort,"[16] was heading for a similar fate, with the Chinese consulate at Hong Kong set up as his goal. His education began at the Merchant Taylors' School, in London, and from 1903–06 he attended a boarding school in Uppingham; "they tried, Heaven help them, to teach me Latin and history and all sorts of things."[55] At the age of nineteen he was taking courses at King's College, London, with the civil service examination the ultimate aim. Actually, though, Karloff wanted to be an actor. "An elder brother had been on the stage under the name of George Marlowe when I was about eight years old. He was the one I knew best when the others were abroad."[108] Unfortunately, George was not a success and so became a businessman. "But I tried to emulate him. There was a church play each Christmas at St. Mary Magdalene's for the parishioners' children. Then the Band of Hope put on an entertainment and I was always in those things, giving everything in me, acting lustily and loudly."[108] At the age of nine, he was in a version of *Cinderella*. "Instead of playing the handsome prince, I donned black tights and a skull cap with horns and rallied the forces of evil as the Demon King."[61]

While studying in London, Karloff realised that the consular service was not for him: "I didn't have enough brains to do the job, and certainly I was not in the least interested. Although my brother George had been dead for a few years, the stage was my only interest."[108] Finally, he decided to leave home. "I felt I had to get away and work things out on my own. Fortunately, there were no brothers at home at the actual time of my departure. I don't remember that any obstacles were placed in my way or that I had to overcome any great difficulties."[108]

Both Canada and Australia were conveniently distant, so in 1909 this youth of twenty-two "tossed a sixpence in a solicitor's office" and set off across the Atlantic. "I had gone to the solicitor about a legacy of £100 from mother. With part of the legacy I bought my steamer ticket for Montreal. I was supposed to work on a farm. I went to Caledonia, Ontario, where I was told there was a job. When I got there, there was no job. They had never heard of me. However, it was the busy season, and they took me on for about ten weeks. Then I set out for Vancouver. When I got there I had just $5 in my pocket. After a day or two I was down to 15 cents. I was wondering what to do next when a man stopped me in the street and asked if my name was Pratt. I said it was . . . The man was a school friend of my brother Jack's at Dulwich, and he recognised the likeness. He gave me a note to the Works Superintendent of the British Columbia Railways, and I got a job at 28¢ an hour with a pick and shovel laying tracks. I wasn't much good at laying tracks."[55]

After about a year, a theatrical opportunity appeared. "One day in an old copy of "Billboard," I came across the advertisement of a theatrical agent in nearby Seattle. His name was Kelly. I went to him and shamelessly told him I'd been in all the plays I'd ever seen, that I was forced to retire to Canada temporarily for my health and was now hale and ready for a comeback."[61] Two months later, Karloff was "up in Camloops, British Columbia, with a survey team, and suddenly I got a letter from this agent inviting me to join a theatrical company in Nelson. It had such a bad reputation that nobody would join it. That's why he sent for me."[55] During the trip, he invented a background for himself and adopted a new name. "Pratt" suggested pratfalls and slapstick comedy, so he selected "Karloff" from his mother's side of the family. "Boris" was arbitrarily added because it fitted the new name better than "William" did. Thus an undying name was born.

"I had finally become an actor, but I mumbled, bumbled, missed cues, rammed into furniture and sent the director's blood pressure soaring. When the curtain went up I was getting thirty dollars a week. When it descended, I was down to fifteen dollars."[61] Karloff remained with the group for two years, touring Western Canada until 1912, when "the manager went broke and stranded us in Regina, Saskatchewan, the day before the famous cyclone, the only cyclone in the history of Canada! By next morning the whole world had blown away—show, manager, week's salary, and the town as well!"[55] He earned some money clearing away debris, then loaded baggage for the Dominion Express Company, and finally joined Harry St. Clair's repertory group in Prince Albert. In 1914, he felt ready for the "big time" and left for Chicago, but the "big time" was not yet ready for him and he couldn't find theatrical work. When the First World War broke out, he tried to enlist in the British army, but was rejected because of a heart murmur.

Eventually hired by the Brinkham Theatre in Bomidji, Minnesota, he later rejoined the St. Clair troupe in North Dakota. "In some towns we stayed a week, in others we settled down for a run. It was in Minot, North Dakota that we stayed 53 weeks and I played 106 parts. I was a quick study and a quick study got the longest parts. So I played leads. . . . We all took turns at being stage manager and we never had a dress or prop rehearsal. We must have done some terrible acting."[22] Karloff again left St. Clair in 1916, this time to join a road company of "The Virginian." When a year's tour of the Western states ended in Los Angeles, he joined a stock company in San Pedro, California, and then shifted to the Maude Amber Players, of Vallejo. He remained there until an influenza epidemic, and the resulting drop in theatre attendance, forced the group to disband in 1918. Remaining in Vallejo, he appeared at the Sperry Flour Mill as a sack-stacker and freight car-loader; two months later, he joined the Lawrence Company in San Francisco. A friend, however, had continued on to Los Angeles, where he was organising a vaudeville sketch. Karloff soon joined him, but the project fell through.

Now stranded in Los Angeles, he applied for work at various film studios as an extra. Some sources list *The Dumb Girl of Portici* (1916) as his first film and others mention a Frank Borzage picture, but Karloff stated that his first screen role was in Douglas Fairbanks's *His Majesty, the American* (1919), as part of a gang of spies. This was followed by a brief appearance in another mythical kingdom story, *The Prince and Betty* (1920). Gradually, Karloff made fewer and fewer stage appearances, as films took up more and more of his time; his gaunt, foreign-looking face caused him to be cast mainly as French-Canadian, Middle Eastern, and Mexican villains. *The Deadlier Sex* (1920), only his third film, gave Karloff "quite a decent role"[108] as a fur trapper who threatens the heroine. In *The Courage of Marge O'Doone* (1920), he again played a dangerous northwoods trapper, and at the end of his first full year in films, he portrayed one of the villainous Indians in James Fenimore Cooper's *The Last of the Mohicans* (1920).

In 1921, Karloff was in a fifteen-episode serial, *The Hope Diamond Mystery,* as well as three features: after being a half-breed kidnapper (*The Cave Girl*) and a Mexican bandit (*Cheated Hearts*), he switched to the mystic East and became a villain named Ahmed Khan (*Without Benefit of Clergy*). This Oriental image was reinforced in 1922 by roles as a Maharajah (*The Man from Downing Street*), and a sympathetic ruler in a tale of Omar Khayyam (*Omar the Tentmaker*). He reverted to type by slaughtering white settlers in *The Infidel,* shifted to the South Seas in *The Altar Stairs,* and returned at the year's end to his familiar performance as a French-Canadian north-woodsman in *The Woman Conquers.*

At the start of 1923, Karloff was almost lost in *The Prisoner.* Perhaps because of this he felt that, having risen from the status of extra to that of bit-player, he now was in danger of slipping back. So he decided not to accept any more work as an extra, and instead took a job driving a building materials truck. "The first thing to do was to learn to drive. I spent Sunday with a friend learning to drive his car. Monday morning I applied for the job and got it. It was one of those simple tasks entailing the handling of a 17-ton truck. After learning the little idiosyncrasies and whimsicalities of this, they told me to take out a speed lorry delivering 300 casks of putty. All I had to do—very simple when looking back—was to carry those 300 casks from the warehouse to the lorry, drive about 27 miles and then unload them."[108] Karloff kept this job for a little over a year, taking a few days off whenever a film role turned up. It was also during this period that he met and married his little-known first wife, Helene Vivian Soule, whose stage name was evidently Pauline (or "Polly").

Late in 1924, Karloff appeared as a villain in *Dynamite Dan,* a contemporary boxing story. This was followed by the larger part of an Apache in *Parisian Nights* (1925); at the climax of this film, a gang of thieves kidnaps the hero, who "is tied to a wooden post and a bald-headed old man is heating a wicked-looking weapon with which, it is inferred, the hero's eyes are to be rendered sightless."[97] Karloff must have seemed at home amid this sadism, for his next film, *Forbidden Cargo* (1925), showed him trying to pour molten lead into the eyes of the hero. As a reward, he was given featured billing. Then his Mexican half-breed performance was revived for *The Prairie Wife* (1925), followed by appearances as a governor in *Lady Robinhood* (1925) and a South Seas villain in *Never the Twain Shall Meet* (1925).

After beginning 1926 by going unnoticed in *The Greater Glory,* Karloff played several varied roles, two of which were quite distinctive. A bandit in a railroad story (*Flames*) became a comic masher trying to pick up Mabel Normand (*The Nicklehopper*); the murder victim in an E. Phillips Oppenheim mystery (*The Golden Web*) was reborn as a pirate (*The Eagle of the Sea*). A dog story (*Flaming Fury*) was also added. In *Her Honor the Governor,* Karloff was Snipe Collins, a cocaine addict who works for the corrupt Senator Dornton. When Adele Fenwick (Pauline Frederick) is elected Governor, Dornton plans to expose her as an unwed mother living in sin, by having Karloff steal the divorce papers of her late husband's first marriage. Later, when Karloff kills a man with a pool cue, the lady's son is convicted of the murder and she herself is impeached for "moral turpitude." Justice is finally done, however, and she re-tires from politics to re-marry. One critic noted that, next to Miss Frederick's performance, Karloff's was "the most authentic piece of work in the picture," and went on to describe his "shaken, jerky figure, the twitching mouth, the vicious anger which vents itself on a helpless man who has tortured him for years."[51]

This frighteningly pathetic character contrasts sharply with the mysterious mesmerist portrayed by Karloff in *The Bells* (also 1926). If Snipe Collins evokes the Frankenstein Monster, this figure suggests the quiet menace found in *The Mummy* and *The Black Cat*. A carnival performer who haunts the murderer Mathias (Lionel Barry-more) like a conscience, Karloff appears in only a few major scenes, but each is important to the plot. Early in the film, he invites the debt-ridden Mathias to be a hypnotic subject, declaring that he can "make criminals confess and the good tell of good deeds." Mathias hesitates, and then refuses. After this, Karloff is not seen again until after Mathias has killed a man and stolen his gold; then he returns with the victim's brother to investigate the disappearance. Karloff smiles knowingly as Mathias, now Burgomaster, orders him to leave. Mathias then dreams of a trial during which he is hypnotised by Kar-loff and forced to tell what he did with the body. A flashback of its destruction in a lime kiln follows, and when the dream is over, Mathias is sitting lifeless in his chair.

At his first entrance, Karloff establishes a sense of uneasiness that is confirmed by the later murder: he backs slowly toward the camera, then turns to reveal his features. This staging resembles James Whale's introduction of the Monster in *Frankenstein*, but without the cuts to closer and closer views, and here Karloff's visage is not as striking. "Because my make-up for this part was a conventional Svengali-like job, Lionel sat down and on an envelope sketched an idea for [writer-director James] Young and the make-up person. What he sketched was Caligari."[107] With top hat, cape, circular glasses, and hair stand-ing out from his head, Karloff does suggest a less exaggerated version of the character in *The Cabinet of Dr. Caligari* (1919), and a similar carnival environment reinforces the parallel. Karloff expected this role to put him in greater demand, but the *tour de force* performance of Barrymore attracted most of the critical attention. The hypnotist, though an impressive figure, is just an intentional cipher possessing little depth or individuality; Mathias, on the other hand, is a kind and dignified character with more personality and several changes of mood.

March, 1927 came in like a lion—Edgar Rice Burroughs's *Tarzan and the Golden Lion,* to be specific, with Karloff playing the Chief of a tribe of African lion-worshippers. Also in 1927, he appeared in two westerns (*The Meddlin' Stranger* and *The Phantom Buster*) and a pair of comedy-adventures with Douglas Maclean (*Let It Rain* and *Soft Cushions*). In *Two Arabian Nights* (1928), an imitation of *What Price Glory,* Karloff portrayed the purser on a Greek tramp steamer. Another feature, *The Love Mart,* rounded out the year with more adventure, this time in Nineteenth century New Orleans.

After playing a pirate in *Old Ironsides* (1928), Karloff performed in *Vultures of the Sea,* the first of four serials he made for Mascot. *Vultures* was followed at the end of the year by *The Fatal Warning,* in 1929 by *King of the Kongo,* and in 1931 by *King of the Wild.* All were directed by Richard Thorpe. *King of the Kongo* appeared in two versions, one equipped with a synchronised soundtrack; while the heroine wanders through ten episodes and a jungle in search of her father, Karloff seems to be the villain, but he is ultimately identified as the missing parent. A second Hoot Gibson western and two Northwoods melodramas were also released at this time, followed by Karloff's final all-silent pictures, *The Devil's Chaplain* and *Two Sisters.* *Behind That Curtain,* appearing two months before *King of the Kongo,* was his first sound feature, a murder mystery that gave him the role of Warner Baxter's faithful Sudanese servant. He played a Hindu servant named Abdoul in another 1929 sound mystery, *The Unholy Night.* Lionel Barrymore was director, and he applied enough old house atmosphere of fog and eerie noises to keep viewers interested.

Karloff (at right) in SOFT CUSHIONS

While the technicians were setting up a scene, Barrymore took time out to fatten Karloff's role and to offer bits of business that improved the still-unknown performer's big scene—the discovery of his dead wife.

During these last years of the decade, Karloff was also appearing in the San Francisco and Los Angeles productions of such plays as *Hotel Imperial* and *Kongo.* Sometime in 1929, he and his first wife were divorced. A blonde professional dancer, Polly was not the ideal mate for a man described in a 1933 issue of *Photoplay* as "introspective, analytical, serious." The writer of that article visualised the marriage as "Frivolity wedded to the Three Fates . . . Red heels in a cathedral. The contrast obviously was marked for disaster from the first. After a time, Polly simply went to Panama as a café entertainer. Divorce followed."[103] In 1930, Karloff married again, this time to Dorothy Stine, a librarian in the Los Angeles public school system. This combination was more fitting, and lasted for fifteen years.

At the start of 1930, Karloff participated in a production of "The Criminal Code" that had been sent to the Coast from New York with several roles to be cast locally. "I ambled into the Actors' Equity office one day to see whether there was any mail for me. There wasn't, but the girl at the desk asked if I was working. When I answered no, she said, 'Go down to the Belasco Theatre. They're casting *The Criminal Code.*'"[106] He did, and was awarded the small but showy part of Galloway, a prison trusty-turned-killer. The producer's decision was a wise one, with Karloff perfect for the following action: "Galloway appears at the entrance to the corridor; in his hand is the haft of a knife, the blade of which is in his sleeve. He stands there for a moment; then, as if impelled by some psychic power, Runch turns deliberately and stares straight into his face. A pause."[39] Martin Flavin's play describes the destruction of young Robert Graham by two impersonal and conflicting codes. First, the law and an ambitious District Attorney demand that he be strictly punished for an accidental killing. While in prison, he witnesses the murder of a dope-fiend squealer by Galloway and is torn between the law's demand that he identify the guilty one, and the equally strict "criminal code" that requires him to protect his fellow prisoner. Placed in solitary confinement, he finally cracks and kills a bullying guard—just as his parole comes through.

This production had a nine month run, after which Karloff played several film roles. In *The Bad One,* he was a sadistic guard at a prison colony. *The Sea Bat* followed, with Karloff receiving sixth billing as a villainous half-breed Corsican. He then played a western bandit in *The Utah Kid,* again working with director Richard Thorpe, and had a bit part in *Mothers Cry.*

When Columbia filmed *The Criminal Code,* Walter Huston played the D.A. who convicts Robert Graham and ends up warden of the youth's prison, and his restrained performance so dominated the reviews that other actors received little official notice. Still, Karloff's role as Galloway was larger here than it had been on the stage: in order to add a happy ending for the hero, the script has Galloway kill the taunting guard, and when the youth is suspected, Galloway reveals the truth ("That kid don't take no rap for me") and is shot. Karloff's lean and merciless looks make a solid impression, his delivery of the line "I've got an appointment to keep" before leaving to commit a murder is ominous, and his menacing presence is enough to keep a threatening guard from entering the cell which he shares with the boy. Like many of Karloff's other characters, Galloway is not a villain just for the fun of it; he is the victim of his own earthy nature. For example, while out on parole he is spotted drinking and sent back to prison ("Twelve years for one lousy beer!").

"It was the first time I ever had played a part which ran through the entire picture," recalled Karloff,[118] and he was disappointed when Columbia's option to sign him to a long-term contract was allowed to lapse. But at the film's release (in January 1931) he started getting calls from other studios. He next appeared in *King of the Wild,* a primitive serial that Mascot released in 1931. He was rather ineffectually Middle Eastern as the sinister owner of the Inn of the Fez who, always thinking about his own profit, co-operates with both the hero and the villain. After this came *Cracked Nuts,* a wacky RKO comedy filmed in November 1930, and released a few months later; Karloff played a revolutionary in the mythical country of El Dorania. *Young Donovan's Kid* (1931), which was sometimes called just *Donovan's Kid,* concerns a criminal's attempt to retain custody of a child orphaned by gang warfare. Karloff, as a dope peddler named Cokey Joe, tries to get the boy (Jackie Cooper) hooked.

Pleased with the success of *Little Caesar* and *Public Enemy,* Warner Brothers teamed Edward G. Robinson and James Cagney for *Smart Money* (1931). As one of Robinson's unsuccessful opponents, Karloff had an unconvincing hangdog demeanour while gambling with money obtained from a girl, who had gotten it from Robinson. In contrast, his next film, *The Public Defender* (1931), allowed him more sympathy than usual; playing "The Professor," he aids "The Reckoner" in solving murders and defending the public against crooked bank officials.

Warners continued its series of "social protest" films with *Five Star Final,* an attack on yellow journalism that went before the cameras in May 1931. The editor of the New York "Evening Gazette" (Edward G. Robinson) bolsters failing circulation by reviving the long-forgotten case of a woman who had been acquitted of murder twenty years before, and who is now a respectable wife and mother. When the story apears, her daughter's wedding is cancelled by the

Karloff with Richard Dix in THE PUBLIC DEFENDER

outraged parents of the groom, and eventually the woman and her husband commit suicide. Disturbed at the results of his work, the editor resigns and the final shot shows an issue of the "Gazette" being swept off the street with other pieces of trash.

Karloff portrays Isopod, the only character with absolutely no redeeming features. Expelled from divinity school for a sexual offense and now on the "Gazette" staff, he is assigned to write the story on Nancy Voorhees. Passing himself off as "The Rev. T. Vernon Isopod," he visits her home and learns of the planned wedding. Since the family assumes he will officiate, Isopod is welcomed and even given a photo of the girl. Karloff's phoney piety here demands our attention, but his second major scene is even more impressive. After celebrating this unexpected scoop, he drunkenly reports it to Robinson. His mock indignation at Nancy's attempt to marry her daughter to an innocent boy, and his gloating self-satisfaction, are at the same time amusing and repulsive. Karloff's acting style, though exaggerated and "theatrical," is quite justified by the character's inebriation. (While the mock indignation was in the original play, the drunkenness was not, and Isopod was considerably less important to the entire scene.) Karloff played his role to the cowardly and hypocritical hilt and was

Karloff with Aline MacMahon (centre), in FIVE STAR FINAL

generally singled out for praise, but this reaction had little effect
on the actor's career: he was already making *Frankenstein* by the
time *Five Star Final* was released.

   I Like Your Nerve opened in New York the day after the *première*
of *Five Star Final,* and Karloff literally was praised one day and
ignored the next. Douglas Fairbanks Jr. starred as a shy, porridge-
eating lad who becomes an audacious, grinning hero in this frank
imitation of his father. Here, Karloff played a butler named Luigi.
He then re-entered the criminal world via *Scarface,* the release of
which would be delayed for nearly a year by censorship troubles, and
Graft, as a murderer pursued by cub reporter Regis Toomey. Karloff
also had a small role in *The Yellow Ticket,* as the orderly of the

lecherous Baron Andrey (Lionel Barrymore), head of the Russian Secret Police.

His next film was made by the Hungarian-born Michael Curtiz, who had been one of Lugosi's European directors. This picture was *The Mad Genius*, an attempt to recreate John Barrymore's success in *Svengali*. In both cases, Barrymore converts an unknown into a brilliant performer: Trilby had been hypnotised into becoming a great singer, and in this new film a young boy, Fedor, is trained to be a ballet star. The film opens with an atmospheric prologue set in the countryside of Czarist Russia, where Barrymore runs a traveling puppet show. Karloff appears here in the brief, almost wordless role of Fedor's father, who catches his son watching the puppets and starts to beat him. The boy flees and is hidden by Barrymore. Karloff, drunken and cruel, speaks his few lines in a gutteral accent and wears a straggly beard; the critics, understandably, failed to notice him. If the film had been made a few years later, he would no doubt have played either the ballet master—a mental and physical cripple—or the drug-addicted assistant who, crazed by an overdose, finally dispatches his boss with an axe.

Like *Frankenstein*, this film deals with a man's determination to "create" a human being. Its author, apparently aware of the kinship, also knew about similar legends found in several German silent films. At one point Tsarakov, the ballet master, asks, "Have you ever heard of the Golem, made of mud and given a human soul? Or Frankenstein, the monster created by man?* Or the Homunculus, the pale being, the product of science? These are all dreams, brought to life by mortals. I will create my own being. That boy—that boy will be my counterpart, he shall be what I should have been. I will mould him—I will pour into him my genius, my soul. In him all my dreams, all my ambitions, will be fulfilled. I will make him the greatest dancer of all time."

In one of its less astute moments, "Variety" questioned the box-office appeal of such a story. "The mob doesn't always react to monstrosities, even when they're magnificent in stature," it said. "This Tsarakov type is too remote from everyday experience to engage sympathetic interest."[109] Less than two months later, however, a film appeared which created considerable sympathy for a magnificent monstrosity and, since Depression audiences were eager for something remote from everyday experience, this film went on to phenomenal success. Its title, of course, was *Frankenstein*.

---

* This clearly indicates that confusion between Frankenstein and his creation existed even before the 1931 film was released, though the later sequels are generally blamed for originating the error. Even the cast list for Peggy Webling's play, "Frankenstein: An Adventure in the Macabre," when presented in London in 1930, called the Monster "Frankenstein."

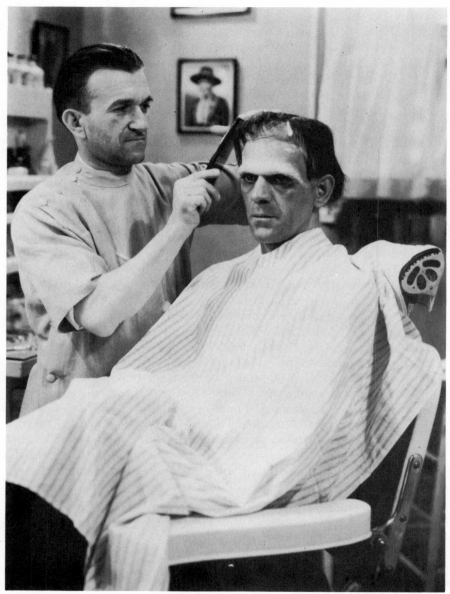

Jack Pierce preparing Karloff's hairstyle in FRANKENSTEIN

2. Frankenstein: The Beginning (1931)

In February 1931, *Dracula* opened to excellent business and grossed half a million dollars. Clearly, Universal's gamble on the popularity of horror films was paying off, so *Frankenstein* was filmed in August-September 1931. The task of adapting Mary Shelley's novel had first been allotted to Robert Florey, a Frenchman working in Hollywood. Florey's autobiography notes that the design of a Dutch pastry shop located outside his window prompted him to use a windmill as one of the film's settings. He also had the Monster's intended brain accidentally replaced with that of a murderer. "The crimes committed by the Monster were relatively easy to imagine, and during an unusual interview, while Carl Laemmle Jr. [production chief at Universal] surrendered his fingers to a manicurist, his hair to a barber, his thoughts to his secretaries, and his voice to a dictaphone, I explained the general plan of the film to him. He told me to type up the story right away and send it to the head of the scenario department."[40]

Using a set from *Dracula*, Florey shot a two-reel test with Bela Lugosi as the Monster. When the production finally got under way, Lugosi had been replaced by an "unknown" named Boris Karloff, and James Whale was the director instead of Florey, who did not receive even a writing credit. (At least four writers besides Florey—Richard Schayer, Garrett Fort, John Russell, and Francis Edwards Faragoh—worked on the script, and James Whale was probably involved as well.) It will doubtless never be known exactly why and how these changes occurred, since parts of the testimony conflict.

Certainly Lugosi was not enthusiastic about playing the Monster. One reason given is that it was not a speaking part, and Lugosi was immensely proud of his voice. The actor himself said, "I made-up for the role and had tests taken, which were pronounced OK. Then I read the script, and didn't like it. So I asked to be withdrawn from the picture. Carl Laemmle said he'd permit it, if I'd furnish an actor to play the part. I scouted the agencies—and came upon Boris Karloff. I recommended him. He took tests. And that's how he happened to become a famous star of horror pictures—my rival, in fact."[16]

Florey's comments, on the other hand, mention only that Lugosi did not want to play the role, but since Lugosi said he didn't like

Florey's script, that writer's further silence is understandable. Lugosi, in turn, failed to state that he had created his own make-up for the test and that it was not well received. Edward van Sloan, who appeared in the test reels, once described Lugosi's appearance as similar to that of Paul Wegener in *The Golem,* with a head "about four times normal size, and with a broad wig on it. He had a polished, claylike skin."[47] Jack Pierce, Universal's makeup expert, reported that Lugosi "had too many ideas of his own that didn't correspond with those of the producer, Carl Laemmle. Lugosi thought his ideas were better than everybody's."[56]

Karloff's own version of his discovery differs considerably. In his view, James Whale had probably seen him in *The Criminal Code;* he wasn't sure that that was the film, however, because "I didn't ask him, and he didn't tell me . . . I was working at Universal at the time" (which must have been June 1931, during *Graft*). "James Whale was in the commissary having lunch. He asked me over to his table to have a cup of coffee and said he wanted me to take a test for the Monster."[54] At another time, though, Karloff implied that the interview with Whale had been set up in advance. When asked to test for the role, he recalled being "a trifle hurt, as well as elated. I was wearing a new set of clothes which I'd bought especially for the interview and I thought I was looking rather smart. Monster indeed!"[92] Of course, Karloff probably met with Whale several times, and after more than thirty-five years it was no doubt difficult to remember each one separately. At any rate, his statements sound more convincing than Lugosi's.

"I had no idea of the importance of the role," Karloff said in 1967, "but Jack Pierce did; he stalled the test two weeks while working on the make-up, and the make-up sold the part."[68] Even after filming began, Karloff was not pleased with the situation. Edward van Sloan recalled, "When he saw the rushes of the picture he mumbled unhappily to me that the film would ruin his career. But I told him, 'Not so, Boris, not so! You're *made!*' "[47]

Florey had expected to direct as well as write the film, but he ran into trouble when James Whale, whom Florey calls "the Ace of Universal," decided that he wanted to make *Frankenstein.* Whale, a young Englishman in his thirties, had previously been a stage actor, designer, and director. In 1929 he staged R. C. Sherriff's war play, "Journey's End," the success of which made Whale, Sherriff, and star Colin Clive famous. He then prepared the New York production, and later became dialogue director on two Hollywood films. Hired in 1930 by Tiffany Productions to film "Journey's End," Whale brought Colin Clive to America to play the lead, and both film and director were listed among the best of 1929–30. Whale then moved to Universal, where he made *Waterloo Bridge* (1931), another successful war story. Now established, he could ask the company for whatever he wanted, and he wanted *Frankenstein*. This did not sit too well with Florey, and in order to make peace, Universal allowed him to adapt and direct Poe's *Murders in the Rue Morgue;* on the basis of that film, viewers should be glad that Whale had enough influence to win *Frankenstein* for himself.

During production, Karloff reportedly had to wear a blue veil to keep his make-up secret; he was not allowed off the set during the day, and two guards kept visitors out. This, however, was probably just the "kind of secrecy that makes publicity,"[135] especially since the original ads for the film carried a clearly-detailed picture of the Monster's face. This kept the big secret from being a surprise, and reduced the effect of the "To have seen *Frankenstein* is to wear a badge of courage" challenge. But the important thing is that the film was made with skill and intelligence. The N.Y. *Times* selected it

Preliminary make-up not used in the final film

as one of the best films of the year, and in 1932 it was even shown at the first Venice Film Festival. To *Frankenstein* belongs the distinction of being the most prestigious horror film ever made. Unfortunately, this implies—and rightfully so—that the rest of the route was downhill. Soon after the release of *Frankenstein,* "horror" became established as a separate movie *genre.* When this happened, the films were no longer considered serious works and critics didn't even bother to distinguish the good from the bad. Instead, they cracked jokes or dismissed the pictures with a casual "here comes another one." Perhaps *Frankenstein* was treated with respect, and accepted for what it was, because of the story's distinguished background. The connotation of "Literature" evoked by the name of Shelley apparently had power to soothe even a reviewer's savage breast.

In 1814, Percy Shelley deserted his wife and ran off with seventeen-year-old Mary Wollstonecraft Godwin. Together with Mary's half sister Jane, the couple toured Europe, and at the end of the trip Jane had a short affair with Lord Byron. Learning that Byron planned to stay at Lake Geneva in the summer of 1816, and hoping to revive their relationship, Jane suggested that she, Mary, and Percy also return to Switzerland. The two groups were neighbours, and spent their evenings talking at Byron's villa. On one cold, rainy night they read to each other from "Fantasmagoriana," a collection of German ghost stories. Afterward, Byron began reciting "Christabel," Coleridge's poem about a female vampire. Suddenly, Shelley ran screaming from the room. Brought back, and revived with cold water in the face and a dose of laudanum, he explained that he had been looking at Mary and suddenly she resembled a legendary woman who had eyes in her breasts.

Instead of forgetting the incident, the friends decided that each would now write a ghost story. Byron's vampire tale was never finished, but a fragment was published at the end of his poem "Mazeppa" in 1819. Shelley began a plot based on childhood experiences, but this didn't get anywhere. Dr. Polidori, Byron's medical attendant, had an idea about a skull-headed lady who spied on people through keyholes, but she was never heard of again. He did, however, publish a short story called "The Vampyre," which sold well because everyone falsely attributed it to Byron. But whether or not the stories were finally finished, everyone had an idea to report the next morning—except Mary. She couldn't think of anything, and so just toyed with an ordinary ghost story until a few evenings later. Byron and Shelley were arguing about whether or not man would ever create life, and the name of Erasmus Darwin was inevitably brought up. Dr. Darwin, who had died in 1802, was a fairly famous but often-ridiculed scientific radical. Known today only as the grandfather of Charles Darwin, he really deserves more credit since he was the first to offer, albeit in rough form, a theory of evolution. But being something of a dilettante, he was content just to set it down superficially in one of his books: "all vegetables and animals now existing were originally derived from the smallest microscopic ones, formed by spontaneous vitality."[64]

It was this reference to "spontaneous vitality" that started rumours circulating that Darwin had tried, perhaps successfully, to generate life. Byron and Shelley discussed one instance, in which the doctor had reportedly kept a piece of vermicelli in a glass case until it began to move on its own. The poets were sceptical of this method of creating life, but theorised that it might be done by re-animating a corpse or by making and assembling new component parts. Such talk continued until after midnight. That was enough for Mary: "When I placed my head on my pillow I did not sleep, nor could I be said to think. My imagination, unbidden, possessed and guided me, gifting the successive images that arose in my mind with a vividness far beyond the usual bounds of reverie." She saw, "with shut eyes, but acute mental vision," the creation of life in a corpse and the creator's terror at the event. By the next morning, she too had a story.[114] Originally intending to write only a few pages, Mary was convinced by Shelley to expand the idea to novel length. No doubt she was sidetracked by Jane's pregnancy, their return to England, her own nineteenth birthday, the death by drowning of Shelley's wife, and her marriage to the widower. Eventually, in 1818, the book was published as "Frankenstein; or, The Modern Prometheus."

According to Greek mythology, Prometheus was an antagonist of the Gods who stole fire from Heaven and brought it to earth. As punishment, he was nailed for ages to a mountain peak. Some ancient writers also say that he moulded man from clay. This story was very popular in the Nineteenth century, and Shelley himself, in "Prometheus Unbound," used the character to represent man's never-ending search for knowledge and freedom from restraint. That work was written at almost the same time as "Frankenstein," and no doubt influenced Mary's ideas; all of the qualities mentioned above are found in Victor Frankenstein, a "modern" Prometheus who creates a man and challenges the Gods by seeking knowledge, and who is severely punished for this.

"Frankenstein" was widely read and widely dramatised, with three different adaptations appearing in London during one year, 1823. The most successful was "Presumption; or, The Fate of Frankenstein," by Richard Brinsley Peake. Mary Shelley herself, who attended a performance, said that T. P. Cooke played the Monster "extremely well; his seeking, as it were, for support; his trying to grasp at the sounds he heard; all, indeed, he does was well imagined and executed."[20] The other versions were "Frankenstein; or, The Danger of

Presumption" and "Frankenstein; or, The Demon of Switzerland."
Then, aside from three burlesques, the Monster lay dormant for over
a century, until Peggy Webling (with John L. Balderston, who had
worked on *Dracula*) wrote "Frankenstein: An Adventure in the
Macabre." This play premiered in London in 1930, and Hamilton
Deane's road company alternated it with "Dracula." Universal Pictures
bought the rights to this play because Webling had modernised the
story, and so the movie is derived as much from her work as from
Mrs. Shelley's. Officially purchased on April 8, 1931, the play cost
the studio $20,000 plus one percent of the gross; the novel, of course,
was in the public domain.

"Frankenstein" had already inspired at least two silent films. The
first was Thomas Edison's one-reel version, made in 1910, which had
its Monster created in a cauldron of blazing chemicals. Another version
appeared in England around 1915, entitled *Life without a Soul*. Of
course, the makers of the 1931 film probably knew nothing about
these pictures. More significant were such German Expressionist films
as *Homunculus,* a 1916 serial in which an artificial man possessing
superior qualities eventually learns the circumstances of his "birth,"
feels himself to be an outcast, runs off, and out of anger causes
a World War. Its ending is similar to the one in Peggy Webling's
later play—both creations are killed by bolts of lightning.

A second influential German film is the 1920 version of *The
Golem,* about a legendary figure of clay brought to life by Rabbi
Loew in the Fifteenth century. This story involves the persecution
of Jews and its atmosphere is that of medieval sorcery, but the basic
situation is still similar to that in *Frankenstein*. In addition, *The
Golem*'s Rose Festival corresponds to *Frankenstein*'s wedding celebra-
tion, and both films have the creator try to destroy his handiwork,
despite the creature's desire to stay alive. The warning in *The Golem*
that "lifeless clay will scorn its master and turn and destroy," and
the presence of a young girl who seems to be the only one not afraid
of the creature, are both directly paralleled in *Frankenstein*. Even
The Golem's "legendary" atmosphere is echoed in *Frankenstein,* which
takes place in a foreign land replete with folk-dancing peasants, and
there are no signs of modernity apart from the laboratory equipment.
The settings of *Frankenstein,* such as a graveyard silhouetted against
the sky and the slightly stylised stone walls and staircases of the tower
laboratory, are not as distorted as those in *The Cabinet of Dr. Caligari,* but sometimes they do verge on abstraction, and the very fact
that most of *Frankenstein* was made in a studio contributes to the
aura of fantasy. (On July 14, 1931, "Variety" reported that Whale did
screen *Caligari,* "to get some ideas for *Frankenstein*." After hunting
all over for a print of the film, absent-minded Universal found one in
its own library. This was about one month before shooting began on

Colin Clive and Edward van Sloan with Karloff in FRANKENSTEIN

Frankenstein.) Herman Rosse, working under art director Charles D. Hall, created the sets. A well-known stage designer, Rosse had won an Academy Award for Universal's *King of Jazz* (1930), and he had also worked on *Dracula*.

Mrs. Shelley's original plot took place over a long period of time, during which Frankenstein and the Monster engaged in a duel to the death, with the latter demanding a mate and the scientist refusing. The Monster, in retaliation, kills off all those whom Frankenstein loves, including his wife on their wedding night. Frankenstein vows to destroy his creation and chases him to the Arctic, where the scientist dies and his foe remorsefully floats away, presumably to his death, on an ice floe. Clearly this story has epic proportions for which the film medium is ideal, but the 1931 movie is derived from the stage version and so has a narrower scope. Still, it never resembles just a photographed stage play, and the differences emphasise the human drama involved and create a faster pace. Because of this, the film should stand or fall on its own merits, and only its basic theme, embodied in the character of the Monster, ought to be judged against Mrs. Shelley's conception.

Universal's uncertainty about the new *genre* of horror films can be seen in the pre-credits teaser (which resembles the vignette originally at the end of *Dracula*). Here, Edward van Sloan walks onstage from behind a closed curtain and offers "a word of friendly warning" that this story about a scientist who tried "to create a man after his own image, without reckoning upon God" is "one of the strangest tales ever told . . . I think it will thrill you. It may shock you. It might even—horrify you."

After the credits, the film wastes no time on stilted exposition but begins *in medias res* with a series of vignettes depicting Henry Franken-stein (Colin Clive) and his assistant Fritz (Dwight Frye) gathering materials for their work. The first scene, a burial at a hilltop cemetery, opens with a long tracking shot that starts at a pair of hands holding a shovel, moves across the faces of the mourners, and continues on past a fence. This shot illustrates Whale's fluid style, which keeps the story's pace brisk: he saves the establishing long-shots for later, lets the camera roam about, and makes liberal use of close-ups.

When the grave is filled in and the site deserted, the two men appear and dig up the coffin. Frankenstein, in his eagerness, unknow-ingly heaves a shovelful of dirt into the face of a nearby statue of Death; such bizarrely comic touches are characteristic of Whale's work. Anticipating today's "black humour," they exist in greater abundance in *The Old Dark House* and *Bride of Frankenstein*. The digging completed, Frankenstein jumps into the grave and stands the coffin on end. With his ear next to the box, as though listening for some telltale heartbeat, he pats the wood almost caressingly and murmurs, "He's just resting—waiting for a new life to come." This reference to resurrection adds a touch of discreet sacrilege to the opening scene.

The film then shifts to the two men arriving at a gallows, which still supports a corpse. Fritz reluctantly climbs the post to cut the body loose, and crawls slowly along the crossbar toward the camera, knife in mouth. But Frankenstein declares that the brain is useless be-cause the victim's neck is broken (hardly surprising, since the man *was* hanged). The final scene in this sequence takes place at Gold-stadt Medical College, where Dr. Waldman (Edward van Sloan) is concluding a comparison of normal and criminal brains. After every-one leaves, a window at the back of the amphitheatre opens and Fritz comes stumbling in. He takes the jar containing the normal brain, is startled by a noise, and drops his plunder; in desperation he picks up the other jar and leaves. This incident, credited by Robert Florey to his own imagination, is the main weakness in the entire film and a key change from the original story. The whole point of the novel was that the creature was normal, even superior, in every respect except for his ugly appearance; that he was not inherently evil, but driven to killing by the failure of others to understand that he was not just a brutal Monster. The addition of a criminal brain to the plot undermines this concept, and makes him a Monster in fact as well as in appearance.

The change may have been deemed necessary in order to justify having the Monster kill someone in a short time, since the complex situations and relationships of the novel were omitted from the script. However, this decision damages the film's logic: viewers are expected to believe that Frankenstein didn't notice the jar's label before or after putting the brain in his being, and that he—an expert in anatomy—failed to perceive "the scarcity of convolutions on the frontal lobe . . . and the distinct degeneration of the middle frontal lobe" that characterise the criminal brain (according to Dr. Waldman's lecture). In addition, it is hardly likely that a pickled brain would produce a sober Monster. The problem, though, is not as serious as it could have been. The plot always provides other, more valid motives for the Monster's acts: the fear of the unknown, the instinct for self-preservation, the mistreatment suffered at the hands of Fritz (who is happy to find someone worse off than himself), and the awkwardness of having an undeveloped, newly-born mind enclosed in a full-grown, powerful body.

Boris Karloff's pantomimed performance as the Monster supports these alternative motivations by adding the element of pathos; the actor's movements and facial expressions leave no doubt about the confusion of a person suddenly brought to life in a strange, unknown environment. Thus Karloff followed the precedent set by the novel, and by Hamilton Deane's stage production in which the character appealed "to our sympathy . . . as a symbol of humanity itself adrift in an uncaring world."[43] Karloff has said, "Whale and I both saw the character as an innocent one. Within the heavy restrictions of my make-up, I tried to play it that way. This was a pathetic creature who, like us all, had neither wish nor say in his creation and certainly did not wish upon itself the hideous image which automatically terrified humans whom it tried to befriend . . . What astonished us was the fantastic number of ordinary people that got this general air of sympathy. I found all my letters heavy with it."[92]

The clearest indication that the Monster is potentially a normal individual appears after his first entrance. Frankenstein opens a window in the darkened laboratory's high ceiling, and the light falls where the Monster is sitting. He slowly rises, straightens, and faces the light; gradually he raises his hands, reaching and stretching to grasp it. Frankenstein, seeing this hopeless effort, has the window shut. With the light gone, the Monster is frustrated and bewildered. He lowers his arms, and extends them in an open, pleading gesture that echoes the questioning expression in his face and eyes. He sits down again, and the sequence is climaxed with a close-up tilt from his face to his empty hands. This scene, referred to by Whale as "an afterthought,"[57] brilliantly characterises the Monster and functions as a small-scale allegory of man's efforts to grasp the intangible unknown, and of his bewilderment at a Creator who keeps him from it.

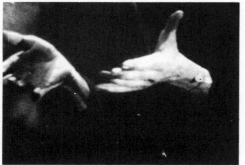

Frame enlargements from the "light scene" in FRANKENSTEIN, *with Karloff*

Another scene that illustrates the humanity of Frankenstein's creation occurs after the two doctors decide to render him unconscious. They administer a drug, and when it starts to affect the Monster his expression again becomes one of quizzical incomprehension that verges on the imploring—his plight is tragic, for he is forced by others into actions which he is powerless to prevent and which he does not understand, in this case the killing of Fritz; these actions then cause others to hurt him, also without explanation. He is caught in what must seem to be an absurd nightmare of the unknown, in which he discovers that he must kill to live. Throughout the film, both actor and director contradict the script's distorted vision of the creature as doomed to a life "of brutality, of violence and murder" (to quote Waldman's description of the brain's former owner).

The film's opening section of Frankenstein and Fritz collecting corpses plunges the viewer directly into the story, and apart from Dr. Waldman's information about the criminal brain, very little overt exposition is presented. It is left to the script's next section to provide necessary background information, as well as to carry the story forward, introduce a parallel plot thread, and allow the viewer to pause and regain his bearings after a sudden exposure to evident abnormality. This opportunity to pause is typical of the film's overall structure, which follows scenes that build in intensity with others that offer temporary relief.

Similar to this technique of opening with action and saving the exposition for later is Whale's tendency to break the traditional rule of establishing the setting with a long-shot before cutting to close-ups; in *Frankenstein*'s very first shot, the director involves the viewer by opening with close observation of the mourners, and only afterwards providing a more objective view of the scene. Another example appears at the start of the film's second section: a shot of a framed photograph of Henry Frankenstein (recognisable from the previous scenes) is followed by a close-up of a maid announcing "Herr Victor Moritz," a close-up of Victor's face, one of Elizabeth greeting him, and only then a long shot of the two in the same room.* This series of faces clearly implies the connection between the characters, and the rest of the scene makes official what the viewer has already concluded.

In this scene, the protagonists (including the absent Frankenstein) are identified, and we learn something specific about their situation. The explanation is logically motivated (after all, Frankenstein *has* left his *fiancée* alone for four months and only now written a mysterious letter about experiments in an abandoned watchtower) and it also carries the plot forward by prompting Elizabeth, the *fiancée*,

---

* For some reason, the scriptwriters saw fit to switch the first names Mary Shelley gave Victor Frankenstein and his friend, Henry Clerval.

and Victor, the friend, to visit Dr. Waldman—who has already been introduced at the brain lecture—and ask him to accompany them to Frankenstein's laboratory. The scene also establishes a potential romance between Victor and Elizabeth: "You know I'd go to the ends of the earth for you." "I shouldn't like that; I'm far too fond of you." "I wish you were!"

The film's pace continues to be rapid. The conversation with Waldman is joined after it has started, and thus we avoid the visitors' introductions and questions and just overhear the important part. Frankenstein, we are told, was a brilliant but erratic student who has gone off to work by himself. Waldman explains that Henry's "researches in the field of chemical galvanism and electrobiology were far in advance of our theories at the University. In fact, they had reached a most advanced stage. They were becoming—dangerous . . . The bodies we used in our dissecting rooms for lecture purposes were not perfect enough for his experiments, he said. He wished us to supply him with other bodies, and we were not to be too particular as to where and how we got them. I told him that his demands were unreasonable, so he left the University to work unhampered. He found what he needed elsewhere . . . Herr Frankenstein was interested only in human life; first to destroy it, then re-create it. There you have his mad dream."*

In its third section the film returns to Frankenstein, and then brings the two plot threads together when the three visitors arrive. It is night and there is thunder: "The storm will be magnificent—all the electrical secrets of Heaven," says Henry as he is about to give life to the body wrapped in white bandages and lying on a table. The inconvenient knocking at the door below irritates him, and he sends Fritz to answer it; the resulting vignette is Whale's grotesque variation on the porter scene in *Macbeth*. The hunchback descends the great stone staircase in his bent-over manner, muttering all the while about interruptions "at this time of night." He opens the door and blurts out "go away," then slams it shut and returns up the stairs, awkwardly pausing to pull up an uncontrollable sock.

Frankenstein finally lets his visitors—Victor, Elizabeth, and Waldman—enter the laboratory only after someone claims he is crazy. (An early plot synopsis reveals that it was first planned to have Henry send Elizabeth away for her own safety.) "Crazy, am I? We'll see whether I'm crazy or not!" He allows them to view his final experiment, and it is here that Colin Clive's performance and Whale's conception of the character are most impressive. In a letter received

---

* This speech is misleading, because there is no evidence that Frankenstein caused anyone's death in order to gain a part for his creation. Evidently Dr. Waldman was not up-to-date on Henry's experiments!

by Clive when he arrived in America, the director described Frankenstein as "an intensely sane person, at times rather fanatical and in
one or two scenes a little hysterical, and a little reminiscent of the
breakdown in *Journey's End*. Similarly to Stanhope, Frankenstein's
nerves are all to pieces. He is a very strong, extremely dominant
personality, sometimes quite strange and queer, sometimes very soft,
sympathetic and decidedly romantic. He hates causing anxiety to
Elizabeth and his father, but his passionate zeal and his invention
forced him to do so. He is pulled two ways—his love for Elizabeth
and his almost insane passion for his experiments. In the first scene
in his laboratory he becomes very conscious of the theatrical drama
and goes a little insane about it. All the time I should feel that
Frankenstein is normally and extremely intelligent, a sane and lovable
person, never un-sympathetic, even to the monster."[41]

Colin Clive fulfilled this description remarkably well. (Actually,
he appeared in *Frankenstein* only because Whale insisted on having
him. Universal's preference had been Leslie Howard.) Both Clive
and Whale deserve credit for creating in Henry Frankenstein a forceful and individual figure who even today avoids the "mad scientist"
stereotype. Especially acute is the creation scene, in which Frankenstein gradually gets carried away by the theatricality of it all. At first
he describes his experiment in a calm, though intense, manner. "Dr.
Waldman, I learned a great deal from you at the University, about
the violet ray, the ultra-violet ray, which you said was the highest
colour in the spectrum. You were wrong. Here in this machinery I
have gone beyond that, I have discovered the great ray that first
brought life into the world . . . At first I experimented only with
dead animals, and then with a human heart which I kept beating for
three weeks. But now, I'm going to turn that ray on that body and
endow it with life . . . That body is not dead; it has never lived.
I created it. I made it with my own hands, from the bodies I took
from graves, from the gallows, anywhere."

Then Henry is struck by his visitors' function as an audience.
"Quite a good scene, isn't it? One man, crazy; three very sane specta-
tors." This feeling increases as they watch him conduct the experiment.
The depiction of it, full of sparks and levers and tubes, is highly
dramatic, with the body raised through an opening in the roof,
left for a few moments, then lowered with one bare hand hanging
free. When the table is back on the ground, this hand slowly rises
and Frankenstein repeats over and over, "It's alive! It's alive!" as he
holds his own hands nearby, without actually touching it (an echo
of his earlier line, "I made it with my own hands"). Finally, he
turns toward the "audience" and almost collapses with laughter. The
scene ends here, before anything really exciting happens, yet the

earlier dialogue and the visual build-up during the creation have so charged the film's atmosphere that such a small thing as a moving hand functions as an excellent climax.*

This sequence, perhaps the film's high point, is followed by a comedy-relief scene at the village between Baron Frankenstein, broadly played in a blustery British manner by Frederick Kerr, and the pompous Burgomaster. They are discussing young Frankenstein's forthcoming wedding, and the Baron is convinced that his son is being distracted by another woman, "and I'm going to find her!"

Then, we are returned to the tower for another major sequence, and again the plot thread established in the preceding "pause" scene merges with it. The sequence starts out quite in contrast to the hysteria of the creation. Time has passed, the Monster has been locked up, and Frankenstein sits at ease, calmly smoking a cigar (and how many young hero-scientists have ever been shown smoking cigars?). But Waldman is worried and paces the floor; he fears that the creature will prove dangerous. Frankenstein replies, "Dangerous? Poor old Waldman! Have you never wanted to do anything that was dangerous? Where should we be if nobody tried to find out what lies beyond? Have you never wanted to look beyond the clouds and the stars, or to know what causes the trees to bud and what changes the darkness into light? But if you talk like that, people call you crazy. Well, if I could discover just one of these things—what eternity is, for example—I wouldn't care if they did think I was crazy." This monologue, and Clive's delivery of it, is the major factor that gives dimension to the character of Frankenstein. While the creation scene could have involved any well-played but conventional "mad scientist," the quiet sincerity of this speech makes the man human, and its content places him in the same category as Marlowe's Dr. Faustus, who also sought the limits of knowledge. The Scientist was probably the last potential tragic hero, for there is grandeur in his aims and hence a great depth to which he could fall.

Frankenstein now learns that the brain he used was that of a criminal, a fact which he counters with the rationalisation, "Oh well, it's only a piece of dead tissue." Waldman predicts, "Only evil can come of it . . . You have created a monster and it will destroy you." He is right, but less because of the brain than because of the treatment the creature receives. The Monster is brought in. His entrance, from the corridor's darkness, is another example of how a scene underplayed in Whale's style does not date in effectiveness, even though we may have seen a thousand photos and imitations of the

---

* This scene originally ended with the following over-explicit dialogue, later removed by a censor in the Thirties: *Victor:* "Henry—in the name of God!" *Henry:* "Oh—in the name of God—now I know what it feels like to be God!"

make-up. First, his footsteps are heard. The door is opened and the Monster enters from a dark hallway, backing into the room with his body gradually emerging into view. A shot of his full figure is followed by one of just his head and shoulders as he turns around, then a close-up of his face, and finally a tight view of only the area from his eyes to his chin. For a change, the make-up and performance of a monster can withstand close scrutiny, so they are revealed slowly to prevent viewers from ignoring their convincing reality.

The scene with the window light follows, and the Monster's fairly calm reaction augurs well for the future, but Fritz enters with a torch and excites him until he must be overpowered. There is a fade-out, followed by a scene of the Monster chained to a wall while Fritz, with whip and torch, continues to torment him. Frankenstein is repelled at this sight, saying, "Oh, come away Fritz. Leave it alone. Leave it alone!" But while Fritz doesn't leave, Frankenstein does and in this way shirks the responsibility for his creation. As a result, Fritz is killed, the two men drug the Monster, and Waldman decides they must kill it "as you would any savage animal."

At this point Elizabeth and Victor arrive with the Baron, and Waldman assures Henry that he will destroy the Monster painlessly, so the distraught Frankenstein allows himself to be taken home. The creature's body is again stretched on a table with a white sheet over it and the right arm hanging free. Dr. Waldman, about to dissect the Monster, faces away from the camera and leans over to reach the heart. Slowly the Monster raises his arm behind Waldman's back, grabs him by the neck, and sits upright. The actual murder is not shown, as the scene dissolves to a later shot of the Monster stumbling downstairs and out the main door. Distinctive is his jerky, surprised reaction to such things as a door that opens when he pulls on it; hesitating which way to go, he passes the room where Fritz had died and shies away, still fearful of what the dwarf represented.

This climax, which sends the Monster out into the world, is followed by a "pause" scene of the wedding preparations, the last such pause until the film's conclusion. The scene ends with a tracking shot along a street filled with dancing peasants, which dissolves into a similar tracking shot that follows the Monster's halting run through a forest. On the shore of a lake, he encounters a little girl who is waiting there for her busy father. "I'm Maria," she says as the creature parts the bushes and enters the clearing. "Will you play with me?" She takes his hand and leads him to the water's edge. "Would you like one of my flowers?" As she gives him some daisies, he compares her hand to his own. Both innocents kneel on the ground. "I can make a boat." She tosses a flower into the lake. "See how mine floats?" He tosses one, too, and looks pleased when it floats. Impulsively throwing in all the flowers she had given him, he glances down at his empty hands, looks up at her, and leans forward. There is then an awkward cut back to the wedding preparations.

Originally, this scene concluded with the Monster mistakenly assuming that because the flowers looked better in the water, Maria would too. Karloff has described this occasion as "the only time I didn't like Jimmy Whale's direction . . . My conception of the scene was that he [the Monster] should look up at the little girl in bewilderment, and, in his mind, she would become a flower. Without moving, he would pick her up gently and put her in the water exactly as he had done to the flower—and, to his horror, she would sink. Well, Jimmy made me do *that* over my head which became a brutal and deliberate act. By no stretch of the imagination could you make that innocent . . . I insisted on that part being removed."[54] Unfortunately, the scene now ends with the Monster reaching out to grab the girl, followed by a "discreet" cut away that creates an equally undesirable suggestion of a sexual attack. For the record, the sequence originally concluded as follows:

> CLOSE UP BESIDE WATER. The monster throws his last daisy into water—he watches it—then looks at his empty hands—he holds his hands out—[This is the final shot in the released version].
> VIEW BESIDE WATER. The monster leans over and picks Maria up—she screams—he rises and throws her into water—the water splashes up as she lights—. *Maria*: "No, you're hurting me! Daddy!!"
> CLOSE UP OF MONSTER. Looking off—puzzled—.
> VIEW BESIDE WATER. The child sinking—Monster watching—surprised—.
> CLOSE UP OF MONSTER. Puzzled—.
> CLOSE UP OF WATER. Smooth—.
> CLOSE VIEW BESIDE WATER. The monster rises—goes to foreground—goes off at side and exits—.
> VIEW IN BUSHES. The monster coming through the bushes—toward foreground—he stops and looks around—walks along—camera panning—he stops beside tree and then goes on again—.

It is not clear exactly when this excision was made, but the scene was described by at least one trade reviewer, who declared, "I won't forgive Junior Laemmle or James Whale for permitting the Monster to drown a little girl before my very eyes. That job should come out before the picture is released. It is too dreadfully brutal, no matter what the story calls for. It carries gruesomeness and cruelty just a little beyond reason or necessity."[82] Incidentally, the episode had its origin in Webling's play, with one London critic describing the Monster as "blunderingly slaying the one human being

Frankenstein with Maria's flower (frame enlargement)

who had taken an interest in him and dared to touch his hand. This was Henry's little crippled sister Katrine, one of whose pet doves is strangled by [the Monster], and hurled down to float upon 'the shining water,' beneath which the girl is afterwards held down till she drowns. Another of the Monster's laments is, 'Why did not he tell me that the shining water could kill?' "[42]

At the castle, Elizabeth feels uneasy, and when Henry learns that Dr. Waldman has been found dead, he locks her in her room. (Why are heroines always helpless and alone at times like this?) While everyone searches the house, the Monster enters by a window and sneaks up behind Elizabeth, until she finally sees him and screams. When help arrives, he has gone without hurting her and she is in a daze. This scene, even to the fact that the creature does not harm the woman, parallels a portion of *The Cabinet of Dr. Caligari*.

Maria's father enters town carrying the girl, and Henry vows to help kill the Monster; "I made it with these hands, and with these hands I'll destroy it." The Burgomaster sends out three search groups, charging them to "get him alive if you can, but get him . . . The Fiend must be found." Men swarm over craggy rocks, and float past in boats mounted with glowing torches. Frankenstein, separated from the rest, encounters the Monster on a rocky outcropping and is knocked out and carried to an old mill. The others, seeing this, follow and the dogs are set loose. (Frankenstein's laboratory was originally

Still of the Monster after he has killed Maria (shot cut from final version of film)

FRANKENSTEIN: in the mill (frame enlargement)

to have been located in the old mill, so when the Monster returns there at the film's end, it is because that is the only refuge he knows. Unfortunately, this plot element was eliminated before production began.)

On the top floor of the mill, Frankenstein recovers, and he and the Monster stalk each other around a rotating, slatted wheel. Again they fight, and Frankenstein falls on to one of the mill's vanes, which supports him for a short distance and then drops him to the ground. The villagers set fire to the mill, and the Monster, trapped beneath a wooden beam, screams with panic amid the flames. Meanwhile, Frankenstein is carried off with a great deal of lamentation. Thus the film climaxes in an extreme case of misjudgement, prejudice, mob violence, and what Whale called "the pagan sport of a mountain man-hunt"[57]; at the finale, the film's sympathies are with the Monster rather than with the lynch mob.

Until the last minute, *Frankenstein* was intended to end with the death of Henry, and the script clearly prepares us for this. The latent romance between Victor and Elizabeth establishes Henry as the eccentric third party whom the script will kill off before the final fade-out. Henry himself states that he leaves his *fiancée* in Victor's care. Several references are made to the fact that the scientist's work will destroy him, which is suitable and required punishment for challenging God's role, and Elizabeth feels that "something is coming between us." Henry's final fall is a substantial one, both literally and figuratively, and one which it would be hard to survive. In fact, Colin Clive originally chose to make the film because it "has an intense dramatic quality that continues throughout the play and culminates when I, in the title role, am killed by the Monster that I have created. This is a rather unusual ending for a talking picture, as the producers generally prefer that the play end happily with the hero and heroine clasped in each other's arms."[27]

When *Frankenstein* was previewed on the West Coast it had "a bigger percentage of walkouts during the running time than any picture for many months,"[136] and the company was seriously worried. In 1939 a trade reviewer recalled sitting in a screening room "when *Frankenstein* first was shown and when the Laemmles, Senior and Junior, did not know what to do about it."[70] Universal decided to put more emphasis on the horrible in their advertising, and to add the prologue in which Edward van Sloan tells the audience what to expect. Then, only two days before the negative was to be sent East, a new ending was added. In this one-shot epilogue, Henry is mentioned as recovering from his injuries and reunited with Elizabeth, while the Baron drinks a health to them in the hallway. This change ill-advisedly contradicts the preparations in the script, but it appears to have occurred at least with Whale's knowledge, for he commented that "the semi-happy ending was added to remind the audience that after all it is only a tale that is told, and could easily be twisted any way by the director."[57] Although "twisted" is the right word, the ending is so short that it barely has a chance to ruin the film's overall impression.

If any single element can be said to determine the success of Karloff's performance, and of the whole picture, it is the make-up. Whale said, "Boris Karloff's face has always fascinated me, and I made drawings of his head, added sharp, bony ridges where I imagined the skin might have been joined. His physique was weaker than I could wish, but that queer, penetrating personality of his I felt could be more important than his shape, which could easily be altered."[57] And his shape *was* altered, with a pair of boots that added height and gave him a heavy-footed appearance; with steel braces for his arms and a five-pound steel spine; with a padded suit and two pairs of pants; and with make-up that added more height to his head. Also, "to fill out my Monster costume, I had to wear a doubly quilted suit beneath it. We shot *Frankenstein* in mid-summer. After an hour's work I would be sopping wet. I'd have to change into a spare undersuit, often still damp from the previous round."[61]

However, Whale ought not to have implied that he created the make-up himself, when most of the credit belongs to a man who had once been a semi-pro shortstop in Chicago—Jack Pierce, the head of Universal's make-up department. (The Monster's final visage, according to Pierce, was "a compromise" between his own ideas and those of Whale.[56]) Pierce and Karloff spent three hours each evening for three weeks preparing the make-up. In Pierce's words, "before I did a bit of designing I spent three months of research in anatomy, surgery, medicine, criminal history, criminology, ancient and modern burial customs and electrodynamics. My anatomical studies taught me that there are six ways a surgeon can cut the skull in order to take out or put in a brain. I figured that Frankenstein, who was a scientist but no practicing surgeon, would take the simplest surgical way. He would cut the top of the skull off straight across like a pot-lid, hinge it, pop the brain in and then clamp it on tight. That is the reason I decided to make the Monster's head square and flat like a shoe box and dig that big scar across his forehead with the metal clamps holding it together.

"Here's another thing. I read that the Egyptians used to bind some criminals hand and foot and bury them alive. When their blood turned to water after death, it flowed to their extremities, stretched their arms to gorilla length and swelled their hands, feet and faces to abnormal proportions. I thought this might make a nice touch for the Monster, since he was supposed to be made from the corpses of executed felons. So I fixed Karloff up that way. Those lizard eyes of his are rubber, like his false head. I made his arms look longer by shortening the sleeves of his coat . . . I cover Karloff's face with blue-green grease paint which photographs gray. I blacken his fingernails with shoe polish. It takes me four hours to build him up every morning and two hours to tear him down every night."[96]

Karloff's only contribution to this design occurred after Pierce had finished. "My eyes seemed too normal and alive and natural for a thing that had only just been put together and born, so to speak. I said, 'Let's see if we can do something about it . . . Let's put some putty on the lids.' He put some putty and shaped it so that the lids were the same . . . and that was it. It was trying to veil them."[54] The actor also mentioned that the make-up's "frightening realism" was partly due to "the look of *pores* in the skin. Jack achieved this by a special technique in which he carefully built the make-up from layers of cheese-cloth. When he was done you couldn't tell where my real face ended and the Monster's began."[94]

The significant thing about Pierce's work is that it left a tremendous amount of flexibility to Karloff's own face. As a result, the actor could employ a natural stream of expressions, instead of being limited to a stiff robot's mask. In this facial and physical pantomime, Karloff's years spent gaining stage presence were put to good use.

Frankenstein is a horror film that rises above its *genre* designation. Whale's presentation is admirable, because all the elements work together smoothly and almost none are potentially laughable. The actors are controlled and talented. The photography is exceptional, and employs the possibilities of lighting to create shadows, of composition to frame the scene, and of close-ups to evoke intensity. The film also reveals skill in devising Gothic humour; in writing a script that convinces despite being scientifically dated; in art direction that balances realism and stylisation (despite an occasional wrinkled sky backdrop); in plot structure and pacing; in inspiring dread without undue violence and gore; and in perception regarding both Frankenstein and the Monster.

The pleasant result was that this skill, including Karloff's, did not go unnoticed.

One trade magazine's review of the film began, "If Universal's production of *Frankenstein* does nothing else it establishes Boris Karloff as the one important candidate who has arisen for the mantle of the late Lon Chaney as a delineator of weird and grotesque roles. Because of his restraint, his intelligent simplicity of gesture, carriage, voice and make-up, Karloff has truly created a Frankenstein monster. Had he yielded to the temptation to melodramatize as the opportunity offered, the character would have been far less formidable, horrible, terrible, and a lot of other 'ibles' which might be added. Karloff has done some excellent things in pictures, though usually in minor roles. This was his big opportunity, and whether you like the picture or not you won't deny his efficacy."[82]

Large sections of the public, having difficulty dealing with the Depression, were glad to spend some time in the company of a monster that could more easily be defeated. At its release in November 1931, *Frankenstein* did Standing Room Only business in many large cities, and was the biggest hit in the history of New York's Mayfair Theatre, where it took in $53,000 during its first week (compared with a puny $19,000 that *Suicide Fleet* had collected there the previous week). The demand was so great that extra shows had to be scheduled and tickets were being sold until 2:00 AM. Considered by "Variety" to be "the biggest money picture in the country,"[137] it grossed almost a million dollars in America alone (about twice as much as did *Dracula*), and it set loose a host of other monster and horror films. Many of these were also made with skill and, surprisingly, very few were outright imitations of *Frankenstein*. (Aside from this picture's numerous sequels, there have been almost no films about the creation of an artificial human.) Many of these future movies were to star Boris Karloff, who was here launched on a career that would give him a place in popular mythology not far from the one he had helped the Frankenstein Monster to obtain.

Last shot of the Monster in the burning mill (frame enlargement)

A portrait of Karloff in the early Thirties

3. The Reign of Terror (1931-1938)

Films were made rapidly during the early Thirties, and an actor could easily appear in five or more pictures every year. As a result, by the time one of these became a hit he might already have finished several insignificant parts in minor films. This was true of Boris Karloff, and it was not until several months after *Frankenstein*'s release that he started getting larger roles in better pictures.

The Guilty Generation (1931), filmed in the same month as *Frankenstein,* featured Karloff as the rival of beer baron Leo Carrillo, and in *Tonight or Never* (1931) he played a waiter. The start of 1932 then found him in *Business and Pleasure,* as a sheik who abducts Will Rogers. Karloff's character in *Alias the Doctor* (1932) is not important to the plot, but it intriguingly anticipates his subsequent career: he plays a pathologist who is fond of his work and "seems to be disappointed when an operation is successful. His presence sometimes is obviously symbolic of death or the shadow of death."[49] *Alias the Doctor* was filmed during December-January 1931–32, and went into release that spring; the same is true of *The Miracle Man,* a re-make of the 1919 feature about criminals who use a faith healer in their racket. The earlier version established Lon Chaney's reputation, via his performance as a fake cripple who is "cured" anew in each town, but since Karloff was not yet associated with the monstrous and mutilated, it did not seem odd that someone else played Chaney's role. Instead, Karloff portrayed the minor character of a tavern owner who is thrown down several flights of stairs when he pays too much attention to the pickpocket "heroine."

In February, "Photoplay" let its readers know the identity of this new performer. "The latest horror sensation, *Frankenstein,* has everyone thrilled and the most outstanding question this month has been, 'Was the Monster real or was it mechanical?' Movie-goers say it seems unbelievable that anything so terrifying and ghastly could be human. But it's true. Boris Karloff was the chap who made you and you and you stiffen with fright each time he appeared on the screen."[8]

Near the start of 1932, Universal's follow-up, *The Murders in the Rue Morgue,* closed in New York after only one week, so the "Times" declared that "the horror cycle isn't doing so well, and is just about

47

demoted to a 'fad.' "[52] This evaluation was slightly premature: Universal had a number of memorable horror movies as yet unmade; Paramount had recently released *Dr. Jekyll and Mr. Hyde* to tremendous success, and was considering an adaptation of Karel Capek's *R.U.R.;* M-G-M had just finished *Freaks,* and a little later would make *The Mask of Fu Manchu* with Karloff; Warner Brothers was about to start on *Dr. X* and *The Mystery of the Wax Museum;* and RKO planned to film *The Most Dangerous Game* and *King Kong.*

Dracula and *Frankenstein* also prompted studios to graft horror material on to otherwise traditional films. One case is Columbia's *Behind the Mask,* filmed in November 1931. Exploited as a horror effort, this was actually a crime story about the Secret Service's attempt to break up a dope ring. For the climax, however, the hero was strapped to an operating table and menaced by an insanely sadistic surgeon (Edward van Sloan). Evoking Lugosi's grandiose Love of Torture in *The Raven* (1935), this scene touches directly on the latent fears that most helpless patients have about their surgeons. Says Dr. Steiner, "Has it ever occurred to you, Mr. Hart, that you can commit almost any crime, *if* you select the proper environment? For example, if I were to stick a knife into you in the street, it would attract attention, I might have to answer embarrassing questions. But when I stick a knife into you *here,* on the operating table, nothing will happen—to me . . . The pain when I am going through the layers of skin will not be unendurable. It is only when I begin to cut on the inside that you will realise that you are having an experience. Wasn't it Nietzsche who said that unendurable pain merges into ecstasy? We shall find out whether that was an epigram, or a fact. For my part, I know it will be ecstasy."

As a member of Steiner's gang, Karloff had nothing to do with the picture's one horror scene. We first meet him as a sullen and angry prisoner in Sing Sing; then, after being "sprung," he reappears with derby, cigar, and jaunty manner. However, this crisp self-assurance exists only on the surface, and whenever Steiner expresses displeasure with his work, Karloff starts to cringe. There is good reason for this, since Karloff is not an effective henchman: he is easily fooled by a disguised Secret Service agent, and after trying to kill the hero he fails to wait and check on the results. Though adequately performed, the character is neither as colourful as Isopod in *Five Star Final* nor as forceful as the Monster, and since *Frankenstein* had increased Karloff's critical standing, the "Times" was able to complain that *Behind the Mask* "does not make any serious demands on his talent."[50]

But Karloff's presence in the film was a good selling point, and a "Film Daily" ad printed his name in letters almost as large as Jack Holt's, without even mentioning Edward van Sloan. Karloff was

Karloff with Jack Holt and Constance Cummings in BEHIND THE MASK

termed, "The man who made America 'monster-minded,' " and the ad continued: "You know the sudden vogue for "shocker' pictures— and how audiences are clamoring for them. Cash in on it now, while the fever is at its height. Columbia looked them all over and decided to go them one better."[38]

After the release of *Frankenstein,* Universal extended Karloff's contract, and soon he was officially designated a "star." His first Universal film under these conditions was *Night World,* shot around March 1932 and released in May. This multi-threaded story of people and events at a night-club during a single evening was a minor echo of M-G-M's current *Grand Hotel,* but at least it gave Karloff a sympathetic role as "Happy" MacDonald, a cuckolded club owner who is killed by gangsters when he refuses to change the source of his liquor supply. Filmed at about the same time, but released a month earlier, was *The Cohens and Kellys in Hollywood* (1932) , the fifth entry in a series about two feuding families. In it, Karloff appeared briefly as himself; otherwise, this weak and hastily-made comedy had little to offer. *Scarface* also opened in May, but it had been completed prior to the making of *Frankenstein.* Numerous censor battles had delayed release of this gangster classic which, at the time, seemed the ultimate in callous brutality. Paul Muni, and the carnage he and George Raft create, so dominated the picture that Karloff remained in the background as Gaffney, a rival gangster who is killed while bowling (his ball continues down the alley to score a strike).

Still at Universal, Karloff followed *Night World* with his second film for director James Whale; shooting on *The Old Dark House* took place in April 1932. This re-discovered classic turns out to be charming, witty, highly individual, and occasionally suspenseful, with the horror element minimised in favour of the eccentric comedy that Whale found in this tale of weird characters inhabiting an isolated mansion. It is this quality that makes Whale's film far different from all other old house, creaky door mysteries.

Driving through Wales, Philip and Margaret Waverton (Raymond Massey, Gloria Stuart) and the cynical Roger Penderel (Melvyn Douglas) are stranded by a storm and forced to take refuge at a house owned by the Femm family. Later, they are joined by two other travellers, Sir William Porterhouse (Charles Laughton) and his current "companion," Gladys DuCane (Lillian Bond). The action of the story is limited to this single night, during which the oddities of the household are revealed and confronted; this provides the mystery, and Morgan (Karloff) —the large butler who is tame when sober but a menace when drunk—creates excitement for the climax.

Karloff with Dorothy Revier in NIGHT WORLD

Karloff with Eva Moore in THE OLD DARK HOUSE

J. B. Priestley's novel, published in 1928 as *Benighted,* is really an examination of post-First World War disillusionment in the guise of a mystery story. Each of the Femms has been affected by a strain of madness that allows him to retreat from the misfortune of two deaths in the family, but it has affected them in different ways. Horace Femm (Ernest Thesiger), now head of the house, is sharp and cunning, but no longer emotionally alive. His nearly deaf sister, Rebecca (Eva Moore), has taken refuge in the religion of an unpredictably angry God. The third, Saul, is a dangerous maniac who is interested only in destruction. These individuals embody, in exaggerated form, qualities that could then (and no doubt can still) be found in the real world. The overall feeling that Priestley creates is the very modern one of a world that is unharnessed, mocking, and anarchic, as expressed in Penderel's toast, while the flood swirls around the house: "Behold two mortals whose hearts were fashioned for your service but who sit in a darkness within a darkness, homeless, lost, the black water rising around them—."[103] Philip Waverton, too, feels "a density of evil, something gigantic, ancient but enduring, only dimly felt before, but now taking the mind by storm; it was working everywhere, in the mirk of rain outside, here in the rotting corners, and without end, in the black between the stars."[103]

Morgan the butler is most completely associated with this quality of unreasoning threat; he is inhuman, anonymous, and described as "that vague mass, that dark hulking shapelessness, like something monstrous spawned by the shadows."[103] Horace Femm states the situation clearly: "Being little better than a brute, he is very close to Nature, and these upheavals [the storms] have a bad effect on him and then he takes to drink and that makes him worse."[103] Unlike Priestley's novel, the picture does not articulate this association of Morgan with Nature; the closest it comes is the addition of an occasional crash of thunder to the soundtrack when he is on screen. Morgan is, in fact, less important, less interesting, and less vivid than most of the film's other characters. He and the Frankenstein Monster are similar in their ugly and imposing appearances and in the fact that neither can talk, but this new character is not as subtle or as memorable as the Monster. Most of the time, Morgan is less an individual than a latent "force," and this requires him to be slow of wit and body, in contrast to the quick-moving, relatively alert Monster. Even when he is drunk, Morgan is not very active, though his long struggle with three men trying to force him into the kitchen conveys some fury.

Morgan's make-up differs considerably from that of the Monster,

Ernest Thesiger, Eva Moore (in background), Melvyn Douglas, and Lillian Bond in THE OLD DARK HOUSE

with "a full black beard and matted hair over a low forehead,"[106] and scars along his right eye and across the bridge of his heavily padded nose. Simpler than the work done for *Frankenstein,* this make-up more fully obscures the actor's own features and interferes with his range of expression. Though this supported the conception of him as an anonymous force, it also prompted the studio to place a printed statement at the start of the film, reassuring audiences that this was indeed the same performer who had appeared in *Frankenstein.* Unfortunately, only one scene really requires Karloff to act; it occurs near the climax, just after Saul has been killed. Morgan goes to the body, embraces it, and cries. Then he carries the corpse upstairs—never to be seen or mentioned again, not even the next morning. (A similar incident would be seen later in *Son of Frankenstein.*)

The script arbitrarily lets Penderel live after his confrontation with Saul, and eliminates many of the book's philosophical overtones, but it does retain an after-dinner conversation in which the characters play a kind of truth game. Thus the film includes more of the original characterisations than might be expected, though the novel's semi-allegorical level remains distant. Even Penderel's toast is omitted.

Still, the film cannot help but retain the central image of the setting, situation, and characters. The qualities of James Whale as a director have ideal material here: his intelligence and sensitivity to symbolism (as in the *Frankenstein* Monster's first encounter with light) surely made him aware of Priestley's intent; his sense of grotesque humour belongs in this houseful of eccentrics; and his often-implied mockery of religion found satisfaction in Rebecca's hysterical evangelism, in Horace's description of saying grace as one of his sister's "strange tribal habits," and in Saul's speech to Penderel just before throwing a carving knife at him: "Did you know my name was Saul? And yours is David. And it came to pass on the morrow that the evil spirit came upon Saul and he prophesied in the midst of the house and David played upon the harp and there was a javelin in Saul's hand and Saul cast the javelin."[103]

Ernest Thesiger was a perfect choice to play Horace Femm, a "thin, elderly man in black . . . His voice was as thin as he was, very dry, and harsh, and he spoke with a curious and disconcerting precision."[103] His eyes were like "two pin-points in a crumpled sheet of paper."[103] It is Thesiger's performance that best reveals Whale's combination of humour with menace and insanity. The actor's precise and haughty delivery gives a strange edge even to ordinary lines. He enters the film just after the visitors have arrived; descending a staircase, with his nose pointing up at a sharp angle, he announces, "My name is Femm! Horace Femm!" As he talks he picks up a bouquet of flowers. "My sister was on the point of arranging these flowers," he says, and then without further comment tosses them into the blazing fireplace. The perversity of this action is typical of Whale, and cannot be found in the novel.

When Rebecca shouts, "No beds! They can't have beds!" her brother turns to the guests and, with civilised irony, adds: "As my sister hints, there are, I'm afraid, no beds." Horace brings out a drink for the visitors and, carrying the bottle and glasses on a tray, he somehow resembles a perverted butler. "It's only gin, you know. Only gin. [Slight pause.] I like gin!" His toast is to "illusion," after which he perceptively identifies Penderel as one of those "battered by the war." During dinner, Horace politely repeats his "have a potato" line several times—always as though implying something more. When the lights flicker, he explains that it is not the storm's fault. "We make our own electricity here—and we are not very good at it."

Although most of the pleasure in these examples comes from the writing and the acting, the individual and consistent tone must be traced to Whale's handling. And while *The Old Dark House* is not as strikingly visual as *Frankenstein,* it is a carefully directed film. Sometimes Whale uses technique for humour, as in the opening scene with the Wavertons arguing while they struggle against the storm's irritations. As Philip complains about a "trickle of ice cold water pouring down my neck," there is an unexpected, almost eccentric, cut to a close-up of the back of his hat brim—as water streams off it.

Much later, the after-dinner truth game is filmed with a variety of close and medium shots, all taken through the blazing fireplace, with heat waves giving an odd texture to the scene. Interestingly, when Morgan first threatens Mrs. Waverton, the editing recalls the introduction of the Monster in *Frankenstein*: Whale cuts from a full shot of the character's face, to an extreme close-up of his eyes, and then to an extreme close shot of his mouth.

Cinematically, the most imaginative sequence begins when Mrs. Waverton enters Rebecca's room to change her wet clothes. Rebecca stays, telling about the past injury of a relative and the wickedness now in the house. As she talks, she is framed by candles on the right and their reflection on the left. There is then a cut to a close shot just of her face, followed by one of her distorted reflection in a mirror. She approaches Mrs. Waverton and examines her dress. "That's fine stuff, but it'll rot." Touching the young woman's chest, the old lady adds, "This is fine stuff, too, but it'll rot too in time." She gives Mrs. Waverton a lecture on the evils of vanity, and then on her way out checks her own hair in the mirror.

Disturbed by the obviously irrational Rebecca, Mrs. Waverton remains in the room. As she looks at herself in the mirror we see her distorted reflection, followed by shots of Rebecca repeating her speech, with cuts between each line from one view of her fragmented face to another. Also intercut here are close-ups of Morgan secretly watching Mrs. Waverton. The entire sequence is a visual and psychological *tour de force* elaborated from a single reference in the novel (". . . she sat down in front of the little cracked mirror . . .") that aims at a completely opposite effect ("The familiar reflection brought comfort to her . . .") .[103]

Even though Karloff is not as important to this film as to *Frankenstein,* the studio realized that he had become a significant selling point and accordingly emphasised him in the publicity. One ad in the trade press included six drawings that showed the Monster's face evolving into Morgan's. It stated, "The man who played the Monster in *Frankenstein* now transforms himself into the mad butler in *The Old Dark House.* A characterization that will make the world talk! Screen acting that lifts the screen to new heights!"[83] Trade reviews, however, found it necessary to warn exhibitors about the film's comedy content, so that they would not sell the picture as another *Frankenstein.* Actually, many audiences were disappointed in this skilful but unpredictable classic.

After finishing *The Old Dark House,* Karloff was loaned out to M-G-M, where he portrayed Sax Rohmer's Oriental evildoer in *The Mask of Fu Manchu* (1932). Warner Oland had already starred in several films about this character, but as M-G-M's advertising campaign claimed, this was "A *new* Fu Manchu . . . not to be confused with the Fu Manchu of other pictures!"[126] Neither was it quite the Fu Manchu of the novels, but nonetheless Karloff's version remains the closest that films have come to that model. This production emphasised the unwholesome side of the characters and situations, as recently explained by Myrna Loy, who portrayed Fu Manchu's daughter: "I carried around a pet python and whipped a young man tied to a rack and all sorts of dreadful things. Now I had been reading a little Freud around that time, so I called the director over one day and said, 'Say, this is obscene. This woman is a sadistic nymphomaniac!' And he said, 'What does *that* mean?' I mean, we did it *all* before these kids today ever thought of it, and we didn't even know what we were *doing*!' "[105]

The script discards much of the novel's plot, and replaces it with a series of tortures inflicted upon the representatives of law and order. In the process, the respect and nobility that Rohmer had carefully created for his Fu Manchu were mislaid, and only once are we allowed to side with him; that is when the captured Sir Lionel Barton crisply demands, "You're Fu Manchu, aren't you?" and his opponent replies, "I am a Doctor of Philosophy from Edinburgh. I am a Doctor of Laws from Christ's College. I am a Doctor of Medicine from Harvard. My friends, out of courtesy, call me 'Doctor.' " But beneath this civilised dignity, he is just another sadist.

Karloff in THE MASK OF FU MANCHU

Sometimes the script, in its determination to emphasise torture, loses track of logic and of Fu's original desire to locate the mask and sword of Ghenghis Khan, possession of which will give him such power in the East that he could conquer the West and wipe out the whites. The first person captured by Fu Manchu is Sir Lionel Barton, the leader of an expedition searching for Ghenghis Khan's tomb. He is tied to a slab over which hangs a large bell. Says Fu Manchu, "Just a bell ringing, but the percussion and repercussion of sound against your eardrums will soften and destroy them, until the sound is magnified a thousand times. You can't move, you can't sleep, you will be frantic with thirst. You will be unspeakably foul. But here you will lie—day after day, until you tell."

Meanwhile, the expedition has discovered the tomb and finds that a curse has been placed on anyone who dares enter. Terrence Granville, the hero, hesitates and says, "Remember the curse on Tutankhamen's tomb; all the people connected with it died soon after its opening." But the curse is disregarded. After the relics are located, a messenger from Fu Manchu convinces Terrence and his *fiancée* Sheila Barton to exchange them for Sir Lionel. When they do so, however, Fu Manchu turns on a machine and directs electricity from his finger to the sword. The object melts, and is exposed as a fake—manufactured, unknown to the others, by Sir Denis Nayland Smith. In reprisal, Sir Lionel's dead body is sent to Smith.

Fu Manchu then concocts a serum from some snakes and tarantulas that he keeps at hand in his laboratory. "Distilled from Dragon's blood, my own blood, the organs of different reptiles and mixed with the magic brew of the secret seven herbs," this liquid makes Granville a slave to his enemy's will. (Apparently no one thought of using this drug on Sir Lionel, and thus saving everybody a lot of trouble.) The helpless hero is sent off to retrieve the original relics, and he soon brings them back, along with Professor von Berg and Sheila. Before long, Smith blunders in and completes the group. (Never did Rohmer's characters act with such inefficiency. In fact, Shan Greville—renamed Terrence Granville by the scriptwriters—was the only one who ever actually met the wily Oriental in the novel.)

Smith is placed on a seesaw structure, and as sand is slowly released from a container at the opposite end, he is lowered head first toward some hungry alligators. Meanwhile, von Berg is to be punctured by two sliding walls covered with spikes; originally the script had scheduled Smith for this torture, but it was felt that more horror would result if a stockier man were placed in the predicament, so Jean Hersholt (von Berg) replaced Lewis Stone (Smith). Elsewhere, Granville is about to be re-injected with the snake drug by Fu's sadistic-amorous daughter, and Sheila is due to be sacrificed by a triumphant Fu Manchu before a crowd of his followers. Needless to say, Smith at the last minute unties his hands, saves his companions, and wipes out the enemy.

The film's main weakness is the contrived quality of its situations and final escapes, all of which lack logic, ingenuity, and an awareness of character. This is not surprising, since the studio even had to halt filming in August 1932, to allow time for some emergency script surgery. Director Charles Vidor was removed from the production, and replaced with Charles Brabin (who in turn had just been removed from *Ras-*

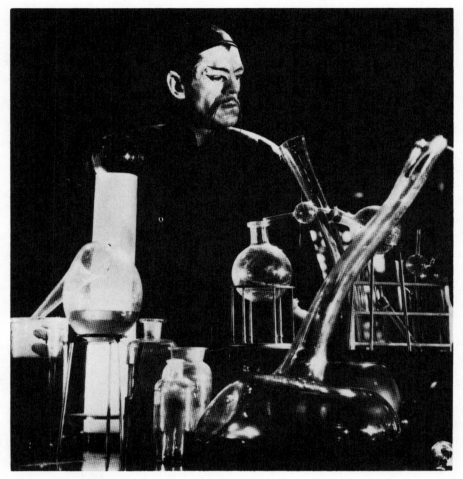

Karloff in THE MASK OF FU MANCHU

putin and the Empress). In order to revise the story, several writers were "formed into a shock-troop to get something filmable out in a hurry."[126] This task was somehow accomplished, shooting was resumed early in September, and the final product entered release one month later— to universally discouraging reviews. "And the cinema goes busily about its task of terrorizing the children," quipped the "Times," with the industry's "Motion Picture Herald" agreeing that only "the juvenile will get real satisfaction from the picture." Even "Photoplay" noted that, "Except for the kids, who cannot seem to get enough thrillers, *Fu Manchu* is a disappointment."[76]

Still, *The Mask of Fu Manchu* has the advantage of M-G-M's lavish settings and dignified actors, and Karloff certainly looks his part and invests it with as much intelligence and impressiveness as the script allows. Though his long, thin moustache was not part of Rohmer's description of the character, it turns out to be an improvement on the original. The make-up took about two and a half hours to apply each day, with much of the time devoted to the actor's eyes. For the first time, Karloff played a horror character who wasn't a brute and who had lines to speak. Success or failure here would affect his future, since an actor cannot play mute monsters forever, but in fact Karloff was able to modulate his voice and use pauses and suggestion in much the same way as Lugosi could (though without that performer's flamboyance). On the other hand, speaking lines also meant that "I could not use any of the many types of false teeth which were such potent parts of disguises in silent days. Lon Chaney once told me speech had made impossible about fifty of his best make-up devices. In *Fu Manchu* we used some thin shell teeth that covered only the front of the natural teeth."[107]

Both *The Old Dark House* and *The Mask of Fu Manchu* were released in the autumn of 1932, while *The Mummy* was in production (during October) at Universal. This picture was originally conceived by Nina Wilcox Putnam as a nine-page story called "Cagliostro," and writer Richard Schayer then worked with her in preparing a treatment early in 1932. This title character was an Egyptian magician who has, by

Karloff in THE MUMMY

Karloff as the Mummy (frame enlargement)

injecting himself with nitrates, been able to stay alive for three thousand years. In revenge for a woman's betrayal, he seeks out over and over again women who resemble his love, and destroys them. In present-day San Francisco he poses as the blind uncle of Helen Dorrington, a movie-cashier who bears a fateful resemblance to the girl. Assisted by a Nubian servant, Cagliostro uses radio and television rays to commit robberies and murder. Also involved are Helen's boy-friend, and a professor of archaeology who learns the truth and helps to destroy Cagliostro. In the summer of 1932, John L. Balderston wrote a screenplay combining this with other plot ideas and removing the "scientific" elements, while retaining some basic situations and names. The script was known at various times as *Cagliostro, The King of the Dead, Im-Ho-Tep,* and *The Mummy,* with the last title the one ultimately used.

The first film directed by Karl Freund, photographer of such German silents as *Metropolis* and *The Last Laugh, The Mummy* is a tense, moody, understated, and slowly-paced classic of horror. Freund has complete control of a camera that glides softly and freely into a scene. Tracking and editing concisely tell the story, with no footage expended on static "paintings" or unnecessary verbiage, and the result is a brooding atmosphere of menace.

The discovery, late in 1922, of the burial chambers of Tutankhamen was impressive news to both scientists and the general public. The first tomb ever uncovered free of plundering by graverobbers, it remained a source of fact and rumour for well over a decade. The vast amount of statuary, furniture, and jewellery found within provided the experts with considerable information about this little-known, eighteen-year-old Pharaoh, and about Egyptian life in general. So packed were these underground rooms, and so fragile and precious their contents, that they were not completely emptied until 1930.

The public's imagination was aroused by this priceless treasure and by the mystery of a vanished civilisation. The excitement soon grew into a fad, with King Tut motifs appearing on everything from jewellery to popular songs. Reporters at the excavation, grasping at both fact and opinion, fed exaggerated stories to the newspapers back home. Naturally, when Lord Carnarvon, the expedition's backer, died within six months of the tomb's opening, this news was elaborated with the idea that he had angered the publicity-shy king and was punished accordingly. The exotic possibility of a "curse" appealed to the sensation-hungry masses and many circulation-hungry editors seized the idea. For the next fourteen years, the death of anyone who had ever visited the tomb, or even just approached it, was immediately linked to the "curse" that had killed Lord Carnarvon. Experts and professors confidently offered theories on the effectiveness of Egyptian magic. Eventually, well over fifteen deaths were attributed to the youthful Pharaoh's unceasing vengeance.

The majority of these "victims" were only indirectly connected with the tomb, however, while most of those directly involved remained unharmed. Even Lord Carnarvon's death was less the result of a mysterious malady than of pneumonia attacking a body already weakened by an infected mosquito bite. As for the curse itself, two different versions were quoted two years apart in the New York "Times": the straightforward "Here lies the great King and whoso disturbs this tomb, on him may the curse of Pharaoh rest"[128] was followed by the more poetic "Death shall come on swift wings to him that toucheth the tomb of Pharaoh."[131] Neither of these had any validity, for official reports declared that no such inscription ever existed. In fact, the late Pharaoh had considerable reason to encourage the excavators, since Tut's successor had reduced his rival's chances for an afterlife by having his name chipped from all carvings and statuary, thus adding the death of the king's immortal memory to that of his earthly body. The attempt was so successful that only a few references to his existence survived. By once again causing this forgotten man's name to be spoken, the archeologists were actually doing his soul a service by giving it eternal life.

But such facts failed to interest a populace intrigued by statements such as those of Dr. J. C. Mardrus, Orientalist and translator of "The Arabian Nights." "This is no mere childish superstition which can be dismissed with a shrug of the shoulder . . . I am absolutely convinced that [the Egyptians] knew how to concentrate upon and around a mummy certain dynamic powers of which we possess very incomplete notions."[123]

The facts and aura of the Tutankhamen discovery inspired the basic plot of *The Mummy*, which begins in Egypt, 1921, just after the tomb of Imhotep has been unearthed. However, the only specific detail of the young Pharaoh's life employed by the script is the name of King Tut's queen, Ankhesenamon, which was given to Imhotep's *inamorata*. Actually, the name Imhotep also belonged to a real person. Architect, high priest, physician, and writer of proverbs under the Pharaoh Zoser, he had the distinction of building the first great structure of stone—the Step Pyramid at Sakkara. But while his cinematic counterpart was punished for sacrilege, the real priest was posthumously elevated to the status of a God and welcomed into the pantheon; he died, it should be noted, at least a thousand years before the real Ankhesenamon's birth. Needless to say, they were never lovers.

In the film, a curse is found inscribed on the lid of a small box and Dr. Muller (Edward van Sloan), an adviser in the occult, tries to talk Sir Joseph Whemple (Arthur Byron) into obeying its warning. As they go outside to talk, young Norton, an assistant, is left alone and curiosity prompts him to open the box. Inside is the Scroll of Thoth, by which Isis had supposedly raised Osiris from the dead. Reading it softly to himself, Norton unwittingly brings to life the mummy of Imhotep (Karloff); the reactivated corpse then takes the Scroll and walks away, as Norton laughs hysterically. When the two older men return, they find their associate completely mad.

Building rapidly to its strong climax, this sequence grips the viewer's attention just as does the pre-credits teaser of a modern TV film. In fact, it is so well made that it threatens to overshadow even the film's conclusion. Karl Freund's knowledge of what *not* to show makes this return to life of a mummy a high point in the history of horror movies. A shot of Norton quietly reading his translation of the Scroll is followed by a close-up of Imhotep, who lies in a mummy case upright against the wall. Though the position is akin to that of Cesare in *The Cabinet of Dr. Caligari*, Freund does not just re-create the somnambulist's awakening, with its emphasis on the face of Conrad Veidt. Instead, after the mummy's eyes open slightly, the director pans downward to its crossed arms; first the right one lowers, slowly straightening out, and then the other follows. There is a cut to Norton's face, as he continues reading, followed by a slow pan to the Scroll at his elbow. The mummy's hand enters the frame and pulls the ancient papyrus away. As Norton turns to see what is happening, his mind snaps at the sight; laughing wildly, he backs against the

Karloff about to strike in THE MUMMY (frame enlargement)

wall. From his figure, the camera tracks across the floor and arrives at the base of the doorway just as the ends of a few strips of gauze drag through. Then, without a cut, it tracks upward to the now-empty mummy case, and downward to the empty Scroll box, as the maniacal laughter of Norton pierces through an otherwise silent sound track. When Muller and Sir Joseph rush in, the sequence ends with Norton's statement, "He went for a little walk. You should have seen his face!"

The effect of this scene is, for the most part, created by the viewer's imagination. There are shots of the mummy's hand and of Norton's reactions, but although stills exist that show Imhotep taking the parchment, the film itself never gives a full view of his moving figure. Instead, we are forced to await his later return in the more human form of Ardath Bey. Because we don't really see his figure here, we feel more fully the uncertainty and dread that it inspires.

After a fade-out the characters are rejoined ten years later. An expedition led by Sir Joseph's son, Frank Whemple (David Manners), is about to return to England in failure when the thin figure of Ardath Bey appears and tells them where to find the tomb of Princess Ankhesenamon; it is Imhotep, but without his mummy wrappings he is accepted as a wrinkled native. He moves and speaks with restrained, distant authority—the embodiment of all the mystery of ancient Egypt. The burial chambers are uncovered, but by then Ardath Bey has disappeared.

Some months later, the contents of the tomb are displayed at the

Cairo Museum. One night Imhotep, attempting to return the Princess's soul to its long-dead body, kneels by her coffin and reads from the Scroll. Elsewhere in the city, a young woman (Zita Johann) suddenly acts as if hypnotised. Leaving a gathering of friends, she heads for the museum and collapses at its door. She reacts to the mummy's call because the soul of Ankhesenamon is reincarnated in her body. The girl, a vestal virgin, and Imhotep, a high priest, had been lovers in the old days. At her death, he committed the sacrilege of stealing the Scroll of Thoth, for use in returning her to life. Captured, he was buried alive, and so the internal organs usually removed during embalming remained intact. His soul was denied eternal rest through the removal of religious inscriptions from his tomb.

At the museum, Imhotep kills a watchman who interrupts him and leaves without taking the Scroll, which is found by Sir Joseph and Dr. Muller. When Ardath Bey shows up to retrieve it, he is recognised as Imhotep; he in turn realises that the woman, Helen Grosvenor, is his long-deceased love. However, he is forced to leave empty-handed, with neither Scroll nor girl. Later, as Sir Joseph is about to burn the parchment, Imhotep causes his death though remaining some distance away. Chanting quietly, he reaches out his hand, fingers extended, and slowly closes it into a fist, drawing and twisting the hand closer and closer to himself. At the same time, the other man clutches painfully at his chest, collapses, and dies. The interplay between these two events creates a feeling of fatality and helplessness that makes the viewer, as well as the dying man, squirm. This remote-control Force that Imhotep exerts lends itself to the film medium, since it demands the intercutting of events occurring in widely separate places, as in the earlier juxtaposition of Imhotep, reading the Scroll in the dark museum, with Helen's reaction to his call.

A Nubian servant who now obeys the high priest retrieves the Scroll and returns it to his master. Meanwhile, Dr. Muller gives Frank a protective charm that wards off the mummy's powers. They decide to let Helen leave the next time she is called, to follow her, and hopefully to destroy her ancient lover. But Frank, protecting the girl he now loves, hangs the amulet from her doorknob and is then "attacked" in the same manner as Sir Joseph. At the last moment he grabs for the charm, is saved, but loses consciousness. Helen leaves and joins Imhotep, who burns her hollow mummy and dresses her in the costume of ancient Egypt. Now completely taken over by the Princess, Helen is to be killed, embalmed, and finally given eternal "life."

During the concluding sacrificial scenes, either the Nubian servant or his shadow hovers constantly within the frame. As the ceremonial knife descends on Helen, shots of it and of the approaching rescuers prolong the tension, and when the men do arrive, Imhotep silences them by holding out his sacred ring. His hand, with its fingers clasped around the sacrificial knife, is thrust out at arm's length; in a close-up, the focus changes from his face, to the ring and knife and fist, which now fill the screen. With his opponents helpless, Imhotep returns to the ceremony, but Ankhesenamon breaks loose and runs to a statue of the Goddess Isis. Kneeling, she begs to remain alive: "I am Ankhesenamon, but I'm somebody else, too. I want to live, even in this strange new world . . . Save me from that mummy—it's dead!" The statue's arm moves, and from it a flame strikes the mummy, who collapses and disintegrates into the dust of centuries. The two men run to the girl, and Frank calls for Helen's soul to return. It does.

John L. Balderston's script for *The Mummy* is really an adaptation of *Dracula*, revived with the new blood of a different environment. This was hardly coincidental, since Balderston had Americanised the British dramatisation of Stoker's novel, nor is it a disadvantage, since *The Mummy* retains the other film's virtues while bypassing its uncinematic, theatrical vices.

Re-animated corpses are featured in *Frankenstein, Dracula,* and *The Mummy,* but while the first film explains everything scientifically, the others demand a total acceptance of supernatural forces. The Scroll of Thoth really does revive the dead, and both hero and scientist are unable to save Helen from Imhotep's blade; Isis alone makes the final decision, and raises the arm of her statue to destroy the mummy. Dr. Muller, speaking on this subject, sounds like a disciple of the aforementioned Prof. Mardrus: "The Gods of Egypt still live in these hills, in their ruined temples. The ancient spells are weaker, but some of them are still potent." This approach differs from that used during the more realistic Forties. In the pseudo-scientific mummy films made then, Kharis "never really died," and so his mummy did not need to be re-born; instead, a priestly cult has kept him alive over the centuries by feeding him the juice of boiled tanna leaves.

Besides sharing a belief in mystic powers, *Dracula* and *The Mummy* contain the same basic conflict. An elderly specialist in the occult (Edward van Sloan in both films) discovers and challenges the sinister aims of an individual who is neither alive nor dead. The menace then sets his "romantic" sights on an attractive girl, and draws her away from the young man (twice played by David Manners) who loves her. An amulet, representing the Goddess Isis, protects its wearer from the mummy in the same way as a crucifix offers security to a vampire fighter. Such ornaments are required because both villains avoid violent physical contact, exerting instead an intangible, hypnotic influence over the will power of others. Each film also contains several confrontations between the professor and the threat, with these articulate opponents fencing in guarded, circuitous conversations. But such scenes are forced on *Dracula* by its stage origins, while *The Mummy* works them into a freer, more filmic framework; since Imhotep controls events from a distance, the technique of parallel editing is well integrated into the plot. The heroines of both *Dracula* and *The Mummy* are torn between two lovers. The young heroes embody health, life, virtue, and normality, while the menaces represent other, more fascinating, sides of existence: death, darkness, and power. *The Mummy*, however, adds the element of reincarnation, so that Helen's divided affection for Imhotep and Frank Whemple is reflected in her struggle with Ankhesenamon for control of her own body. Necrophilia, or love of the dead, is quietly present in both *Dracula* and *The Mummy*, since the heroine's relationship with Dracula or Imhotep can only be consummated through death, followed by a re-birth into perpetual life and love.

Imhotep seems based on the same Romantic image as Bela Lugosi's suavely appealing Count Dracula. Such doomed figures radiate a hypnotic appeal that captivates the weaker sex; with tortured souls and long, cloudy pasts, they have seen, experienced, and suffered all. Face and voice reveal the disillusionment of a dangerous, yet refined and inherently noble, individual. Lugosi's personality clearly defined this style, but it is more fully developed in *The Mummy*'s script: Imhotep challenged the Gods and risked their wrath for the sake of a beautiful woman, while the vampiric Count is not even allowed an explanation of his state. "No man has ever suffered for woman as you've suffered for me," declares Ankhesenamon (via Helen), and Imhotep echoes this thought with, "My love has lasted longer than the temples of our Gods. No man ever suffered as I did for you."

In contrast to Karloff's violent (and mute) performance in *Frankenstein*, his Imhotep is virtually immobile, but this lack of activity contributes to the characterisation of age and fragility. Clumsiness and inarticulate violence have become subtlety, suavity, and clear but muted strength. The pathos that had been created solely by physical means is now achieved through a few graceful, formalised movements and a deep and burning gaze, combined with meaningful pauses, accented syllables, and the hollow, cultured tone of time and infinite sorrow. But dominating all, even a voice that echoes the desert's dry precision, is Karloff's quietly dynamic presence, which is threatening although he barely raises a hand. The brute is now a figure of distant, dangerous, haughty dignity.

Although Boris Karloff is known for playing "monsters," *The Mummy* was almost his last heavy make-up job (the two Frankenstein sequels are the only major exceptions). It was reported that for one week, during the filming of Imhotep's return to life, the actor spent eight hours a day having his face covered with clay, sprayed with collodion, and wrapped in one hundred and fifty yards of gauze. "When it was completed, he was unable to move a muscle of his withered

Karloff made up as the Mummy

face!" claimed "Photoplay."[98] For the remaining seven weeks of work, the relatively human form of Ardath Bey required only a skin of painted-on cotton that had to be melted off each day.

It was just before the release of *The Mummy* that Karloff was "officially" accepted as a star by "Photoplay," and accorded the honour of a fan article that described him as having "suffered none of the usual symptoms of picture success. He drives a battered old Ford coupe, and his friends are the same ones he made fourteen years ago when he arrived in Hollywood."[104] In one trade magazine, a reviewer cautioned exhibitors not to advertise *The Mummy* as another *Frankenstein,* stating that the new film "does not depend upon gruesomeness of horror for its entertaining punch. Weird, to be sure, and unreal, this story is . . . highly imaginative melodrama about which an interesting romance is woven. Because the name of Karloff has been associated with several gasp provokers and because of the title, it would seem that the first thing to do would be to impress upon your patrons that *The Mummy* is not a horror picture."[80]

Inevitably, the public was disappointed that *The Mummy, The Mask of Fu Manchu,* and *The Old Dark House* were less sensational than *Frankenstein,* and by the end of 1932 the horror film vogue had been replaced by one for musicals. Though these three pictures did well at the box-office, business was not as impressive as the studios had hoped. *Fu Manchu*'s week at New York's Capitol Theatre took in $46,000, while *Prosperity* preceded it with $62,111 and *Flesh* followed with $52,504. Similarly, *The Mummy* (at the Mayfair) took in $21,250 in contrast to $24,750 for *The Half-Naked Truth* just before it. *The Old Dark House* stayed at the Rialto for three weeks, but its receipts were no better: $24,500 for the first, $13,600 for the second, and $6,200 for the third. From here on, only novelties like *King Kong,* and to a lesser extent *The Invisible Man,* were able to challenge the records of *Frankenstein* and *Dr. Jekyll and Mr. Hyde.*

The Invisible Man was intended as Karloff's next film, but when the production was postponed, he returned to England for the first time in twenty-four years. Leaving America in March 1933, he spent three months abroad. "It was thrilling to be on English soil once more. I wanted to see London and to know all about the changes. I drove all over London with my brothers, and it gave me one of the greatest moments of my life."[2]

Karloff was uncertain about meeting his brothers again—after all, they were dignified diplomats who had spent years becoming important but comparatively unknown figures, "whereas I, because of a series of lucky accidents, have been granted fame and fortune" as an actor in horror movies.[2] These two worlds threatened to collide during a reception given for Karloff in London; when a photographer asked the actor to pose in the next room with his brothers, Karloff

Another portrait from the early Thirties

feared that they would not approve. "Well, you never saw such a stampede. The three reserved, distinguished elderlies—Ted, who'd been judge of the High Court in Bombay; Fred, who'd administered an entire province in India; and Jack, who'd been Chief Magistrate of the Consular Court in Shanghai—all but got stuck in the door getting through. And there was quite a to-do about who was to stand where."[61] "No sooner was the picture taken than all three brothers began to inquire how soon they could secure prints—and by this time I was in a positive glow of relief."[2] On another evening, the Karloffs attended a play at the Drury Theatre. "There was a tremendous crowd gathered round the entrance. As I got out of the cab, many of them shouted in a most friendly fashion: 'Welcome home,

Mr. Karloff, welcome home.' They came around, some wanting auto-graphs, some more simply to extend friendly greetings. A welcome to me! I was overcome almost to the point of tears."[2]

Karloff's excuse for visiting England was to star in *The Ghoul*, an American-style horror film made by Gaumont-British in March-April 1933 and released during October. He played an Egyptologist who be-lieves that if, at the first full moon after his death, his soul brings a jewel called The Eternal Light to Anubis, the God will reward him with eternal life. When the professor dies, the jewel is bandaged to his wrist, a light is left flickering within the tomb, and a key to the door is placed inside. Unfortunately, one of his servants (Ernest Thesiger) steals the jewel, and from then on the film is devoted to attempts by several others to locate this treasure. Eventually, an angry Karloff returns from his tomb to retrieve the bauble and kill a few people in the process. A final struggle in the tomb sets the building on fire, causes a dynamite explosion, and dispatches Karloff empty-handed while his two heirs end up with the jewel.

The basic situation of Karloff, the jewel, and the Egyptian Gods has potential, and could have been handled in at least two ways. In one, emphasis would be on Karloff, with his eventual death and re-turn as the climax. Unfortunately, *The Ghoul* resorts to the less in-teresting option: the jewel itself takes precedence, and the film be-comes a variation on the familiar reading-of-the-will, eccentric house-hold, non-supernatural melodrama. As if they didn't trust the horror style or couldn't decide what it was, the writers used Karloff as back-ground for a rather ordinary story that is hardly a star vehicle, since he is on-screen for only a fraction of the running time, has very little dialogue, and is allowed no characterisation at all.

Karloff is first seen on his death-bed, muttering some lines about what to do with the jewel and already looking a bit decayed. So we "meet" him when he is hardly a person at all, and we never get to know him any better because he dies right away and is not seen again until the last reel or so. For the rest of the film, we are treated to lots of skulking around in shadows after the jewel. Finally, when Karloff does return from the tomb, his make-up is gaunt and frightening, but the handling of the sequence is curiously uncertain. Karloff is menac-ing enough, as he appears before members of the household and lopes across a room to head off an escape, but once he grabs someone, he seems incapable of an efficient strangulation. Either the victims are held limply and awkwardly or they manage to pull loose with little effort, and when he finally seems to have done the job, they later re-appear quite alive. Also, these serious scenes are intercut with others that are too comic for this point in the story.

After Karloff is finally killed, the film develops into a game of jewel, jewel, who's got the jewel—an anti-climax so extreme that it becomes pleasantly amusing. Karloff returns to the tomb and places the jewel in the hand of a statue of Anubis. He waits, kneeling. The statue's hand moves, grasping the jewel. Karloff rises triumphantly, and is shot. The local vicar (Ralph Richardson), who had been hidden behind the statue, now possesses the jewel; he is spotted by the male heir, and the two fight until another character, an Arab, enters and takes the jewel at gun-point. He leaves, locking the two in the tomb, but as he runs off, a girl who is infatuated with him grabs at his coat, ripping the pocket and causing the jewel to fall to the ground. When Karloff's lawyer (Cedric Hardwicke) stops the Arab, the two realise what has happened and chase the girl, who holds them off by threatening to drop the jewel down a well. Meanwhile, back in the tomb, a stray bullet has weakened Karloff's perpetual flame, which falls, spreads to the door, and sets off some dynamite that the vicar had planted there long before. The police arrive at the well to save the girl, and despite the explosion, the hero survives.

The best scenes of conscious humour in *The Ghoul* involve the Arab and the gushing, gullible friend of the heroine, who is impressed at the thought that he rides a white stallion. Later, the Arab orders her around and she loves it. Also interesting is Cedric Hardwicke's caricature-like performance, creating a figure straight out of Dickens. He resents the vicar's presence, so when the latter remarks, "After all, we are only ships that pass in the night," Hardwicke snaps back, "You want a drink or will you pass now?"

The direction by T. Hayes Hunter is unimpressive, with the scene of Karloff breaking out of his coffin, handled too straightforwardly. In a simple long shot of the coffin, the lid is awkwardly thrown off from the inside, then one arm extends upright into the air and pauses strikingly. There is a cut to the tomb's exterior and, after a pause, the door opens and Karloff appears. He stops to check the hand bandage that should hold the jewel—but why has he waited so long to do that? He finds the jewel gone, and there is a close-up of his face as it grows hard with fury. Here, Karloff's expression successfully carries the full burden, and at a few other points the actor's skill at pantomime almost rescues the film. Wandering in the house, he comes upon the spot where the statue of Anubis had stood. He stretches out his arms and puts his hands against the wall. This gesture, and his kneeling, rising, and collapsing at the very end, are visually dramatic but excessively operatic, as though Karloff had to resort to this style because the situations or the direction lacked substance. Two of the film's stars, Dorothy Hyson and Kathleen Harrison, recently agreed "in their dislike of T. Hayes Hunter . . . [He] seemed to have the tyranny of a Stroheim, without the talent to match."[36] A reporter on the set reinforced this view: "T. Hayes Hunter summoned Anthony Bushell and Harold Huth for a desperate hand-to-hand scuffle. 'I've had 43 falls in the last 24 hours,' cheerfully confessed Mr. Huth. 'Now, you guys! This is no pink tea,' exhorted 'Happy' Hunter, dominating everybody. 'All right? Turn 'em over.' Strenuously, grasping and snarling, the two men grappled fiercely, stumbling and hitting . . . 'I'm afraid that's no good,' was the director's comment. 'Just a couple of tame wild cats.' "[74]

Though catalepsy is provided as a logical explanation of Karloff's return, the plot remains farfetched, and contemporary critics praised only the photography and sets. The talent, however, was more Germanic than British, with the photographer and art director imported to work on the film. One reporter described Karloff being made-up by "a brace of intensely serious German experts . . . The old Teuton bending over him was snipping transparent wrinkled cellophane into patches and plastering it over the entire facial area. 'Leave the mouth till last,' said the victim. It looked as though it must itch terribly. 'It doesn't really,' Karloff reassured me. "Just burns a bit, that's all.' "[73]

By 1934, horror movies had fallen into such disrepute that *The Ghoul* opened in New York at the Rialto Theatre, an exploitation house specialising in cheap action-adventure films. It did capacity business at first, but the viewers were of the kind that got their kicks from booing the human villains and hissing Karloff's corpse. They evidently agreed with one American critic who said that "a newsreel of a Sunday School picnic would have been more thrilling."[129] The picture took in $18,500 for the first week, and $8,000 during an additional five days.

On his return from England in May 1933, Karloff was still to star in *The Invisible Man*, but in June he encountered salary troubles with the studio. As "Variety" reported, "Universal is continuing its policy of dumping contract players as soon as they reach the big money class and substituting them with new people at less money. Latest Universal star to go off the list is Boris Karloff. At the studio 18 months, Karloff had been drawing $750 per week, and was scheduled to get $1,250 on his coming option jump. The sum represented a jump of $500 or $250 each for two option periods. Karloff waived the previous option increase, which would have boosted his salary to $1,000, on condition that he would get the full amount on the next option. Universal refused to meet the figure, which came due Thursday, and Karloff walked."[138]

James Whale went ahead on *The Invisible Man*, with Claude Rains in the lead, and other projects planned for Karloff faded out: *Bluebeard* or *Bluebeard's Eight Wives* (to have been directed by Karl Freund), *The Wizard* or *Wizard Man* (John Huston was to write this adaptation), and *The Mystery of Edwin Drood* (in which

Rains eventually starred). Universal soon realised its mistake, and in July a new contract was signed and new projects were announced. These included *Bombay Mail* (which was made in October without Karloff), *The Return of Frankenstein*, and *A Trip to Mars*.

First, Karloff spent part of October at RKO, filming *The Lost Patrol* for director John Ford. This tale of British soldiers lost in the Mesopotamian Desert was a grim one, though weakened a bit by some overly sentimental dialogue. When the only commissioned officer is killed, the Sergeant (Victor McLaglen) takes charge. In addition to the heat and a lack of water, the group is tormented by Arab snipers who steal their horses and pick off the remaining soldiers. When Karloff, as the Bible-quoting Sanders, badgers another soldier for "repentance," McLaglen orders him into a hut. As he walks away from the camera, Karloff's stooped back is restrained, physical evidence of chastisement. This is probably Karloff's best moment in the film, for otherwise his passion and hysteria are excessive. Third from the last to be killed, he finally cracks under the tension and, looking like an Old Testament prophet, marches up a sand dune and into rifle fire. When *The Lost Patrol* was released in February 1934, one trade reviewer called it "a courageous picture; one that courageous, resourceful

Karloff (at right) in THE LOST PATROL

showmen should welcome"[79] and the New York "Times" declared that it was, "with the exception of Boris Karloff, who plays a religious fanatic, an exceptionally well-acted production."[130] Also in the "Times," a British soldier who had served in Mesopotamia wrote that he could easily recognise all the characters in the film; "though it was my good fortune never to run across the religious fanatic," he said, "I can well believe he existed."[53]

Also in October, Karloff and several other actors decided that the Academy of Motion Picture Arts and Sciences did not offer them sufficient protection and support. Rumours of government attempts to limit "excessive" star salaries proved to be the last straw, and this group, resigning in protest from the Academy, formed a separate Screen Actors Guild. By the end of the first week, 529 members were enrolled. At the time, this professionally risky undertaking was called "one of the most sudden and decisively effective steps ever taken in the unionization of a group of motion picture employees."[84] The Guild's executive secretary, writing at the time of Karloff's death, said, "Boris was not the type to go along for the ride. He was a courageous and aggressive force. He felt injustice and he reacted to it. He continued to serve his fellow actors as an active member of the Guild Board until the early 1950s. He served on every negotiating committee during that period—an outspoken, challenging advocate for the many who dared not speak for themselves, innovative, intelligent and articulate."[2]

The House of Rothschild, Karloff's next picture, was the first made by George Arliss for United Artists. It was filmed in December–January, 1933/34. Although Karloff had by now achieved star status, he agreed to play a featured role in support of Arliss, supposedly out of admiration for the other actor. It also was good for his own image to appear in such company, and the fact that *The Lost Patrol* and *The House of Rothschild* appeared on most ten-best lists increased Karloff's prestige. Arliss, who had never met "the terrible Karloff," was "considerably surprised to find him one of the most retiring and gentle gentlemen it has ever been my lot to meet."[7] Set in the early Nineteenth century, *Rothschild* was a well-acted attempt to comment on growing anti-Jewish feeling in Nazi Germany. It shows banker Nathan Rothschild (Arliss) risking his fortune to prevent war, and to establish an atmosphere in which Jews could live and work with dignity. To an extent, historical accuracy was sacrificed for the rhetorical purpose of contrasting the noble Arliss with Baron Ledrantz (Karloff), a Prussian tyrant who opposes the Rothschilds and supports his country's anti-Semitism. The elaborately costumed Karloff was an impressive figure, but again he was accused of being "perhaps the only member of the cast guilty of overacting."[116]

In February 1934, James Whale returned from England with R. C. Sherriff's completed script for *A Trip to Mars*. Karloff was set

Karloff with George Arliss in **THE HOUSE OF ROTHSCHILD**

to star, and he even declared that in *Mars* he would avoid elaborate make-up and depend entirely on his acting ability. Nothing more was heard about the project. *The Return of Frankenstein* was also announced, but this time it was postponed in favour of a property with far less advance publicity. *The Black Cat* (filmed in February–March 1934, and released in May) was originally to be based on Poe's short story, but after several plot revisions, the studio settled on a hastily evolved script inspired by a current scandal about Aleister Crowley and a young couple that had become involved in his magical ceremonies. Karloff and Lugosi were co-starred for the first time, and although they received equal billing, Karloff's first name was dropped while Lugosi's was not. Bela was cast only after Boris had been set, with Universal imagining that two horror stars would double the business. The picture was plugged as: *"The Daddy of 'em All!* The Monster of *Frankenstein* plus the monster of *Dracula*, plus the 'monstrousness' of Edgar Allan Poe—all combined by the master makers of screen mysteries to give you the absolute apex in supershivery!"[85]

In Hungary, Dr. Vitus Werdegast (Lugosi) returns, after fifteen years in a military prison, seeking revenge on Hjalmar Poelzig (Karloff); during the First World War, Karloff had betrayed the fort he commanded, allowed the men under him (including Lugosi) to be

Karloff in THE BLACK CAT (frame enlargement)

captured, fled for his own life, and stolen Lugosi's wife. Because of a
bus accident, a young American couple, the Alisons, are forced to stay
at Karloff's house. Lugosi wants the couple set free, so he can get on
with his mission, but Karloff wishes to keep the girl. The resulting
struggle is almost entirely covert, and the film is an extreme model of
the "gentlemanly" school of horror films. Both men hide the real
situation from the Alisons for as long as possible, and between themselves they are coolly polite and end by playing chess for the heroine.
This metaphor reappears occasionally during the film: the actual game
is interrupted, then resumed, and Lugosi finally comments to the dying
Karloff, "It has been a good game." So abstract a depiction of the
struggle between life and death is a cultured, eminently civilised, and
(yes!) slow-moving form of conflict, but if a viewer approaches the
film without expecting much action or even explanation, he may be
satisfied with the subtler rewards of atmosphere.

   Karloff and Lugosi are about evenly matched here. Vitus Werdegast
does most of the talking and is generally more sympathetic. Hjalmar
Poelzig is passive and quiet, with a predominantly still face that suggests power and superiority; the character is intended to be an enigma,
a man of mystery, an unknown quantity. This lack of individual identity does dissipate interest by keeping the character from being "human," but in the light of the entire film, the approach establishes
Poelzig as part of the overall atmosphere.

   A brooding sense of death permeates *The Black Cat*, and pains

Karloff in the cellar, with preserved victim, in THE BLACK CAT
(frame enlargement)

were taken to have its settings and situations reinforce that feeling. Most of this was the work of Edgar G. Ulmer, an Austrian who had been an art director on some of F. W. Murnau's German films, and who was an assistant on Murnau's American pictures. Besides directing and co-authoring *The Black Cat*, Ulmer designed its sets and costumes; in his words, "Karloff kept insisting that he didn't want to make any more horror pictures . . . One of the things he found most exciting in the film was the wardrobe . . . He knew he would be playing 'Karloff,' but also felt in these duds, he could employ a sort of 'out of this world' appearance. That, as you know, was exactly as he appeared. In preparing the script, which I also had a hand in, we had come up with some very interesting, very supernatural undertones that had to be cut from the original. Censorship in the Thirties was even worse than now, and people couldn't take things like the character of Karen resembling the physical characteristics of a cat. There were several other items of important interest to the story that have been cut, and for me, let us say, how I feel, this has injured the story in many ways."[71]

What is left, though perhaps incomplete, is quite consistent. Lugosi has an intense fear of black cats because he believes "that the black cat is the living embodiment of evil"; Karloff sometimes carries a cat around with him, always dresses in black garments, and has a somewhat feline haircut. In addition, death and evil permeate his home, which is built on the ruins of the fort he had betrayed. ("A masterpiece of construction built upon the ruins of the masterpiece of destruction

—the masterpiece of murder!") The cellar is a chart room for long-range guns, and here Karloff keeps several women, including Lugosi's wife, preserved in glass cases. Even the land beneath the house remains studded with live mines. The bus driver, early in the film, provides a graphic description of the area. "All of this country was one of the greatest battlefields of the war. Tens of thousands of men died here. The ravine down there was piled twelve deep with dead and wounded men. The little river below was swollen, red, a raging torrent of blood. That high hill yonder, where engineer Poelzig now lives, was the site of Fort Marmaros. He built his home on its very foundations. Marmaros—the greatest graveyard in the world!" So, Karloff represents Death and Evil, which justifies his somewhat stylised performance. Even the characters are aware of this association, so that when Karloff is told that his telephone will not work, he says, "You hear that, Vitus? The phone is dead. Even the phone is dead!"

Earlier, in a long monologue, Karloff speaks some lines that are surprisingly mature in their thoughtfulness, and which use horror themes (vampires, the living dead) to deal in a symbolic, cynical, even poetic way with realistic death and the violence in life. After Lugosi has temporarily lost control and attacked him, the world-weary Karloff says, "Come, Vitus, are we men or are we children? Of what use are all these melodramatic gestures? You say your soul was killed and that you have been dead all these years. And what of me—did we not both

THE BLACK CAT (frame enlargement): "Even the phone is dead!"

die here in Marmaros fifteen years ago? Are we any the less victims of
the war than those whose bodies were torn asunder? Are we not both
the living dead? And now you come to me—playing at being an aveng-
ing angel, childishly thirsting for my blood. We understand each
other too well; we know too much of life. We shall play a little game,
Vitus. A game of death, if you like. But under any circumstances we
shall have to wait until these people are gone, until we are alone."

But they are unable to wait, since Karloff decides to use Mrs.
Alison in that night's black mass, and when he wins the chess game
he also wins her. The ceremony begins, but when a participant faints,
Lugosi manages to free the heroine. Then, after some struggle, Karloff
is tied to his own embalming rack and Lugosi proceeds to tear the
skin from his body, slowly, bit by bit. Pausing in his task to help the
Alisons escape, he is shot by the hero, who misinterprets his actions.
Seriously wounded, Lugosi orders the couple to leave, then pulls the
inevitable switch that destroys the building.

Despite its extreme subject matter (black masses and human sacri-
fice, skinning alive, Poelzig's marriages to Werdegast's wife and daughter), *The Black Cat* is austere enough to keep from offending. None
of the violence is shown directly: the camera focuses on Joan Alison's
reactions when Karen is killed, and Poelzig's torture is seen in shadows
and in shots of his agonised, manacled hands. However, the reviewer
on "Variety" called the final skinning-alive scene "a truly horrible and
nauseating bit of extreme sadism."[67]

Karloff is not allowed much characterisation and motivation, but
Poelzig is still a striking antagonist in this struggle between two giants.
In his disturbing politeness and hypnotic influence over women, he is
similar to Imhotep, but enough details differ for this role to be independent. Though Karloff wears less make-up than usual, his appearance is striking. His mouth seems to lack teeth, so that the lips curl
slightly inward and create an evil, reptilian look. Unlike Imhotep,
this character breaks out of his almost inhibited self-control and resorts
to physical violence, as in the final fight with Lugosi. When such
action occurs, Karloff's manner is quick, lithe, and as lizard-like as
his appearance. (Unfortunately, in some close-ups his face seems covered with an excess of white powder and lipstick.)

Either hasty writing or pre-release editing have caused *The Black
Cat*'s plot to be less than satisfying, with contemporary reactions emphasising that the story "is so confused that it is difficult to pick up
its various threads . . . It does seem a pity that with several good
ideas started none of them is ever carried out to the end. The moment
you feel that the film is getting somewhere it simmers out to nothing."[144]
The public seemed to agree, and one Minnesota exhibitor complained
about the negative comments the picture received, calling it "one of
those dizzy things with a foreign setting. No one seemed to know what

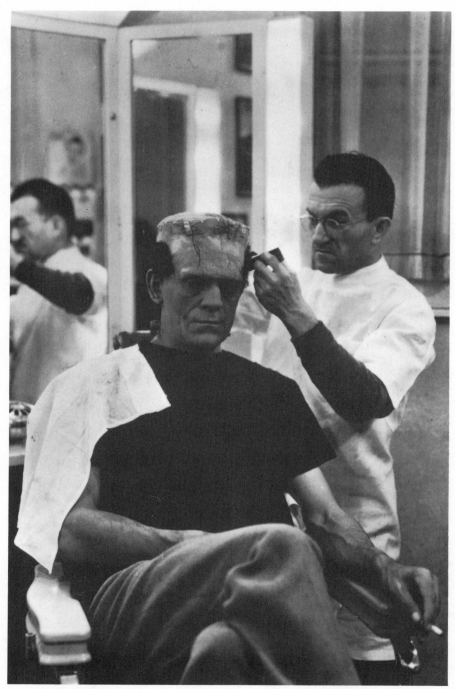

Jack Pierce attending to Karloff's make-up for BRIDE OF FRANK-ENSTEIN

it was all about."[86] But although its conflict is probably too covert, *The Black Cat* has a basic idea that is original and its treatment is above average; it clearly belongs in this golden age of Hollywood horror.

★ ★ ★

In the summer of 1934, Karloff and Lugosi played guest roles in Karl Freund's *The Gift of Gab*. During one sequence of this musical comedy, several Universal players enact a burlesque murder mystery in a radio studio. Karloff's make-up here looks hasty, and consists of dark shadows around the eyes, a top hat and cape, and a wig of long, scraggly hair. Then, in January 1935, *The Return of Frankenstein* finally entered production, and was released the following April as *Bride of Frankenstein*. James Whale again directed, and Universal allowed him more money and freedom than ever before. The result is far more ambitious than *Frankenstein*, and this is both its strength and its weakness.

Since *Bride* begins exactly where its predecessor left off, it was necessary to summarise the earlier film. To do this, Whale and his writers (including the ubiquitous John L. Balderston) constructed a prologue in which Mary Shelley discusses the novel with her "husband" and Lord Byron, though the incongruity of having Mary refer to a modernised version of her book is ignored. This sequence is an efficient but extraneous source of exposition, as Byron vocally savours certain highlights of the story, while we view scenes from the previous film (along with one or two shots prepared especially for this flashback). Mary now reveals that the burning mill was not the end, and agrees to tell the rest. Here the scene shifts to the mill, where the flames are dying down, and the film's main portion begins. The badly-burned Monster has survived in the water beneath the mill, and when the father of the girl drowned in the other film falls through the collapsing floor, the Monster kills both the man and his wife—as an owl looks sleepily on. (The script, however, had the more ordinary idea of intercutting the Monster with a beady-eyed rat.) In all the later Frankenstein sequels, the Monster survives simply because he is "indestructible"; this is the only time when a normal human might have lived under similar circumstances. Naturally, the character is not given the elaborate introduction he received in *Frankenstein*, but his emergence from behind a wooden beam, with only an arm and shoulder seen at first, is a well-staged entrance.

Henry Frankenstein (Colin Clive), whose body has been returned home in a beautifully-staged procession, is discovered to be still alive, although one wonders why this was not noticed right away. Some time later, he and Elizabeth are planning to leave the area, and an eerie mood is created as she cautions Henry, "When you rave of your insane desire to create living men from the dust of the dead, a strange apparition has seemed to appear in the room. It comes, a figure like Death, and each time it comes more clearly, nearer. It seems to be reaching out for you, as if it would take you away from me. There it is. Look! There! It's coming for you. Nearer! Henry! Henry!!" There is a loud knock on the door. Dr. Pretorius, one of Henry's old teachers, has arrived! Once a Professor of Philosophy, Pretorius had been booted out of the University. "Booted, my dear Baron," he says, "is the word—for knowing—too much." (Pretorius mentions that Henry has become Baron, but the fate of his crusty old father is never specifically mentioned. One version of the script, though, had him die off camera just before Henry regains consciousness.) Hoping that Henry will work with him, Pretorius reveals his own creations: the living, miniature figures of a King, Queen, Archbishop, Devil, ballerina, and mermaid. Achieving normal size has been Pretorius's problem, and to solve it he needs Frankenstein's help. "Alone you have created a man. Now, together, we will create his mate!" It is odd, though, that Pretorius should think of doing this even before he learns that the Monster is still alive.

Meanwhile, the Monster has been roaming the countryside. When he pauses at a stream to drink, a shepherdess sees him and, startled, falls in. The Monster saves her, she screams again at the sight of him, and he is shot at by some hunters for his trouble. The men report this to the villagers and a mob chases the Monster. Whale's earlier reference to "the pagan sport of a mountain manhunt" is especially apt here, with the Monster cornered on a rocky outcropping, tied to a long pole, and carried off like a captured boar or a primitive Christ, to the accompaniment of a victory march. Jeered at and painfully chained to a chair in an old dungeon, he has complete audience sympathy, and when he breaks loose the viewers relish his almost superhuman power over the townspeople. This whole sequence, starting with the chase, is one of the finest in all horror films.

Eventually the Monster blunders upon the cabin of an old blind hermit, who welcomes the mute figure. "Perhaps you're afflicted, too . . . I shall look after you, and you will comfort me." After feeding the Monster and giving him a place to sleep, the man prays, thanking God for sending him a friend, and the Monster sheds a tear. This episode verges on the maudlin, but is effectively moving because of its frankness and sincerity; even the *Ave Maria* on the soundtrack "works" because the old man had been playing it on his violin earlier.

Later in the film the hermit teaches his new friend to speak, and to understand the meanings of both concrete and abstract words. He is sitting at his teacher's feet, smoking and listening to music, when two hunters enter and destroy this Utopia. They panic at the sight of the Monster and the cabin is accidentally set on fire, so the bewildered and protesting hermit is led away by the hunters. When

BRIDE OF FRANKENSTEIN: "tied to a long pole, and carried off like a captured boar or a primitive Christ"

Another frame enlargement from BRIDE OF FRANKENSTEIN

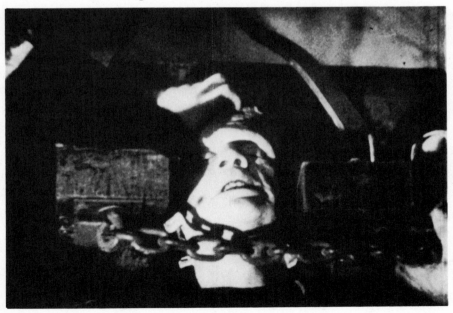

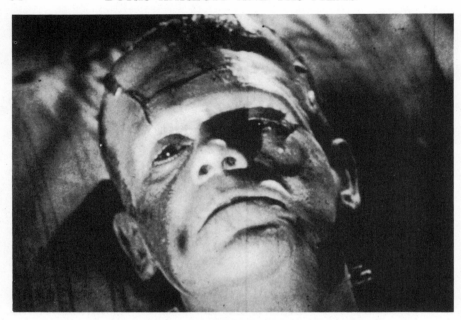

Karloff in BRIDE OF FRANKENSTEIN (frame enlargement)

the Monster finally evades the flames and reaches the door, his call of "Friend?" goes unanswered. Pursued once more by the populace, the Monster runs through a cemetery, where he resentfully knocks over a religious statue. Below is the entrance to a tomb, and as he descends, his form resembles that of a crucifix placed starkly and significantly nearby. Within the tomb, the Monster examines the face of a deceased girl and asks, "Friend?" By chance, this is also the place where Pretorius and two assistants have come to obtain the skeleton of a girl to be used in his new creation. The two helpers leave as soon as they can, but Pretorius remains. The Monster then steps forward and Pretorius, showing only a slight trace of surprise, tells him that a companion is in preparation. The Monster is pleased, and takes in his hands the skull of his intended.

When Henry tries to back out of their partnership, Pretorius has the Monster kidnap Elizabeth. Then, in a scene filled with more shots, angles, and flashing machines than the one in the earlier film, the bride is given life. In every respect, from the size of the set to the use of light and shadow to mould faces, this version is superior, except that just as the body is raised to the roof of the laboratory and the tension should be building to its climax, the background music shifts into a quiet, almost-romantic melody that short-circuits the emotional effect. When the now-living woman is finally helped to her feet by the two scientists, there is a dissolve from her bandage-covered figure to her in a long white dress, with white-streaked hair standing directly out from her head. This coiffure is pure indulgence, as is Pretorius's announcement that she is "the bride of Frankenstein." At this point, composer Franz Waxman continues to undermine the film by including wedding bells, a touch of self-conscious kidding that is out of place. On the other hand, the bride's quick, jerky head movements are strikingly weird and logically convincing.

When the Monster clomps forward, the bride sees him and emits a hissing scream. The two are then seated together, and again she looks at him and screams. "She hate me. Like others!" says the Monster, and in a rage he starts smashing the laboratory. "Get away from that lever. You'll blow us all to atoms," shouts Pretorius. This gives the Monster an idea and, after letting Henry leave to join Elizabeth, destroys himself, his bride, and Pretorius. It is hard to say why Henry is allowed to live, since the Monster has as much reason to hate him as he does Pretorius, so the action must be attributed simply to contrivance, especially since the original script had Henry and Elizabeth perish with the others.

Bride of Frankenstein is much more expensive and elaborate than its predecessor. To the extent that this allows Whale to use more complex camerawork, the investment is a great advantage, and the director does not lose track of his characters in the larger settings. But the ambitions of *Bride* lie less in its size than in the way humour is employed. In *Frankenstein*, the scenes of outright "comedy relief" were carefully set apart from the rest of the picture, while similar parts of *Bride* are included in scenes that also involve the Monster. Especially unfortunate is the extensive use made of Una O'Connor (as the servant, Minnie), who offers raucous, whooping screeches and interrupts the action with such comments as, "I'd hate to find him under my bed at night. He's a nightmare in the daylight, he is." This low-grade farce seriously detracts from Whale's quieter brand of bizarre humour. The fact that she appears in almost every major sequence is an incredible lapse of judgement, particularly as her most obnoxious moments could have been cut without damaging the continuity.

Soon after *Frankenstein*, horror was established as a separate *genre*, and with this came a critical tendency to sneer at the films. Whale, an intelligent and skilled director, had to be aware of this situation and so *Bride*, unlike *Frankenstein*, seems self-conscious, almost embarrassed, about its identity as A Horror Film. It is a serious picture that refuses to take itself seriously, as though the director wants to assure us that he isn't being fooled by his material. In *Frankenstein*, his whimsy appeared in small doses (Fritz pulling up his sock, for instance) and this added zest, but Whale's discretion and sensitivity made it a success. In *Bride,* whimsy is dominant, and Whale arouses two contradictory feelings in viewers: a sense of the gravity of the Monster's plight, and an amusement at the way in which events are depicted. When a balance is not maintained, the tone veers into self-parody. It is remarkable that this approach works as often as it does, creating scenes that are complex and modern, anticipating the black comedy of the Sixties. Some of the attempts, however, are just bad, such as the low comedy of the lecherous miniature King. As a result, many viewers fail to make distinctions, and underestimate the whole film by calling it "camp."

There are inside jokes and references, such as having the miniature King resemble Charles Laughton as Henry VIII, because Laughton had been in *The Old Dark House* and his wife, Elsa Lanchester, was in *Bride.* Another such joke, written into the script but happily eliminated, concerned a seventh tiny figure: "In the jar is a baby—already twice as big as the Queen, and looking as if it might develop into a Boris Karloff. It is pulling a flower to pieces." Off-screen, Pretorius was to have said, "I think this Baby will grow into something worth watching." The fact that Elsa Lanchester played both Mary Shelley and the Bride might seem just another coy joke, but Miss Lanchester herself relates it to the fact that Whale was intrigued by the seeming contradiction of a young, refined girl writing *Frankenstein,* and he "felt that frustration and wrath in a woman often lay under an excess of sweetness and light."[66] The prologue supports this theory: Lord Byron calls Mary an "angel," and she replies, "You think so", then shifts to, "You know how lightning alarms me." A little later, Byron says: "And it was these fragile white fingers that penned the nightmare."

The film also contains verbal humour in its often well-written dialogue. The announcement by Pretorius that he has come "on a secret matter of grave importance" might be an accidental pun, but the fact that Minnie immediately repeats it suggests that it was intended. Some of the comments Pretorius makes about his miniature people are intelligently and satirically phrased. "My little ballerina is charming . . . but such a bore—she won't dance to anything but Mendelssohn's 'Spring Song' and it gets so monotonous." In this context, the claim that "science, like love, has *her* little surprises" is strangely humorous. Much more obvious is the dialogue given to the murderers who help Pretorius in the tomb: "If there's much more like this, what do you say, pal, we give ourselves up and let 'em hang us? . . . This is no life for murderers!"

Perhaps the key reason for this dominant strain of humour is Dr. Pretorius, to whom Henry Frankenstein plays second fiddle. Colin Clive's interpretation of Henry as enthusiastic but not mad helped make the first film convincing. Here, Henry's footage is reduced, the character changes moods suddenly, and Clive is not as forceful as before. While Henry is a normal man whose nervousness makes him seem insane, Pretorius *is* mad, but he does outrageous things as though they were everyday occurrences. Ernest Thesiger's performance, far more stylised and arch than Clive's, creates considerable macabre amusement. Very little is told about Pretorius; he enters from nowhere and is given minimal motivation. Despite this, or perhaps because of it, he is a fascinating individual deserving admission to anyone's gallery of classic cinema eccentrics. His formal, dignified appearance and precise, effete speech create the impression of refined charm. Amusement stems from the contrast between this manner and its context: in one of the film's finest scenes, he sits in the girl's tomb, unfolds his lunch, and pours a glass of wine—all the while framed by the Gothic paraphernalia of candles and a foreground skull. He is the polished host of a dinner party who has been whisked to this gruesome setting, and who discovers that he enjoys being here. When the Monster steps forward, Pretorius casually accepts his presence. "Oh," he comments, "I thought I was alone. Good evening." Always the gentleman, he offers the Monster a cigar; "they're my only weakness." (Earlier, he had treated Henry to some gin with the same observation.) Carefully treading the thin line between eccentricity and caricature, Thesiger never lets himself or his character descend to burlesque.

BRIDE OF FRANKENSTEIN: the Monster guzzles wine (frame enlargement)

Although he is always reserved, Pretorius unintentionally gives a few hints about his inner character. A certain vague degeneracy is suggested when he talks of creating a woman and adds, "That should be *really* interesting!" He is almost disgusted by Henry's "dirty" method of creating life. He prefers a "natural" approach, but at the same time mocks religion. "While you were digging in your graves, piecing together dead tissues, I my dear pupil went for my material to the source of life. I grew my creatures like cultures; grew them like Nature does—from seed . . . Leave the charnal house and follow the lead of Nature—or of God, if you like your Bible stories. Male *and* female created he them." Here and elsewhere, Pretorius is an outlet for Whale's evident scepticism about religion. Speaking of a tiny Devil that he has created, Pretorius says, "Very bizarre, this little chap. There's a certain resemblance to me, don't you think? Or do I flatter myself? I took a great deal of pains with him. Sometimes I have wondered whether life wouldn't be much more amusing if we were all devils, and no nonsense about angels and being good." He then laughingly toasts to "a new World of Gods and Monsters."

Pretorius uses people for his own purposes. When he wants the secret of achieving size, he suggests that Henry become his partner, so that they might work together, "No longer as master and pupil, but as fellow scientists." Later, angered by Henry's accurate description of his work as "like black magic," the pose slips and he calls his partner "my dear pupil." He also takes credit for the Monster's ability to talk, and treats him kindly only as long as he is useful for kidnapping and threats. When the unsuspecting Monster is no longer needed, Pretorius callously drugs his drink without even hiding the action.

Another reason for *Bride's* unusual tone is a change in the Monster. In *Frankenstein,* he had just been born and was dazed and bewildered most of the time. Whale, in this sequel, dares to take the next logical step and educate the Monster. He now smokes, drinks, talks, laughs, and cries; he discovers beauty though music, and good and evil though the different uses of fire; he has become relatively alert and aware. It is risky thus to humanise the Monster, because the scenes in which he laughs, puffs on a cigar, or guzzles wine all have a light touch that could affect a viewer's reaction to the more serious scenes. The humour is again that of incongruity, with the appearance and mythical aura of the character failing to fit his mundane actions. This Monster is still less educated and talkative than Mary Shelley's, but compared with his other screen incarnations, he possesses a PhD.

The role is now an even more challenging one, with hesitancy of action and dimness of mind replaced with awkwardness and awareness. Since the Monster is no longer helplessly bewildered or ani-

malistically frightened, it is more difficult to maintain the proper
balance of sympathy and terror. Karloff himself did not like having
the character speak, and claimed that "if the Monster had any impact or charm, it was because he was inarticulate."[54] He also said,
"I don't know but that that was a mistake, that building up of
sympathy for the Monster. I think maybe they lost the excitement
of the picture."[29] The points are valid, because the scene with the
blind hermit is sentimental, and speech *does* eliminate some of the
expected mystique. Still, this is a natural step forward in the character's development and, as a completely new stage, it goes against
expectations. Though uncertain about the role, Karloff gives an impressive performance: one still feels that the Monster is suffering indig-
nities, despite his increased alertness. Pantomime and facial expressions explicitly and movingly reveal the Monster's fear, confusion, pain, and pleasure. The only possible criticism is that Karloff and Whale resort too often to the helpless, questioning, open-
handed gesture used in *Frankenstein*.

To his original Monster make-up, Jack Pierce here adds burns
from the mill fire, "a mangy, frizzled wig that covers only the top of
the square skull,"[95] and an open wound on the right cheek. Every
day for about thirty-two days, Karloff was awakened at 4:30 A.M.
After a cold shower and infra-red ray treatments for his left hip,
which had been dislocated during the first week of shooting, he had
black coffee and left for the studio by 5:20. At 6:00 a cosmetician
started work, and from seven to twelve the make-up was applied.
At 12:30 he got into his heavy, elevated boots and was strapped
into leg and body pads. At 1:30 he paused for tea and a sandwich,
and a half hour later began work. Because the make-up kept his
pores closed under the hot lights and, with the costume, weighed
sixty-two pounds, he lost twenty pounds during filming, and had to
lie down and rest between scenes. After he had acted for five hours, his
make-up was removed with oil and acetic acid. At 8:00 he had a cold
shower, tea, more infra-red treatments, and a massage that aided
circulation in his legs and relieved the pain of his injured side. By
9:30 he was in bed, studying the next day's script.[35] This typical
day was enlivened by incidents like the following: "The watery opening scene was filmed with me wearing a rubber suit under my costume to ward off the chill. But air got into the suit. When I was
launched into the pond, my legs flew up in the air and I floated
there like some sort of an obscene water lily while I, and everyone
else, hooted with laughter. They finally fished me out with a boat
hook and deflated me."[132]

Though *Bride of Frankenstein* lacks the solidity, impact, unity
of purpose, and tragic sense of *Frankenstein*, these qualities are replaced with its own tragedy of self-awareness and with a highly in-

dividual style. Thanks to the hermit scene, the female creation, and the humanisation of the Monster, it is the only Frankenstein movie that comes close to following the book. It is an audacious, and sometimes reckless, feature, with both superb and unbelievably awkward aspects.

Financially, *Bride* started out well. Its Saturday opening in Los Angeles took in $2,700, which was comparable to one week's take for an ordinary feature. In New York, its first week at the Roxy Theatre attracted $38,000, which was good but not outstanding, with the second week of *G-Men* amounting to $36,000 at another house. *Bride* played a second week, but was not kept over for a third. Interestingly, the trade seemed unwilling to admit the extent to which the film contains humour. The "Motion Picture Herald" reviewer, for instance, beat around the bush in his comparison of *Frankenstein* and *Bride,* saying that "in its own way" the latter "is equally daring, yet at the same time so widely different in its scare-power that it demands showmanship consideration and respect in its own peculiar way, putting audiences in the proper mythical mood to look upon the picture as novel entertainment, without becoming too serious minded about what they see and feel."[77] One theatre manager was more precise in describing audience reaction, but without quite knowing its cause: "Those who seek shocking entertainment will find this to their liking, even though it is not the shocker they expect to see. For some reason, the Monster has lost his ability to bring on the goose pimples and spine tingling, and while this pulled a nice business, it did not prove too satisfactory to our patrons."[87]

The next Karloff film followed quickly after *Bride*. This was *The Raven*, which was filmed in April 1935, just before the release of *Bride*, and was itself released that summer. *The Raven* played eight days in New York and did good business, but it hardly outdistanced other now-forgotten films. As in *The Black Cat,* Karloff and Lugosi were co-starred, but while they had been evenly matched before, this film is clearly Lugosi's. Both roles are typical of their actors' film images: Lugosi's Dr. Vollin, an amoral superman who is a law unto himself, contrasts with Bateman (Karloff), who is an earthy human being with a sense of values and morality. For example, Bateman's killing of a bank cashier is purely a reflex action:

> *Bateman:* Well, he tried to get me into trouble. I told him to keep his mouth shut. He gets the gag out of his mouth and starts yelling for the police. I had the acetylene torch in my hand—
> *Vollin:* So you put the burning torch into his face, into his eyes!
> *Bateman:* Well, sometimes you can't help things like that.

Karloff in THE BLACK ROOM

Bateman explains his own criminal deeds in terms of his physical appearance. "I'll tell you something, doc. Ever since I was born, everybody looks at me and says, 'You're ugly.' Makes me feel mean . . . Maybe because I look ugly, maybe if a man looks ugly he does ugly things." Bateman does not want "to do them things no more" but Vollin forces him into torture and murder by making his face even uglier than it was, and refusing to repair it. Now, says Vollin, "You're monstrously ugly. Your monstrous ugliness breeds monstrous hate. Good! I can use your hate."

Bateman is a "normal" but inarticulate human whose situation

is very much like that of the Frankenstein Monster: he is forced
by his abnormal appearance to act against his own feelings, his real
self is trapped beneath a distorted exterior; like the Monster or
Quasimodo, he is moved when someone (the heroine) sympathises
and tries to accept him as he is. This kinship with the Monster is
clearest when, alone in the operating room, he first sees his new
face. Vollin, from above, opens the curtains that had covered a
series of full-length mirrors set into the wall. Bateman rushes from
mirror to mirror, horrified at what he sees. Furious and frustrated,
he shoots out the mirrors one by one as Vollin laughs sadistically
in the background. The gun is empty by the time Bateman notices
his tormentor peering down at him, so all he can do (because the
operation has affected his speech) is shake a fist and growl. This
sound and the horizontal sweep of the hand he uses when later refusing to let the girl be crushed to death are both borrowed from
Karloff's earlier performance as the Monster; in fact, they are so
similar that here they become flaws. But the scene as a whole is so
well acted and edited that it evokes both terror and pity.

Aside from this mirror scene and the acetylene torch dialogue,
Karloff remains in the background as a stooge for Dr. Vollin. But
despite his minor role, Karloff still received top billing, and only
his last name was used. Critical reaction to *The Raven,* even more
condescending than usual, centred around the misuse of Edgar Allan Poe's works. No one could accept the fact that the scriptwriters were not even attempting to adapt a story or, much less, a
poem.

Released at almost the same time as *The Raven* was *The Black
Room,* which Karloff made for Columbia in May-June 1935 (with
the title originally planned as *The Black Room Mystery*). This time,
he completely dominated the film by playing a dual role. *The Black
Room* has a different tone than the Universal films, blending popular menace with the sets and aura of an historical romance. The
bewilderment of the Frankenstein Monster, the muted Romanticism
of Imhotep, the sullen rebellion of the servant Morgan, and the
smooth sadism of Fu Manchu are all missing from Karloff's por-
trayal, and that is just as well; rather than repeat an already successful style, as he had done in *The Raven,* he again tried something different and added still another facet to this period in his career.

A pair of twins had founded the house of Berghman, after which
one murdered the other in the Black Room. Many years later, a
long-standing prophecy ("I end as I began") and the birth of another set of twins create a fear that the same incident will happen
again and end the family. To prevent this, the room is sealed and
the brothers separated. Twenty years later, Anton (Karloff) receives
a letter from his brother, Gregor (also Karloff), requesting his re-

Karloff with Marian Marsh and Katherine de Mille in THE BLACK ROOM

turn from self-exile in Budapest. Anton is soft-spoken, cultured, and pleasant, despite his paralysed right arm, while Baron Gregor is boorish, sinister, and hated by the populace. Sprawled across a chair in a vaulted Gothic castle, a goblet of wine in his hand, Gregor has the aura of an especially disheveled, debauched Byron or Heathcliffe. These two brothers were clearly conceived as opposites, and this is their major weakness, since there is no explanation of why they are so different. Such an extreme contrast causes a feeling of contrivance, though each individual character is played with skill and subtlety.

Gregor, it seems, has called Anton home because he fears assassination and trusts no one but his brother. The twins have dinner with Colonel Hassel, whose daughter Thea sings and plays the harp, and Anton enjoys the music while Gregor leers at the girl. That night a servant, jealous of Thea, visits the evil one and sings for him. As she searches for praise, Gregor ignores her and alternates bites of a pear with such comments as, "A pear's the best fruit . . . There's lots of juice in a pear . . . I like the feel of a pear, and when you're through with it—" (he tosses it away). In desperation, the girl declares that she has seen him use a secret entrance into the

Black Room. Gregor, surprised, kills her and hides the body. Another servant finds her shawl and notifies the townspeople, who an-
grily enter the castle. The Baron greets them, sprawled in his usual chair, and calmly announces his own retirement and the appointment of the well-liked Anton as his successor.

Later, Anton is guided into the Black Room by his brother,
shown the onyx walls, and tossed into a pit—which already contains
several bodies. Pierced by the blade of a knife he had been holding,
Anton gasps that he will fulfill the prophecy, "even from the dead".
Gregor then poses as his dead brother, assumes control of the estate,
and arranges to marry the un-enthusiastic Thea. But one of Anton's
dogs dislikes its "new" master, and chases the carriage that takes
him to the wedding. During the ceremony the hound attacks "Anton,"
who instinctively protects himself with his "paralysed" right hand.
Exposed, he flees to the castle and the Black Room, but the dog
bounds in and knocks him into the pit, where he lands on his brother's dagger. The prophecy has been fulfilled.

After the death of Anton, Karloff's performance becomes quite
intricate. Having played two separate individuals, he now portrays
one of them posing as the other. He could have taken the easy way
and just repeated his own performance as Anton, but instead he
shows us Gregor impersonating his brother. Karloff's skill in this
Gregor-as-Anton interplay is first seen immediately following Anton's
death. Gregor sees his reflection in the gleaming walls of the Black
Room and, testing his pose, he changes stature, appearance, and tone
of voice before our eyes and ears, after which he resumes his own
manner. It is a tribute to Karloff's pantomime that this transforma-
tion is completely convincing.

Director Roy William Neill gratefully uses the photogenic arches
and columns of the lavish settings, tracking his camera past pillars,
cemetery monuments, chandeliers, and candlesticks. This placement
of objects or figures in the foreground creates attractive composi-
tions and gives depth to the characters' environment. Shadow and
light are knowingly used, and the trick photography in scenes between Anton and Gregor is smooth. Neill's style is seen in the discreet
depiction of Colonel Hassel's murder. Having discovered Gregor's
masquerade, Hassel runs to call the servants for help. The camera
tracks along with him, continues on when he stops to reach for the
cord, and remains on a close-up of his hand, the actions of which
reveal that Gregor has caught up with him.

The Black Room is not a masterpiece of originality, but its
story is fleshed out with mood, milieu, and characterisation, and
Karloff's accomplishments stand out sharply. The gothically degener-
ate Baron may be grouped with his most distinctive portraits, while
Anton is one of his earliest normal and sympathetic roles. And the

complex, but clear, Gregor-as-Anton variation is an even greater achievement.

Karloff spent most of October 1935 making *The Invisible Ray* for Universal, and it was released at the start of 1936. Again only his surname was used in advertisements, and he was billed in larger letters than his co-star Bela Lugosi. The two had been evenly matched in *The Black Cat, The Raven* was Lugosi's showcase, and now *The Invisible Ray* is dominated by Karloff. As Dr. Janos Rukh, he is so contaminated by a new element called Radium X that he glows in the dark and destroys any living thing that he touches. The film's opening, at Rukh's home in the Carpathian Mountains, is typically devoid of time-wasting. There are a few expository exchanges between Rukh's wife and his mother, and then visitors arrive to view a demonstration. Janos, informed of their presence by his wife, is first seen looking though a telescope with his face hidden; thus Karloff gets to make an "entrance" as he turns around to speak. His make-up is not unusual, consisting of a mustache and curly black hair, but these changes make him appear more vital and vigorous than usual. After he greets his guests, the film moves right to the demonstration, in which Rukh catches a beam of light from Andromeda, travels backward in time and space on it, and at a certain

Karloff in THE INVISIBLE RAY (frame enlargement)

Karloff with Bela Lugosi in THE INVISIBLE RAY

point turns to watch as the earth of centuries ago is struck by a meteor.

Karloff varies his performance several times during the film, and even in this opening sequence he moves from an initial burst of enthusiasm and anger, to a reserved greeting of the sceptics ("Sir Francis! To see you again after so many years is—interesting"), and finally to a calculatedly terse "That is all," after he has dumb-founded the guests. Rukh's personality is here firmly established: he is stubborn and determined about his work, and the fact that he invites his opponents to view his success indicates a certain vin-dictiveness. At first these qualities are virtues, since his energies are applied to a scientific enterprise possessing real grandeur. His geographic

Karloff's reaction to Lugosi's discovery of the antidote in THE IN-VISIBLE RAY (frame enlargement)

and professional isolation goes beyond the usual horror *cliché* because it is also psychological and emotional, and therefore helps to explain his impatience and inability to work with others. As his mother warns, "You're not used to people, Janos, you never will be. Your experiments are your friends. Leave *people* alone."

After discovering Radium X in the meteor that had landed in Africa, Rukh builds a machine that focuses its strength into a ray. The natives, frightened by smoke and sparks rising from a crevasse, threaten to leave, and so Rukh asserts himself by disintegrating a large boulder. This action and his manner during it reveal Rukh's enjoyment of power and his tendency to use force as a first, not last, resort. When he first discovers that his skin glows in the dark, Rukh says, "It's poisoned me," and he is right in two senses. Not only are his body and mind affected by Radium X, but it has poisoned his personal life by drawing him out of his safe scientific castle, and placing him in contact with people and their unpredictable actions. After Rukh has experienced complete success, everything around him starts falling apart in a reversal of the familiar Midas touch. He first realises that his presence is poisonous when he pets his dog and it dies; this is a literal echo of his psychological situation. From here on, his inability to deal with people and life escalates (as predicted by Madame Rukh).

Professionally, Rukh has never been accepted in scientific cir-
cles ("I believe I have even been called unorthodox"); romanti-
cally, he is mismatched with his wife and, despite her great respect
for Janos, she soon sends him a letter admitting her love for another;
his discovery is "stolen" from him by Dr. Benet (Lugosi), who
does not want to wait for his rival before beginning to help humanity, so both the element itself and full credit for its use are denied
Rukh. The combination of all these things, together with the effects
of the antidote developed by Benet, proves too much for Rukh,
and mental degeneration results. As this happens, Rukh's resentment and stubbornness are channeled into harmful acts. His venge-
fulness and tendency to employ force result in a plan to eliminate
all those who "came like thieves in the night to steal everything from
me." After faking his own death, he selects six statues at the church
where his "widow" has been re-married, and melts one after each
killing. When a party is given as a trap to lure him to the scene,
the fugitive arrives and kills Benet. At the last moment, Mme Rukh
knocks the vial of antidote from her son's hand. This brings Rukh
to his senses and he admits the rightness of her action. He then
jumps from a window, bursts into flame from within, and goes up
in a puff of smoke before reaching the ground. Here, Madame
Rukh's black-hooded cloak and contrasting white face evoke the traditional image of Death, which is what she represents to her son.

Superficially, Karloff's role is a precursor of his later Columbia
scientists who mean well but are forced by society to turn anti-
social. However, Janos Rukh is motivated less by outside forces
than by his own personality and background, and the "touch of
death" is less a cause of events than a literal image of what happens
to his life. The character is solidly written, and Karloff treats it
with the care it deserves through numerous changes of expression
in his face and voice. Near the beginning, when Benet admits that
having Rukh accompany him to Africa is an honour, there is a shot
of Karloff in which he raises his eyebrows slightly—Rukh's feeling
is controlled, but it is also precisely revealed. Two later scenes are
made moving by the distress and pain in Karloff's expressions: one
is the first time he examines his glowing face in a mirror, and
the other occurs when, just after discovering his problem, he forces
himself to send away his unknowing wife.

Although Rukh's personality grows less rational, Karloff's performance never loses such humanising details as his exasperation at
having to do such a mundane thing as pay rent to a talkative land-
lady. The performance, however, never becomes as "grand" as
it would have been if Lugosi had been given the role. Karloff even
underplays, with telling effect, his main confrontation with Benet
in Paris: as he walks around the medical office, Rukh's anger is

Karloff bent on revenge, in THE INVISIBLE RAY (frame enlargement)

held in and his politeness is cool, artificial, ironic. Unlike Griffin in *The Invisible Man,* whose sanity is also affected by a drug, Rukh is aware of the change at the same time as he is its victim. This knowledge increases the pathos of a situation that is typical of Karloff. Lugosi's characters are of another world, oblivious of or pleased by their strangeness, while Karloff's are earthy men who know that something unusual is happening and yet are tragically unable to prevent it.

During December and January, 1935/36, Karloff made *The Walking Dead* for Warner Brothers. This distinctive picture combined that studio's speciality—the gangster film—with the horror *genre,* and the two turned out to be fairly compatible. One of the company's top directors, Michael Curtiz, handled the film, and was reunited with Karloff after having worked with him briefly on *The Mad Genius;* the overall production was skilful, with atmospheric photography that includes some of Curtiz's large, Germanic shadows.

When a judge fails to acquit a racketeer, the gang has him killed and frames John Ellman* (Karloff) for the deed. Ellman is convicted, and electrocuted just as new evidence proves him innocent. His body is brought to the laboratory of Dr. Beaumont (Edmund

---

*The film itself is unsure whether the name is spelled with one "l" or two. The version seen in the credits and that shown in a newspaper headline during the film are contradictory.

Gwenn), who succeeds in bringing him back to life, but in a zombie-like state. Though he did not know it before death, Ellman is now aware that it was his lawyer who framed him. The doctor invites a number of people to hear the dead man, previously a pianist, perform; when Ellman stares intently at his enemies, they grow uncomfortable and leave. One by one these men die, but in each case the death is an accident that occurs as the individual backs away from the advancing Ellman: one falls on his own gun and is shot, another is hit by a train, and a third falls out of a window. Ellman eventually goes to a cemetery, where he is killed by the remaining gangsters (who then die themselves in a car accident).

The Walking Dead is actually a very quiet film, containing no overt "horror" scenes. Music is blended smoothly into the plot, with Ellman's piano-playing adding to the atmosphere and sensitivity. There are also mystic overtones, with Dr. Beaumont trying to find out what death is like but never quite getting an answer. Ellman's actions and manner, and the fact that he knows more than he did before death, create the impression that he is being used by some Higher Power to bring justice to the criminals. It is as though he has returned to haunt them in place of their missing consciences; "You can't escape what you've done," Ellman says while advancing toward one of the gunmen.

Karloff has little dialogue or action to perform, and his only unusual make-up is a streak of white in his hair, but still he dominates the film with unassertive authority, as his eyes bore into each of the gangsters. Once again Karloff is not playing a "monster," but rather a fall guy who is naïve and just a trifle bewildered by what has happened. He is more like Bateman (*The Raven*) than Hjalmar Poelzig (*The Black Cat*). Ellman enters the film after serving a ten-year prison sentence for second degree murder. Asked about the woman in that case, he explains, "It was my wife. I struck a man, but I didn't mean to kill him." He is honest, sincere, and naïve and does not even notice the frame-up in which he is caught. When Ellman returns to life with new knowledge, he is still bewildered. He knows that his lawyer is an enemy, yet when asked why he believes this, or whether he recalls anything about the Other World, he can only answer, "I—don't know."

Ellman's death house scene could easily have been maudlin or melodramatic, but Karloff's underplayed irony makes his lines moving. He refuses to shout or sob.

> *Ellman:* But you can't kill me for something I didn't do; you can't, I tell you, you can't. I don't want to die; I want to live.
> *Warden:* Well, Ellman, it's within my power to grant any last request you'd care to make.

Ellman: You take away my life, and offer me a favour in return. That's what I call a bargain.
Warden: Anything you want, within reason.
Ellman: Anything I want—I'll give you something easy, warden. I'd like music. Have you anyone here who can play a violin, or a cello?
Warden: Yes.
Ellman: I'd like him to play my favourite piece—as I walk out there. It'll make it easier. Is it such a strange request, warden? I always think of Heaven like that.

After being revived, and despite his compulsion to punish the gangsters, Ellman still remains gentle. Near the film's conclusion, he wanders for the second time into a cemetery, and when the doctor's assistant, Nancy, asks him why he returned there, he replies, "It's quiet. I belong here." Ellman is almost immediately shot by the lawyer, and because the bullet strikes his skull in the area of a brain-damaging blood clot, as he dies he may finally remember what occurred during death. Dr. Beaumont questions him about this in a scene which inevitably tells us very little, but is interesting in its moral overtones, its sensitivity, and its reserve.

Beaumont: Try to remember—you must!
Ellman: It's so strange, remembering.

Karloff with Addison Richards as the Warden in THE WALKING DEAD

Karloff with Marguerite Churchill in THE WALKING DEAD

Beaumont: What, John?

Ellman: All the things you wanted to know. How I knew I had been framed.

Beaumont: But how did you find out? You knew nothing before your execution. How do you know now?

Ellman: It's hard—to explain.

Beaumont: Try, John, try. That's why I brought you back from death.

Ellman: Leave the dead to their Maker. The Lord our God is a jealous God.

Beaumont: But John, what *is* death? Can't you put it into words? (*Thunder.*) Tell me—tell me, you must. What is death?

Ellman: I think I can. (*pause*) After the shock—

Beaumont: Yes—

Ellman: I seem—feel—

Beaumont: Yes—

Ellman: Peace—and—and— (dies)

(*A single violin starts the theme which Ellman had played on the piano, and which was associated with Heaven during the execution. Nancy cries quietly.*)

The Walking Dead was Karloff's last American horror film until

Son of Frankenstein. By 1936, the *genre* had developed unsavory connotations that bothered some audiences and producers. Universal tried to vary its product by basing *The Invisible Ray* on an outer-space, science-fictional premise, and then including a bit of jungle adventure. The last portion of that film is structured like a mystery, with several seemingly-inexplicable murders solved through the investigations of Dr. Benet: he photographs, in close-up, an eye of one of the victims, and discovers that it still retains its last image— that of Rukh's menacing face. But then he accidentally breaks the plate, destroying the proof that his rival is not dead. Benet finds more evidence when he notices a glowing handprint on another victim's throat. Eventually, like all good detectives, he plans to trap the murderer by calling together a group of people for a midnight meeting; this time, however, it is the potential victims rather than the suspects.

Universal also tried to give *The Invisible Ray* prestige by hiring an unusually prominent supporting cast (including Frank Lawton, who had played David Copperfield for M-G-M, Beulah Bondi, and Violet Kemble Cooper) , and by having the screenplay written by John Colton, whose work for the stage in the Twenties had included the adaptation of Somerset Maugham's story *Rain*, and the scandalous *The Shanghai Gesture*. To clinch the image, Universal added a dignified foreword to the film itself: "Every scientific fact accepted today once burned as a fantastic fire in the mind of someone called mad. Who are we on this youngest and smallest of planets to say that the INVISIBLE RAY is impossible to science? That which you are now to see is a theory whispered in the cloisters of science. Tomorrow these theories may startle the universe as a fact." The advertising department then attempted to gain general acceptance of the film with the claim, "Not a Horror Picture! But a Revelation in Thrills and Terrific Suspense."[88]

In *The Walking Dead*, Warners also made a film that was different from the popular conception of "horror," and one trade reviewer noted that "although the picture is up to previous Karloff efforts, the desired result is obtained without outright shocking."[15] But the studio ended up mishandling the film by exploiting it like just another fast-buck horror entry. Patrons and others were misled into their usual conditioned response to the *genre,* exemplified by one small-town exhibitor's opinion that it was "much too gruesome and unsavoury for good entertainment."[90] However, a Nebraska exhibitor did complain about the company's publicity campaign. "All of their advertising leads patrons to believe that it is a horror picture. The trailer has nothing in it except horror and even goes so far as to entirely misrepresent one of the best scenes in the picture. Karloff plays the role of a grossly wronged man who was brought back to life through no efforts of his own. At no time after his return does he show any signs of wishing to harm anyone except to bring to his enemies, the men who wrongfully sent him to the chair, the realization of their misdeeds and their stricken consciences brought about their own deaths. Karloff was a kindly man and, in his own way, loved his nurse, whom the trailer led us to believe was in terror when he was around."[89]

One of the factors that killed off the horror film cycle was undoubtedly the "too gruesome and unsavoury" attitude common among people of influence. Perhaps even more significant was the British censor's reaction against such films, and the resulting loss of income from the English market. Another reason was the takeover of Universal by a group of bankers in April 1936; this resulted in a complete executive reorganisation. Carl Laemmle, the company's founder, gave up his position as President, and Carl Laemmle, Jr. was replaced as Vice-President in charge of production. Bankers are notoriously wary of how they invest depositors' money, and the films of what was advertised as "the New Universal" lacked the imagination and creativity of the early Thirties, and reduced the studio's importance.

The *genre* still possessed some momentum, though, when *The Invisible Ray* and *The Walking Dead* were released early in 1936. In February, Karloff sailed to England, where he was scheduled to act in a Gaumont-British horror film. But before leaving America he signed to appear in several thrillers for Warners and Universal. One of those announced by Universal was called *The Man in the Cab*, and the actor, or his publicist, described it in the N.Y. "Evening-Journal": Karloff was to play a man experimented on by Professor Einmetz, who charges his subject with electricity, like a battery. When the professor is murdered, Karloff is convicted of the crime and sentenced to the electric chair, but of course this punishment doesn't have the expected effect. Karloff reported that the laboratory and prison sets were already being designed. "The studio electrical department has rigged up a huge, copper-sheathed chamber. In the middle of this room, standing upright on tall cement bases, are two big electric coils, as thick as barrels, and bigger than anything we had in *Bride of Frankenstein*. The coils toss sparks fifteen feet long, back and forth with a rip and snap like miniature thunderbolts. When the sparks contact at both coils, the flashes seem to revolve and it looks as though the coils were turning an electrical skipping rope. [The plan was for Karloff's make-up] to be the most ponderous I've ever worn on the screen—fifteen pounds heavier than the monster rig-out which weighed over eighty pounds. But very little . . . is to be visible. It will be worn mostly underneath my clothes and is to be made chiefly of metal and insulation. Some of it will be aluminum, other parts will be glass and still others, rubber and steel. This is because it must carry electric equipment so I can shoot sparks in every direction, like the rays of the sun."[63] Ultimately, Universal did film this as *Man Made Monster,* a 1941 vehicle for Lon Chaney, Jr.

During 1936, Gaumont-British imported several American stars, hoping to produce films with international appeal. Karloff was one of these, but although the company announced that he would appear in *Dr. Nikola* (from a novel by Guy Boothby), that picture was not made. Prior to sailing for England, the actor revealed that the film would be called *The Man Who Lived Again,* but all he knew about it was that no elaborate make-up was required. He spent eight days in New York City, in constrast to the two hours his schedule had allowed in 1933, so this time he managed to tour the city and attend a few plays.

The Man Who Changed His Mind (called *The Man Who Lived Again* in the U.S.) had its London *première* in the early autumn of 1936, and Gaumont-British released it in the States shortly after. Karloff portrayed Prof. Laurience, a scientist who learns how to transfer the energy of living brains from one body to another. His work is sponsored by Lord Haslewood, a wealthy newspaper publisher, but when the patron causes a premature disclosure of the work, Laurience is laughed off a speaker's platform and the publisher withdraws his support. Unbalanced by this, Laurience places the mind of his clever but crippled assistant in the body of Lord Haslewood (and, reciprocally, Haslewood's mind in the other's body). Then, because Dr. Clare Wyatt refuses his advances, Laurience places his own mind in the youthful body of her sweetheart, Lord Haslewood's son. At the end, the heroine runs the machines to get her lover back intact before Laurience dies.

According to one reviewer, "The change, effected with considerable display of electrical pyrotechnics and a volume of sound suggesting the ascent of many giant elevators and recorded by the sinking and rising of fluids in giant test tubes, is a striking, if crude, screen effect. It is most impressive, perhaps, in the original experiment with two chimpanzees: the amiable seeker of nuts in the scientist's pockets becomes a screaming and biting savage; the savage monk placidly seeks the nuts."[5] Old horror hand John Balderston worked on the script, and the director was Robert Stevenson, a young man who later came to Hollywood and gave a Gothic atmosphere to *Jane Eyre* (1944), and more recently made some of Walt Disney's better comic fantasies.

While in England, Karloff took the opportunity to captain a cricket team that played against the local one where he was living. Cricket had always been his favourite sport; in Hollywood, he often

A portrait dating from the mid-Thirties

played with his friend C. Aubrey Smith, and the two coached teams at U.C.L.A. Admitting that he was not a good player, Karloff commented, "I was just a happy rabbit, playing for the fun of the game."[81]

Before returning to America, Karloff signed for a second picture, this one with Twickenham films, and his wife Dorothy wrote to a group of their friends in the States that this "will keep us here longer than we had at first planned—probably three months. So, as a result, we are house-hunting these days. We drove through Surrey and Sussex with Sir John Pratt, Boris' brother, and Lady Pratt, through the most beautiful country, and ended up at an old Inn in Mayfield, where we sat before a roaring fire toasting ourselves, and drinking good English Ale—don't you envy us? It was a *real* English Inn—the kind you read about—and they are truly hospitable and filled with the atmosphere of good comfort."[2] A few days later they discovered just the right building: a three-hundred year old house in "the loveliest, tiniest village you can imagine."[2]

Karloff's second British film was *Juggernaut*, and it too opened in London during October 1936. It was not, however, as well received (at a trade screening, "there was an obvious and general disposition to take it as a burlesque"[4]). The film did not reach America until Grand National released it six months later, in April 1937. In it, Dr. Sartorius (Karloff) meets the young wife of an old but rich Englishman, and is offered £20,000 to arrange for the death of her husband. Needing the money to continue his experiments in finding a cure for paralysis, he agrees and becomes the couple's resident physician. Sartorius eventually kills the man with a hypodermic injection, only to discover that the widow's inheritance is small and under her stepson's control. The doctor then unsuccessfully tries to protect his investment by killing the son and a suspicious nurse; when the facts are discovered he poisons himself and, being very dedicated, takes the opportunity to dictate a subjective report on the drug's symptoms. A reviewer for the "Motion Picture Herald" found this to be "a study of a warped and repellant type."[4]

The horror cycle was now over, and when Karloff returned to America there were fewer jobs awaiting him. Still, he kept active in non-horror roles. In October 1936, he made *Charlie Chan at the Opera*, which was shown one month later but not officially released until January 1937. Karloff played Gravelle, an escaped lunatic who is really a famous baritone thought to have been burned to death in a dressing room fire years earlier. He has returned, seeking revenge on his unfaithful wife and her lover. Reviewers considered this the best of the Chan series to date—it is one of the few stories in which the detective is confronted with a worthy opponent—and their judgement still has validity.

It took less than the month of February 1937 for Universal to film *Night Key*, which reached theatre screens barely two months later. This is an efficient but minor mystery about Dave Mallory (Karloff), an elderly, trusting inventor whose burglar alarm system was stolen and marketed as Ranger Protection Services, with no royalties to its creator. Now, after fifteen years, Mallory has perfected an even better device just before his weak eyes give out entirely. Again, however, he is victimised by Ranger, who wants to keep the new invention off the market.

Mallory decides to force Ranger into adopting his new alarm by causing a loss of faith in the old one. Using his knowledge of the mechanism, he builds a neutraliser that matches the frequency of the current, so that the alarm circuit is not broken when a door is opened. Mallory's actions are merely mischievous; in one store he and Louie, a petty thief who has befriended him, open umbrella after umbrella and toss them all into a pile. When the Gang decides to move in, the inventor deliberately breaks the device and only builds another when his daughter is kidnapped and held hostage. While "The Kid" and his associates are out on a job, Mallory and Louie get rid of their guard by wiring his chair, and then escape by rigging up some sort of wand that spews forth little lightnings. At Ranger Headquarters, he reverses the alarm board so that all the warning lights go on. Then, when a circuit is completed (instead of broken), a light will go *off* and indicate where the robbery is occurring. The climax is complete with a shoot-out and car chase.

Though *Night Key* is neatly made, Karloff's performance is its only memorable aspect. In small ways, he creates a convincing image of old age: his make-up—white hair, mustache, glasses, and wrinkles at the cheeks—contributes to the effect, but it is his manner that establishes the character's reality. He is frail, with hands that shake and fingers that inadvertently rub together, and his body really seems to belong to an elderly man in the way he kneels down on the floor, or sinks into a chair as though immensely tired, or gropes

Karloff with Warner Oland in CHARLIE CHAN AT THE OPERA

about with stooped back and shoulders after breaking his glasses. The film is unimportant, but Karloff's performance is one of his most sympathetic in a starring role, and it illustrates his close observation of detail and ability to pantomime a great variety of actions.

Karloff's films for Warner Brothers were also part of a trend away from horror. The first of these was *West of Shanghai* (1937), which was originally called *The War Lord.* Its story was taken from an old play, *The Bad Man,* about a Mexican bandit, but the studio, inspired by such major releases as *The Bitter Tea of General Yen* (1932), *Shanghai Express* (1932), and *The General Died at Dawn* (1936), changed the play's locale to China and gave Karloff the leading role of a war lord named Wu Yen Fang (yes, Fang!). This character becomes involved with a group of Americans trying to out-cheat each other for the rights to a Chinese oil field, and in the process he plays both ends against the middle while also dodging provincial officials. Eventually, he is captured, and executed by a Nanking firing squad. Bosley Crowther, then beginning to review for the New York "Times," spoke of this character's "infinite gallantry and urbanity" and emphasised that "it is the subtly comic work of Mr. Karloff, the nice inflections, the war-lordly economy of gesturing, which gives to *West of Shanghai* its modest value as a comico-melodramatic, if not, perhaps, as a strictly contemporary document."[31]

In this film, Karloff's Chinese appearance was quite acceptable. "The make-up I wear naturally includes slant eyes, which are effected by a powerful constriction at the outer corners of each eye. This constriction, produced by invisible tape, causes the lower eyelid to press against the eyeball, distorting vision so badly that people only a short distance away appear as indistinct blurs."[100] He also had to put up with the inconvenience of having his eyebrows shaved off.

The Invisible Menace (1938) was Karloff's next film for Warners, and it too originally had another title—*Without Warning.* Completed by October 1937, this short (fifty-six minutes) murder mystery was released in January of the next year; it was written by Crane Wilbur and directed by John Farrow, the same team that had made *West of Shanghai.* This story takes place at an island military post, where a murder is committed. During the investigation it is discovered that Karloff, a civilian supervising some construction work for the Army, is also an ex-convict with good reason to have wanted the victim dead. He is arrested, but the guilty party turns out to be an officer who had tried to cut in on the dead man's gun smuggling racket. Back in the early Thirties, Karloff's best roles often had been casually dismissed by critics, but now—in these low-budget films—he was fully accepted, as stated in Bosley Crow-

Karloff (centre) in THE MYSTERY OF MR. WONG

ther's review of *The Invisible Menace*: "We can admire Mr. Karloff, as usual (everybody admires Mr. Karloff)."[30]

With horror movies still on the wane, Karloff found a new niche for himself as Mr. Wong, the Oriental detective, in a series made by Monogram Pictures. Five Wong films were made from 1938 to 1940, and though the studio was known for its tiny budgets, these pictures compare favourably with the Charlie Chan and Mr. Moto films then current. The first was *Mr. Wong, Detective,* and it appeared in September 1938, only a few months before the release of *Son of Frankenstein* revived the Monster and his *genre.* Still, Karloff continued to play the character in *The Mystery of Mr. Wong* (1939), *Mr. Wong in Chinatown* (1939), *The Fatal Hour* (1940), and *Doomed to Die* (1940).

Like other detective films, these pictures had interchangeable plots of minimal importance and originality. The main emphasis was always placed on the leading character, who had to be unusual and appealing enough to hold interest and attention by himself. In this department Charlie Chan is of course the champion, but among the challengers Mr. Wong, as played by Karloff, certainly holds his own. A scholar and criminologist, James Lee Wong possesses degrees from Heidelberg and Oxford, and is one of the five foremost authorities on just about anything. Karloff's make-up emphasised slanted eyes, a mustache, and slicked-down hair; though not extreme, these changes make him quite convincing. A dapper dresser, the lean Mr. Wong generally appears with hat, umbrella, suit, vest, tie, and button-hole carnation. In keeping with this image, his manner is dignified and austere, his comments are calm and a trifle wry, and he wears glasses for reading. Actually, he is the only controlled personality in these films, especially in contrast to the detective (Grant Withers) with whom he usually works. Withers, the cliched stupid policeman, is irritating and overly-excitable.

In *Mr. Wong, Detective,* our hero solves the murders of a chemical manufacturer and his two partners who had stolen the killer's formula and were making millions from it (shades of *Night Key* and Lugosi's *Devil Bat*). *The Mystery of Mr. Wong* (first scheduled as *Mr. Wong at Headquarters,* and filmed early in 1939) involves another murder, this one inspired by a rare Oriental jewel called the Eye of the Daughter of the Moon, which bears the curse of Emperor Hong Chong Chu! After catching the guilty person at a dinner party—it was a fellow criminologist, as a matter of fact— Wong has the jewel returned to China. A poisoned dart is used to kill a Chinese princess in *Mr. Wong in Chinatown* (made in the spring of 1939), and in *The Fatal Hour* (filmed in winter, 1939) Wong becomes involved with diamond smugglers and four more deaths. *Doomed to Die* (made in the summer of 1940) is a complicated tangle of steamship magnates, fires at sea, and unwelcome lovers; Wong doesn't even enter the story until fifteen minutes after its start. William Nigh directed all five films.

Devil's Island was finished by Warners at about the same time as the first Wong film, but it was not released until several months later (in January 1939). The picture was timely, in the light of a recent escape from that prison, the publication of the book "Dry Guillotine," an announcement that France would send no more convicts to French Guiana, and the later rescinding of that plan. Nonetheless, it lacked originality—*The Life of Emile Zola* (1937) and *The Prisoner of Shark Island* (1936) had similar situations— but it did function as a retrospective prison *exposé*; that is, it criticised what was wrong in the past, but stressed (in an introduction) that modern France was committed to "the task of remaking men, not breaking them." This statement and several deletions from the original version had been requested by the French government.

When a man convicted of treason is shot escaping from prison, Dr. Charles Gaudet (Karloff) is brought to attend him. Followed and interrupted by the police, the doctor refuses to leave the operation unfinished, and so is accused of aiding the escape. There is no one who can testify in his favour, since the patient died and all the others fled, so Gaudet is sentenced to ten years on Devil's Island. The context is different, but this development is very close to that in Karloff's later Columbia films: he is a well-meaning doctor who is interrupted during what others consider an "illegal" operation. His trial resembles a scene in *Before I Hang* (1940), only with an impassioned plea instead of a calm and quiet one.

Most of the film takes place in prison, under the rule of Colonel Lucien, a sadist who, evidently unhampered by a castration complex, uses a miniature guillotine for cutting off the ends of his cigars. His subordinates include some strait-laced French officers, and a prison doctor who ignores the obvious illness around him. Because Gaudet is a famous surgeon, he is removed from hard labour when the warden's daughter needs an emergency operation; the child is saved, and Madame Lucien finds herself becoming sympathetic to the prisoner's problem. With her help, Gaudet and others escape in a boat, bringing along proof that the officials are guilty of graft. Ironically, they run out of fuel and are rescued by a ship carrying new convicts to the island. Because Gaudet knows too much, the Colonel sentences him to death, but the combined efforts of a lawyer, the Minister of Colonies, and Madame Lucien result in a successful last-minute-rescue.

Considering that it was just a minor picture in the Warners schedule, *Devil's Island* was given a solid production, and its director (William Clemens) provided efficient camerawork and set-ups. It is a typical programmer in which the star is asked not to *act*, but to *be*; Karloff can contribute only a presence, not a performance, but he does that effectively with his haunted intonations and gaunt figure. The result is inoffensive if a viewer has an hour to spare and a tolerance of occasional lapses in interest.

Karloff also made his presence felt in other areas during this period. In January 1938, he appeared on NBC radio's "Chase and Sanborn Hour," reading Poe's "The Tell-Tale Heart" and bantering with hosts Edgar Bergen and Charlie McCarthy. (A few days later, an Iowa Senator named Herring claimed that this reading was one of the most gruesome things he had ever heard. He feared its effect on children, and suggested that the F.C.C. keep a close watch on radio!) Karloff later performed this reading on stage, and "Variety" reviewed the act from Detroit. As part of a fifty-five minute show that included a female psychic and assorted singers, dancers, and acrobats, Karloff was "a bit disappointing, chiefly through unfortunate selection of dramatic vehicle, Edgar Allan Poe's 'Telltale Heart.' Characterization is far from being the grotesque stuff patrons would naturally expect, but Karloff does nicely with that at hand."[139]

The actor was also hired to inaugurate the fourth year of "Lights Out," a late-night mystery show on NBC radio. He made five appearances in March-April 1938, and Arch Oboler, the show's author, prepared original half-hour melodramas especially for the star. The first, about a man who hears voices telling him to kill, was virtually a Karloff monologue and was quite well received.

Horror films were to gain new life a few months later, but though this second cycle produced several superior films, the sense of innocence, experiment, and discovery that characterised the works of the early Thirties would never be recaptured. That was when horror films reached their highest point of originality, and it was also the high point of Karloff's career; he was never again to have such a series of consistently superior roles, vehicles, and directors. Still, his presence continued to lend dignity to numerous otherwise-minor pictures, and occasional films (such as *The Body Snatcher*) deserve to be ranked among his best. Though Karloff's abilities did not decline, it might be said that the ideas and approaches and creators surrounding him did, too often isolating him as a movie's sole virtue.

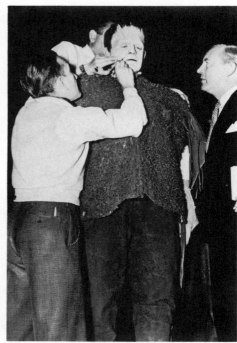

*SON OF FRANKENSTEIN: top, the Monster screams in agony at
the discovery of his friend's corpse; left, above, the Monster compares
his image to that of Wolf von Frankenstein, and below, he is repelled
by his own image; right, with Jack Pierce and Rowland V. Lee*

4. Monster into Father Figure (1939-1968)

At the end of 1938, Universal reissued *Frankenstein* and *Dracula,* and this double feature was so successful that the studio decided to father a *Son of Frankenstein.* During filming (on November 23, to be exact) Karloff's only child, Sara, was also born. By January 1939, *Son of Frankenstein* was in general release, and with it Universal inaugurated a whole new cycle of horror pictures. The last of the three major Frankenstein films, *Son* is a transitional work: though superficially resembling the classics of the early Thirties, it replaces poetic suggestion with a literal approach that caused a decline in both the series and the *genre.* Reminiscing years later about why he ceased playing the Monster after *Son,* Karloff claimed (with the clarity of hindsight) that he had anticipated this change. "I thought I could (and I was right as it turned out) see the handwriting on the wall as to which way the stories were going . . . that they would go downhill. There was not much left in the character of the Monster to be developed; we had reached his limits. I saw that from here on, he would become rather an oafish prop, so to speak, in the last act or something like that, without any great stature."[92]

The story of *Son* begins as Baron Wolf von Frankenstein (Basil Rathbone) returns with a wife and son to the town bearing his family name. Soon after, the shepherd-graverobber Ygor (Bela Lugosi) shows Wolf the unconscious Monster, and the doctor promptly decides to reanimate him, since "*that* would vindicate my father, and his name would be enshrined among the immortals." The attempt seems to fail, but later the Monster recovers and, under Ygor's influence, kills some of the jurors who had sentenced the graverobber to death. Wolf eventually shoots Ygor in self-defence, and the Monster vengefully kidnaps the doctor's son. In the final confrontation, the Monster stands in the laboratory with the boy trapped under one foot. Wolf, grabbing a nearby chain, swings down Tarzan-style and knocks the Monster into a convenient pit of boiling sulphur. The family then donates its castle to the town, and leaves.

In this film, not only is the Monster of secondary importance, but he has lost some of his humanity. When Ygor sends him out to kill the jurors, the creature is nearly an unfeeling automaton with no will of its own. Karloff still uses the same rapid movements as he had in the first two films, but his thick, woolly garment makes him look immobile. Here the Monster is on the verge of being just another goon, a muscleman of horror tossing a few trees around. Wolf's son, in describing the giant who had visited him, is the first of thousands to use the stifflegged shuffle that has become permanently identified with the Monster.

Only two scenes in *Son* are consistent with the earlier conception of the Monster. In one, repelled by his appearance in a mirror, he pulls Wolf over as a comparison, and again turns away from his own reflection. This shows that some feeling still exists beneath the ugly exterior—but such self-discovery had already occurred in *Bride*, and the Monster's open-handed, imploring gesture is also familiar. Just before this incident, Wolf panics when he first sees the Monster conscious; as if to cheer him up, the creature awkwardly pokes Wolf's face into a smile, then he starts to strangle the doctor, and finally he steps aside and puts a hand to his own head as though seized by dizziness, a headache, or nervous tension. These unmotivated actions make little sense and weaken the episode. The second significant scene occurs when the Monster discovers the dead body of Ygor, his only friend. He examines the corpse uncertainly, but when his hand touches blood he looks at it, then rears back and screams; the moment is moving and chilling—and unforgettable. Then, out of rage and sorrow, he furiously heaves giant pieces of laboratory equipment into the bubbling sulphur pit. For the last time in the Universal series, the Monster—a fast-moving creature out of control and impossible to evade—is really frightening.

Except for these two segments, Karloff is given very little to do and even less chance to act. As he correctly described, the tendency here is to use the Monster as a dormant prop that is reanimated at the last minute, only to be destroyed a short time later. *Son's* script blocks out a plot that would be used in most subsequent Frankenstein sequels: the Monster is taken to or discovered by a scientist, who becomes obsessed with the idea of bringing him back to active life. In *Son*, although the Monster is important to the unfolding of the plot, he remains unconscious for nearly half the film, and even afterwards receives limited footage. The filmmakers appear to be far more interested in Wolf, Ygor, and Inspector Krogh (Lionel Atwill).

Son also contains other, smaller deviations from the original concept which lead toward the later, lesser films. The setting is now clearly Germany, rather than the anonymous, Gothic environment created by James Whale. The distant tower that had been the laboratory is now located near the castle, and there is a new sulphur pit that has supposedly existed since the days of the Romans. A change that considerably limits the Monster's humanity is the discovery that he is indestructible. In *Bride,* there was a natural explanation for his return. Here, no attempt is made to explain how the Monster survived the explosion at the end of *Bride.* His unconscious state is not even a result of that event, but rather is the aftereffect of being struck by lightning while out on one of Ygor's errands. The first mention of indestructibility is Ygor's rather unscientific claim: "He cannot be destroyed, cannot die! Your father made him live for always!" This is followed by Wolf's examination of the Monster, during which his great size is explained as some sort of hyperpituitary problem, his heart (containing two bullets) is found to beat more than 250 times per minute, and his blood cells are different from those of a normal human ("as if they had a conscious life of their own"). Wolf concludes that his father had used cosmic rays, "which neither he nor anyone else in the world of science at that time even knew existed. Of course since then many of our most profound scientists have come to believe that these rays are actually the very source of life itself. This creature is indeed a monster. There's not one part of his physical being that's like that of human beings. From his warped brain down to the tiniest argumentative cell of his huge carcass, he's unearthly." Unfortunately, this superhuman quality contradicts the original vision of the Monster as a symbol of "humanity"; it limits what can be done with him, and paves the way for the subsequent series of facile re-reanimations.

Still, the script does employ new concepts and characters instead of rehashing what had been used before, a tendency that would begin when *Ghost of Frankenstein* (1942) borrows from *Son.* An especially imaginative creation is Atwill's Inspector Krogh, with his artificial arm and vivid description of having the original "torn out by the roots" by the Monster. The production given *Son* is dignified and intelligent, substantial and elaborate, and the settings, while inconsistent, are imaginatively grotesque. Whale's individual style has been replaced with the more ordinary, yet careful and discreet, work of Rowland V. Lee. The two murders, for example, are depicted indirectly. In one, the Monster plucks his victim off a wagon, and a horse is shown casually turning his head to watch the killing. The other death is shown in full, but via the characters' shadows on a wall. Lee, whose work is competent but not creative, must however be blamed for not varying the film's pace, for ignoring the possibilities in scenes between the Monster and the boy, and for Basil Rathbone's embarrassingly hysterical acting later in the film.

Though *Son* received an "A" production, most critics continued to look down on horror movies. Even "Variety," which tried to be fair, misinterpreted the concept, saying that Karloff "has his Mon-

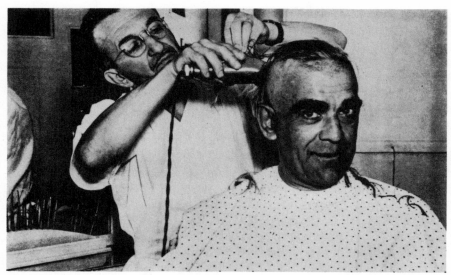

Karloff with Jack Pierce preparing for THE TOWER OF LON-DON

ster in former groove as the big and powerful brute who crushes and smashes victims."[119] But how could a reviewer be blamed if even the film's main character notes, "It wasn't my father's fault that the being he created became a senseless, murderous monster." The script seems written from the viewpoint of the misguided towns-people, rather than from approximately that of the Monster as in *Frankenstein* and *Bride*. Therefore, *Son of Frankenstein* is a big, solid, and respectable picture that does excessive damage to the subtler qualities of the Frankenstein story.

Later in 1939, Universal again teamed Karloff with Rathbone and Lee. This picture was *Tower of London,* an extreme case of injecting horror material into a different context, in hopes of gaining respectability and wider audiences. This became a trend in the Forties, when horror was often diluted with songs, comedy, history, or rational explanations. To the story of Richard III (Rathbone), *Tower* adds the fictional character of Mord the Executioner (Karloff). Conforming to the usual legends of Richard's villainy, the film is made interesting only by the strength of the actors' personalities. Rathbone's Richard is hard but human, a master of dissimulation whose hunchback is minimised by the studio make-up man, and Karloff cuts a fine bald-headed and club-footed figure as the sadistic headsman who runs the Tower's torture chamber and obeys Richard slavishly. A young Vincent Price also appears, as the weak and effete Duke of Clarence.

Why is it that Mord, a minor character, is almost the only one to arouse a viewer's sympathy, even though he clearly enjoys his villainy? The reason is perhaps that the others are sane enough to know what they are doing, to recognise their weaknesses, and to scheme toward some goal. Unlike them, Mord acts instinctively and is incapable of comprehending, much less controlling, his desires and destiny. To Richard, he says, "You are more than a Duke, more than a King—you are a God to me," and Richard replies, "Crookback and drag-foot! Misfits, eh? Well, what we lack in physical perfection we make up here, eh? [pointing at his brain]," establishing a reason for the relationship between these physically warped but otherwise dissimilar men. Because deformity is offered as a motive for violence, Mord is akin to Bateman and the Monster, but this aspect is only hinted at. Later, Mord asks for permission to fight in a battle. "Let me go with you. I've never killed in *hot* blood. It must be different, more—more exciting. Many men are killed in battle. Please let me go!" This speech suggests that there is more to Mord than the scriptwriter bothered to develop.

Between *Son* and *Tower*, Karloff made three other films. Two of them were in Monogram's Mr. Wong series (*The Mystery of Mr. Wong* and *Mr. Wong in Chinatown*); the third was *The Man They Could Not Hang*, filmed in July and released in August 1939. He followed this with three other Columbia pictures (*The Man with Nine Lives*, *Before I Hang*, and *The Devil Commands*) and two for other studios (*Black Friday* and *The Ape*), all of which were distressingly similar. Each employs the same basic situation: Karloff is a middle-aged or elderly scientist, a kind man working for the good of humanity on some experiment generally considered radical. The authorities do not see things his way, and because of accident or an outsider's stupidity, the experiment goes awry and Karloff is executed for murder. Revived by his own apparatus, he takes several lives through revenge or an excess of scientific zeal, but ends up regretting his actions and dying a final death. Three of the films follow this pattern closely, and the others offer only superficial variations.

In *The Man They Could Not Hang*, Karloff is Dr. Savaard, a professor-scientist who has invented a mechanical heart. A student volunteers to test it, and so death must be induced before the new heart can restore life, but the police interrupt and refuse to let the operation be completed. Convicted of murder, Karloff wills his body to another student, vows vengeance, and is executed. Returned to life by the student, he kills six members of the jury that had sentenced him, but when his daughter accidentally dies, his revenge goes sour and, after reviving the girl, he commits suicide.

Nick Grinde directed and Karl Brown wrote *The Man They Could Not Hang*, and since they did the same for *The Man with*

Karloff with (at right) Ann Doran, in THE MAN THEY COULD NOT HANG

Nine Lives (1940), it is no surprise that the films are similar. In that story, Dr. Kravaal (Karloff) is working on a way to arrest cancer and prolong life by freezing the patient into a state of suspended animation. Naturally, he is interrupted and held in custody until he produces the patient's body, but when he does so the village doctor declares that the man is dead and Karloff is charged with murder. By accident, he and four others are trapped in his freezer, and they are not discovered and thawed out until ten years later. The patient's angry nephew then destroys Karloff's formula for keeping a body alive while frozen; trying to save his work, Karloff shoots the youth and again faces arrest, so in order to experiment while the formula is still fresh in his mind, he refuses to let anyone leave and uses his prisoners as guinea pigs. Just after he successfully tests the gas on the heroine, the police arrive and kill him. To give some individuality to this carbon copy, the writer structured *Nine Lives* from the point of view of Dr. Tim Mason, a young scientist interested in the missing Karloff. On his vacation, Mason and the heroine make a pilgrimage to Karloff's home, where they fall through the floor and enter his secret laboratory. Here Karloff is found encased in ice, and after being thawed out he brings everyone up to date on his story. From then on, the picture remains in the "present."

Before I Hang (1940) also was directed by Grinde, from an original story co-authored by Brown. Sentenced to death for the mercy killing of a patient, Dr. Garth (Karloff) continues his work with the help of the prison doctor (Edward van Sloan). His aim is to find a serum that will nullify old age, and since he is scheduled to die anyhow, he uses himself as a subject. After his sentence is unexpectedly commuted to life, he finds that the serum has made him younger—but it also causes him at times to lose control. He kills van Sloan, and then murders a prisoner, blaming him for the first deed. Considered a hero, Karloff is praised and later pardoned. Once free, he volunteers to make three old friends younger, but they reject the offer. After killing two of them, Karloff realises during a period of lucidity that he has a problem, heads for the prison, suffers a relapse, and finally is shot by a guard. His daughter and her boy-friend, however, vow to carry on his work.

These films signal both an advancement and a decline in the horror genre. They are repetitious, cheap, and peopled with mostly minor performers; they are directed in a steadfastly stiff and unimaginative manner. And, perhaps most significantly, they bring down to earth-level what had previously attained heights. It was inevitable that time would evolve a new outlook on the experimenter; Doctors Savaard, Kravaal, and Garth are a step closer to the scientists in *2001: A Space Odyssey* (1968), in which the Technician has overshadowed the Dreamer. True, they are still outsiders and viewed as slightly "different," but they are no longer passionate and individualistic giants. They still strive to achieve the unthought-of, but their vision is bounded by practical minds and aged, vulnerable bodies. The films' attitude is expressed by a hospital administrator in *Nine Lives:* "The day of the lone wolf experimenter is dead. Vast organisations are today fitted with every conceivable device to check, test, prove, and verify every step of a new treatment. And that, Mason, is what we are going to do with your frozen therapy—turn it over to an unbiased staff of experts to re-perform all your experiments and check their independent findings with yours."

Frankenstein was interested in the audacity of creating life, the reasons for doing so, and the results of success. It was not concerned with exactly how to go about it. In these Columbia films, the larger issues are skirted in favour of the specific methods for accomplishing a lesser, more reasonable feat. A mechanical heart was conceivable in 1939, especially in the light of a 1936 kidney transplant, and in 1969 a man survived for 63 hours with only an artificial heart at work. Also during the Thirties, two doctors experimented with the freezing of animals, and today the Cryonics

Society has taken a leaf out of Kravaal's book. There is not, however, any sign of a youth-inducing serum in the works.

But at least these Columbia films avoid the "mad scientist" *cliché*, thanks to scripts that establish the main character as a dedicated and sane man who for some reason (often, in context, a justified one) develops a distorted sense of values. Dr. Kravaal, for example, feels that the potential benefit of his discovery is so great that risks should be taken and sacrifices made. Still, his aim remains unselfish and the logic of his coldly objective outlook is clear. Similarly, the killings in *Before I Hang* are caused by something outside Dr. Garth's personality; since the blood of a multiple murderer had been used in the serum, its effect is not really Garth's fault. Unfortunately, this makes the doctor a passive victim and limits the dramatic conflict: there is no uncertainty within Garth, and as soon as his lucid side realises what his "Mr. Hyde" has been doing, he tries to turn himself in.

The director, intentionally or not, avoids outright horror. His effects are muted, with mood and atmosphere limited to an occasional bit of flickering firelight, or a straightforward shot of Karloff being overcome by the "urge." *Before I Hang*, for instance, ends quietly, without a big crescendo, but because everything is shallowly developed, the conclusion is uninvolving. When the direction is inconsequential, the star must, by himself, command attention. Karloff is the kind of actor who can survive without skilled support, and these pictures rely almost entirely on his presence for whatever subtlety they possess. In *Before I Hang*, he uses certain mannerisms to indicate that Dr. Garth is about to change. "Something terrible happens," he says, as one hand moves to the back of his neck. "Something that I can't control," he adds, while unknowingly taking a handkerchief out of his pocket and twisting it. In these roles, Karloff usually employed a variation of his make-up for *Night Key*. In *The Man with Nine Lives* he is visually convincing with round spectacles, a white beard and moustache, and a shock of hair across his forehead. And it is evident in the film's numerous long shots that stage experience had given him "presence" and the ability to control his body and use it expressively; even when standing still, he is physically "in character" and visually dynamic, while the other actors seem to have stepped aside until they are needed. If nothing else, and often there is nothing else, these movies offer the sight of a thoroughly professional performer hard at work on inferior material.

The remaining Columbia film is *The Devil Commands* (made in December 1940 and released two months later). This story retains the dedicated scientist who loses control of his experiment, but now he is trying to contact the dead. The method Dr. Blair

(Karloff) devises for speaking with his late wife involves sensitising human minds with high frequency radiation, and then using them like tubes in a radio receiving set—a none-too-convincing way for the script to combine science and the occult.

The early scenes are the most pleasant and natural, establishing a relaxed relationship between Blair and his wife, and with Karloff projecting an aura of irony with his associates, who discourage his plans: "We don't know what evil may be lurking behind the veil." "This is not science!" "There are things human beings have no right to know." Karloff replies, "Poor, frightened little people! I don't need you. I don't need anybody!" He's right to feel superior, because the script is completely one-sided. Blair then moves to a large country house and teams with a medium, Mrs. Walters, who for some unexplained reason believes that "if you can do what you're trying to do, you'll own the world," and is determined to be in on the deal.

Under Mrs. Walters's influence, Karloff reluctantly becomes more and more enmeshed in evil. When a man working with them is seriously injured, he says, "We can't hide him. He has to have care!" But Mrs. Walters convinces him that that would stop the experiments. Later, a snoopy housekeeper is accidentally killed and, on Mrs. Walters's advice, the conspirators arrange for her to be found at the foot of a cliff. Says Blair, "We could have told them it was an accident. Now we're as guilty as though we planned her death." Near the end, when the hero discovers that corpses are being used as tubes in this radio, Karloff hangs his head slightly, as though realising for the first time the shamefulness of what he has done by seeing it through the eyes of another. But he tries to experiment once more, and this time is killed in the attempt.

Like the other Columbia films, *The Devil Commands* tries to be a horror picture while denying the existence of an Unknown. Near the start, Blair states that his aim is to "wipe out the horror that superstition conjures up out of fear of darkness." Later, he declares, "This is science, Mrs. Walters! There's nothing of the occult about it." Yet the situations and handling are definitely intended to appeal to a viewer's fascination with the mysterious. Unlike the others in the series, though, this picture has a director, Edward Dmytryk, who reveals a sense of visual form in his use of close shots, and of the foreground to frame the action and give it depth. Also, the script implies (or sidesteps) the theme of Blair being trapped between two forceful women: his wife and Mrs. Walters. And of course there is Karloff's usual fine performance, as he progresses from a happy, moderately youthful man with black hair and moustache, to an older one with wrinkles in a greying, worn face, and with the stooped body of a sleepwalker who is alive only in the eyes.

Karloff with Stanley Ridges in BLACK FRIDAY

Between these films, Karloff made two features that are similar to the Columbia quartet. The first, *Black Friday*, was filmed and released early in 1940 by Universal, and Karloff again played a kindly college professor whose experiment goes out of control. As with *The Man with Nine Lives* and *The Devil Commands,* the story is told in flashbacks, this time via the diary of Dr. Sovac (Karloff), who gives it to a reporter while walking to the electric chair.

When a wildly-driven car injures George Kingsley, a professor of English literature, Karloff concludes that it would be tragic for the injured driver, a gangster, to live if Kingsley dies, so he gives the stranger's brain to his friend. Speculation about the effects of a brain transplant can be fascinating: Which personality would dominate? How much might be remembered from each life? *Black Friday* arouses this interest, but gratifies it only through the familiar Jekyll-Hyde situation in which Kingsley occasionally "becomes" the gangster, Red Cannon, in manner and memory. Another equally ordinary plot development involves $500,000 that Red had hidden before his death. Karloff wants the money so he can build an experimental laboratory, but a gangster named Marney (Bela Lugosi) is also after it. A further complication is Red's determination to

Karloff in THE APE

get revenge on the remaining members of his gang. Several deaths result, the money is found, and Kingsley returns to his classes—until once again he comes under Red's spell, while delivering a lecture, and Karloff is forced to shoot him, for which he goes to the chair.

In *Black Friday*, it is Stanley Ridges who must give a multi-levelled performance as George Kingsley (a role originally conceived for Karloff), and he does a good job, though without the intensity that Karloff would have contributed. The latter rounds out the less complex character of Sovac by including actions and glances and expressions—such as his manner of lighting a cigarette, or the way he surreptitiously looks at Kingsley to check on his condition—that make the man live. Overall, the film is sympathetic, somewhat absurd, and disappointingly minor.

Karloff's last film in this group was Monogram's *The Ape* (1940). He plays Dr. Adrian, who is unfairly gossiped about for "giving Red Creek a bad name." Actually, he is kind and gentle, but so serious about his work that he makes everyone else uneasy. He is especially kind to his crippled neighbour, Frances, because his own daughter and wife had died of polio, and he has spent the past ten years seeking a cure for that disease. When an ape escapes during a circus fire, his injured trainer is taken to Karloff. Seeing

Karloff in THE FATAL HOUR (with Grant Withers at left)

this as a chance to get the human spinal fluid needed for his serum, the doctor lets the man die. The serum is given to Frances and it works, but more is needed. So Adrian kills the ape and, dressed in its skin, commits murder for the fluid. Eventually he is shot while on a raid and his formula dies with him, but at least Frances is cured.

This basic plot about someone who kills people to get their "precious bodily fluids" and then needs more and more was often used during the Forties, although it wasn't fresh then, either. Most of the time it failed to convince, and *The Ape* didn't break this pattern. Filled with rear projection backgrounds and stock circus footage, its sole point of interest is the presence of Karloff, who in his now-familiar spectacles, white hair, and moustache somehow seems believable despite a script loaded to excess with awkward expository dialogue.

In these movies, the lead characters are no longer men far above the average; they are normal people who simply run into unexpected technical problems, and they never come within shouting distance of being classically tragic heroes. The films contain enough entertainment, intelligence, and reserve for an occasional hour's diversion, but they offer little else except a sense of how the social attitude toward science had changed in less than ten years. For Karloff, this batch of consistently minor films proves that he was more than capable of surviving the incompetence of others, and of bringing individuality and subtlety (on a human if not an intellectual level) to *cliché*-ridden characters.

In addition to his kindly-scientist roles, 1940 provided Karloff with two more cases as Mr. Wong (*The Fatal Hour* and *Doomed to Die*), a final film for Warner Brothers (*British Intelligence*), and one for RKO (*You'll Find Out*). *British Intelligence*, set during the first World War, gave him the non-horror role of a German spy posing as a butler in the home of a British cabinet member. When the film was shown at New York's Globe Theatre, the audience was "fascinated by the spy antics and outspoken with 'Bronx Cheers' during German sequences."[28] *You'll Find Out* illustrates how depleted horror movies had become. Karloff, Lugosi, and Lorre all appear in it, but the star of this comedy-mystery-musical is bandleader Kay Kyser. Most of the film is an inconsequential reprise of the old plot about a rich woman being conned by a phoney spiritualist (Lugosi) in league with a phoney scientist (Lorre) and the family doctor (Karloff). There is never any suggestion of a real supernatural, and the audience gets its kicks from Kyser's mockery of the occult: when Lugosi asks for some mood music, the bandleader offers a circus march.

With thoughtful and original horror films no longer being made, Karloff's opportunities grew limited. Clearly needing a change of

pace, he returned to the stage, only now as a star who could headline a Broadway production. The play which turned up was *Arsenic
and Old Lace,* and Joseph Kesselring's comedy about murder was
the perfect vehicle for Karloff. In 1940 its approximation of black
humour seemed radical, and critic Joseph Wood Krutch wondered
whether the public's laughter, indicated a "moral degradation."[65]
But Karloff bought about $5,000 worth of stock in the production.
Since *Arsenic* was an instant hit, he regained his investment in three
weeks, and eventually earned a profit of several hundred percent—all
in addition to his salary as an actor.

For some time, producers had been urging Karloff to capitalise
on his movie fame by starring in a Broadway play. "But I wouldn't
stand for that. Who am I to get a billing like that? I am just a provincial actor, unsure of myself, and I may be a complete flop. It
frightens me—the thought of facing that opening night audience."[117]
Even so, "in the back of every actor's head is the notion that he's
no success until he's had a Broadway smash."[18] During the first
days of rehearsal, Karloff feared the worst. He arrived at the theatre
after an all-night flight from California, whereupon "they handed
me a script, and we did something I'd never done in stock or
repertory—we sat down, cast and director together, and read cold
turkey. I was so tired, and so frightened of my New York role,
that I began to stutter—something that always besets me when I'm
tired. I rehearsed in stutters for three days, continually thinking
that it would cure itself. But instead, it grew worse.

"The third night I wandered the streets of Manhattan wonder-
ing what to do. I thought I'd have to walk up to the management
and say, 'I'm very sorry. I've made a mistake, and so have you.
I've got to get out of your play. Do I owe you anything?' I walked
some more and thought, 'If I do that, honest though it is, I've
certainly had it in New York and haven't done myself an awful
lot of good in Hollywood either. Somehow I've got to go through
with the play. At 5:30 AM I returned to my hotel, catnapped
briefly, then went to rehearse. I'd always stuck on the word 'Come'
in my first line. Now I walked on, took a deep breath and said,
'Come in, doctor.' Not a stutter. By that evening all was OK."[61]

After a ten-day tryout in Baltimore, the play opened at New
York's Fulton Theatre (where Lugosi had played in "Dracula") on
January 10 1941. Karloff rapidly re-discovered his fondness for live
performances: "An audience is wonderful after the cold camera.
If you're playing it decently you get an immediate response and you
gain momentum; if there's no response you know it, and you can
get back on the right track. In a sense, the audience directs you.
And it's a good director."[72] He was also pleased that his role was
not the most important one in the play, since responsibility for

success or failure did not rest solely on his shoulders. "The character itself is really so masterfully conceived by the author that the audience is practically at my mercy from the moment of my first entry. It would be better for my professional pride, as a matter of fact, if it were a far harder characterisation. I'm surrounded with so many dramatic safeguards in the form of lines, situations and business that the thing is practically a pushover."[18]

This old dark house story about a crazy family is played for farce, rather than subtle shivers. It exemplifies how fully Karloff, in developing a household name, had evolved into his own *cliché*: the play's basic concept and many of its specific jokes rely on the public's knowledge of his image. In fact, dialogue and stage directions specify that an alcoholic plastic surgeon has made Jonathan Brewster's face resemble that of the real-life Karloff. Since everyone had become more aware of the actor than of his characters, the only practical solution was to roll with the punch and accept the new situation. Luck was with him, because *Arsenic and Old Lace* allowed him to spoof his image while also using it. The play does not condescend to what it satirises; instead, the character of Jonathan and the situations involving him are handled quite straight. The menace he presents is real and undeniable. What has happened is that the kind of character associated with Karloff has been transferred almost intact to this play, with the tone changed by a conscious acknowledgment of the Karloff image and all it evokes. This allows Karloff to arouse a few shivers that might otherwise have become snickers of superiority. By anticipating viewer reaction and making his own references to the *cliché*, the playwright lets his audience enjoy an "inside joke," and Karloff can set about his intended slow torture of Mortimer Brewster in deadly earnest.

While Jonathan, the epitome of a traditional villain, is quite aware of the difference between good and evil, his kindly aunts see themselves as blithely innocent. They view their plying lonely old men with poisoned elderberry wine as a charitable activity. Jonathan is shocked to discover their accomplishments, and even more disturbed to learn that they have killed as many people as he has—twelve. The professional and the middle-class amateurs have exactly equal results, except that Jonathan is recaptured, while the two women remain completely "innocent" to themselves and to others. Clearly, everyday people can commit, without any sense of evil, crimes which would repel them if attributed to known villains.

Karloff was scheduled for a leave of absence from the play in June 1941, to make a picture for Columbia, but *Arsenic* was so popular that the film was postponed until February, and then again until June, 1942. In order to keep Karloff, the show's producers had to pay a cash settlement to Peter Lorre, his scheduled co-star, for the time he had relinquished. During this long New York run, Karloff appeared on radio's "Inner Sanctum" series, and played Santa Claus at a hospital Christmas party for Lower East Side children. In 1942, he was an air-raid warden in New York City, and Nancy Farrell recalled working with him: "As Karloff entered, he said, 'Good evening. I've brought my *suppah*.' His voice, with its variety of pitch and its resonance, was friendly and reassuring . . . In the air raid post, Karloff kept on his conservative coat of good British tweed. He wore rimless glasses. He looked thin and not especially tall. He urged us two wardens to hurry home and assured us he was glad to go on duty early . . . I felt that he would rather be an air-raid warden in London and that he was imposing on himself the same discipline that he would have observed in the blitz."[37]

In June 1942 the original cast of *Arsenic* moved to the West Coast, where Karloff fulfilled his Columbia commitment. The movie he made that summer was *The Boogie Man Will Get You,* directed by Lew Landers (who had directed *The Raven* as Louis Fried-lander). An imitation of *Arsenic,* it was amusing despite a lack of originality. Larry Parks played a "normal" young man who en-counters a group of eccentrics when his ex-wife buys an authentic Colonial tavern and plans to turn it into a modern inn. Back in his *Man They Could Not Hang* make-up, Karloff is Nathaniel Billings, an engaging and moderately befuddled Professor of Bio-chemistry who conducts basement experiments on traveling salesmen, trying to turn them into eternally young and disease-immune Super-men; the failures are stored in a refrigerated wine cellar. Peter Lorre plays the local mayor-coroner-sheriff-moneylender-justice of the peace who helps the professor, since success will aid our side in the war effort. The film offers very little, but it is inevitably well-played by the two leads, who are obviously enjoying themselves. Karloff in particular seems to relish this change to a light role, even though it involves giving comic emphasis to a characterisation he had pre-viously declined to mock. Charmingly and impractically idealistic, he is oblivious of any moral problem caused by the deaths of his subjects. Typical is his detached reaction when one man falls dead: "Cold as a mackerel. Dear, dear, dear. I wonder what could have gone wrong this time." Then he writes in his record book, "Results negligible." Lorre is equally amusing as an eccentric who carries a small cat around in his inside coat pocket. At the end, the dead bodies turn out to be in a state of suspended animation, and Kar-loff is taken to an asylum—which is run by Lorre, so all is well. The comedy is derivative, wacky, forced, and sometimes successful, not unlike a skit in a television variety show.

His filming commitment out of the way, Karloff began a sixty-six-week tour with "Arsenic and Old Lace." He also visited the Pacific

Karloff with Margaret Lindsay in BRITISH INTELLIGENCE

Islands, to appear in a G.I. production of the play for Major Maurice Evans. Altogether, he logged over 1,400 performances and spent a total of three years as one of the Brewsters. While appearing in "Arsenic," Karloff edited (for World Publishing Company) an anthology entitled "Tales of Terror." This well-selected group of fourteen "horror" stories appeared in 1943, and boasted such distinguished authors as Faulkner, Conrad, O. Henry, Poe, Bierce, and Stoker. In his introduction, Karloff described the book's orgin. "An old friend of mine, Edmund Speare, a college professor of English Letters and now, to my undoing, a publisher's editor as well, suggested that I help in compiling an anthology of terror stories. His bait was: 'It'll be amusing to have a collection of bogey stories selected by a professional bogey man.'" Not realising the amount of work involved, Karloff agreed to read whatever stories Speare suggested and then say "yes" or "no" to them. "We exchanged dozens of letters, conferred into early morning hours in various cities where I was on tour, and in a fine frenzy of egomania I was merrily lopping off the literary heads of my betters. I hoped it would go on forever."[60]

Since "Tales of Terror" was a success, World decided to issue a sequel. This volume, called "And the Darkness Falls," was over six hundred pages long—double the size of its predecessor—and

Karloff with Peter Lorre in THE BOOGIE MAN WILL GET YOU

Karloff edited it while on the road with "Arsenic." "The publishers sent me boxes of books while we moved from town to town on the tour—and I would read through a volume and select a story to go into my collection. It was quite a task but great fun."[94] The final choice of sixty-nine stories and poems produced a wide-ranging anthology of greater scope than most such: included were tales by Yeats, Turgenev, de Maupassant, Galsworthy, Maugham, Crane, and Gogol, as well as Algernon Blackwood, H. P. Lovecraft, Lord Dunsany, and August Derleth. The book, which appeared in 1946, is permanent evidence of its editor's literary alertness and gentle frankness. His few sentences introducing a story by Frederick S. Greene are perhaps typically concise and informative. "Greene can upon occasion exhibit a directness and power in telling a horror tale that is almost classical in its logical unfolding. That was my reason for choosing 'The Black Pool' for this collection. The writing is a little florid, and I must apologize for saying that some of the sentiments expressed are a bit schoolboyish. Nevertheless, there is an original plot, well-handled suspense, and a natural denouement. It is a truly gripping tale with three good shocks in it!"[59]

Early in 1944, after a three-year hiatus broken only for *The Boogie Man,* Karloff returned to Hollywood and to Universal. On arrival, he declared that while he was willing to accept villain roles, he would no longer play heavily made-up monsters, and in his subsequent films he stuck to this rule. The studio immediately cast him in *The Climax* (1944), an unusually lavish production for Universal and Karloff's first in colour. This "dignified" and "prestigious" horror picture clearly imitated the studio's re-make of *The Phantom of the Opera* (1943). Actually, since *The Climax* also used the Paris Opera House as a setting, this new film wasn't really as expensive as it might have seemed.

Both pictures describe a demented individual's involvement with a young female opera singer, played each time by Susanna Foster. In *The Climax,* Karloff is the quiet physician of the Paris Opera who had once loved and killed a singer there. The storyline deals with his determination to keep Miss Foster from singing, because she resembles the earlier woman. The romantic triangle in *Phantom* of Claude Rains-Miss Foster-Nelson Eddy has merely been replaced with one consisting of Karloff-Miss Foster-Turhan Bey. As had happened with *Phantom*, this film's effect is dissipated by weakly depicted normal characters and an excess of "spectacle" and music; the on-stage sequences used melodies adapted from Chopin and Schubert, with lyrics by the film's producer-director, George Waggner.

Though Karloff had left the Frankenstein series in 1939, Universal continued the films with Lon Chaney Jr. (*The Ghost of Frankenstein,* 1942) and Bela Lugosi (*Frankenstein Meets the Wolfman,* 1943). The latter confrontation of monsters was a crowd-pleasing device, so the studio decided to star Karloff in a film that would include Kharis the mummy, the Mad Ghoul, and the Invisible Man. The vague title *Destiny* was soon changed to *The Devil's Brood,* and then to *House of Frankenstein* (though no such building or family tree was evident). The cast list was altered, too, with a semi-mad doctor named Gustav Niemann (Karloff) joined by Larry Talbot, the Wolfman (Chaney, repeating his usual tortured routine), Count Dracula (John Carradine, for the first time), the Monster (Glenn Strange, also for the first time), and a hunchback named Daniel (J. Carrol Naish, stealing what acting honours were available). *House of Frankenstein* was filmed at the end of 1944, and officially released in February 1945.

The film's seventy minutes are so crammed with incidents and characters that there is no room for thought or psychology or emotion; it almost takes longer to synopsise than to view. Dr. Niemann, whose brother had assisted Dr. Frankenstein, and the hunchback, Daniel, are released from prison by a providential storm. The two men happen upon a travelling Museum of Horrors and, after Daniel kills the owner, Niemann takes over and they travel to Reigelberg to take revenge on the Burgomaster there. The oversimplification

Karloff with J. Carrol Naish in HOUSE OF FRANKENSTEIN

that had now become common in horror pictures is evident in the character of Dr. Niemann. The honest scientist who gets carried away by enthusiasm has become a fanatical madman who betrays all his agreements. Niemann had promised to help the hunchback and the Wolfman escape their abnormalities, but ignores this assurance in favour of a game of musical minds that would give him revenge on others: he plans to punish two of his many enemies by imprisoning the mind of one in the Monster's body and by giving the Wolfman's brain to the other, after which he would put the Monster's brain in Talbot's body. The change here is from valid drama to contrived "horror" hokum. Even Karloff, with his dignified silver hair and dangerous eyes, can add little beyond a presence to the trite role.

The biggest weakness of the film is its reason for existence—it is constructed solely to combine and exhibit the studio's stable of horror characters. This motive is paltry, and the resulting plot is just a set of limited, isolated anecdotes that re-heat all the old Universal chestnuts instead of providing something new. Despite this, *House of Frankenstein* contains several effective touches, each possessing quality beyond its context. Among these are Daniel's first naïve and lonely conversation with a young gypsy girl, and his shouting at the Monster after being rebuffed by the girl, "She hates me because I'm an ugly hunchback! If it weren't for you I'd have Talbot's body," whereupon he whips the still unconscious creature, ugliness accusing and attacking its own "reflection." Talbot's first metamorphosis is handled neatly: as he runs off into the night, the camera tilts downward and follows the tracks he has left, which change from footprints to paw-marks; it then tilts up to glimpse the fully altered Wolfman just before he darts out of sight. There is also an excellent shot of the Wolfman half-thawed from his prison of ice, with only his hairy hands protruding free. On such small pleasures are the merits of Universal's Forties horror films based.

The new Monster, Glenn Strange, once commented that "Nobody ever helped anybody as much as Boris Karloff helped me."[120] "I remember, for instance, that he was sick during some of the filming. He had finished his scenes and could have gone home, but he stayed on and worked with me. He showed me how to make the Monster's moves properly, and how to do the walk that makes the Monster so frightening . . . When people congratulated him, he always took the trouble to tell them my name and give me the credit. I really appreciate it."[45] Unfortunately, Strange must not have been a good student, for it is his acting style that has given the Monster a bad name. He played him like a dumb brute who has been knocked out and jolted back to consciousness so often that his mind and physique have deteriorated completely. This is the version imitated by comedians and children, and as a result the public has a narrow conception of the character. Perhaps Karloff was not entirely unselfish in making sure that the performance was credited to Strange.

Though the realism of the Forties inhibited horror films, the fault was less in the style than in the directors, competent men who might make a tight action Western but who failed to realise that horror films need a different approach. They resorted to literal, straight-on shots of man-wolf and man-bat transformations, with special effects replacing mood and atmosphere. In contrast was the series of films created by producer Val Lewton's low-budget unit at RKO. These pictures were made by people with technical skill and artistic feeling who were not content with the fair or the average. It was therefore fitting that Karloff should join Lewton in 1944 and star in three of these films—*The Body Snatcher*, *Isle of the Dead*, and *Bedlam*—all of which are intelligent, efficient, and well worth a viewing. Even *Bedlam*, the least of the three, stands up well against the films being released by Universal.

Isle of the Dead began shooting first, but production was suspended at the start of November 1944 because Karloff had become ill. Certain scenes of *The Body Snatcher* were then started, and that film was completed after about a month of shooting. Some weeks later, during December, work on *Isle* was resumed; the picture was finished early in January 1945. *The Body Snatcher* was released immediately, in February 1945, so RKO avoided competing with itself by holding *Isle* back until the next September. The final film, *Bedlam*, reached audiences a discreet period of time after that, during spring, 1946. Ironically, 1945/46 was the start of a new arid period for horror films, and these works were both the best and the last of the second cycle.

The Body Snatcher is probably the high point of Lewton's career, and it is still one of the best films of Karloff and of director Robert Wise. The script, intelligently elaborated from Robert Louis Stevenson's story, describes the relationship between John Gray (Karloff), cabman and grave-robber, and Dr. MacFarlane (Henry Daniell), for whose medical school Gray supplies cadavers. And since the setting is Nineteenth-century Scotland, the dialogue is written with an ear for both colourful phrasing and character revelation. Unfortunately, the film possesses a sticky centre involving a naïve medical student, a crippled child, and the latter's marriageable mother. The injured girl epitomises sweetness and bravery, and the young man is a callow milksop, the kind of person who antagonises viewers, and makes them hope that his encounter with Cabman Gray will bring him down to earth. The sentimentality of these characters and actors prevent *The Body Snatcher* from being a total success, but fortunately Karloff and Daniell dominate the film.

MacFarlane is the pivotal character, a man unable to escape his past, represented by Gray. He had once been an assistant to Dr. Knox, and thus was involved with Burke and Hare, two Resurrection Men who murdered people to sell the corpses to Knox. During Knox's trial, MacFarlane paid Gray to protect him because, as Mrs. MacFarlane says, he "couldn't swallow the shame of it." Gray saved MacFarlane's reputation by going to prison for him, and now he haunts the doctor, refusing to let him forget his weakness. If *The Body Snatcher* is a tragedy, it is MacFarlane's, for although he possesses knowledge, he is emotionless. As Fettes, the young student, puts it, "He taught me the mathematics of anatomy, but he couldn't teach me the poetry of medicine." Thanks to Henry Daniell and the writers, MacFarlane has a complexity and fullness rare in horror films; his coldness is a flaw resulting from excessive practicality, from the incidents in his past, and from his current dealings with Gray. But at the same time, his connection with the graverobber is justified by the needs of his medical school and the limitations of archaic laws.

Gray is at least as important to the film as MacFarlane, and his character contains even more facets. Karloff inseparably combines the more superficial techniques of menace with a rounded personality. We are continually offered contrasts and flashes of psychology which, while not strictly required to move the story forward, do make John Gray a portrait and not just a type. Gray fits the Karloff style perfectly. He is an earthy, poor, and ordinary man, in no way sophisticated or suave or even educated, and he handles his traffic in bodies with business-like efficiency. He is kind and humble, as befits his station in life. At times, such as when he speaks to the crippled child and lets her visit his horse, he seems to be sincerely nice. He seldom uses words that are not flattering and gentle, and rarely does he acknowledge his true feelings about Mac-Farlane. Threat is masked behind politeness; when Fettes visits his meagre domain, Gray greets him with ironic solicitude: "The young doctor, come to see me. I'm honoured. Come in, come in. Here, sir, take this, the most comfortable chair. To what do I owe the honour of this visit? Some business, was it, of Dr. MacFarlane?" Actually Gray, more sensitive than the doctor and quite intelligent in his own right, realises that he need only remain in the doctor's vicinity, and MacFarlane's nagging conscience will do the rest.

Gray's psychological torture of MacFarlane even takes the form of endearments. He uses the nickname "Toddy" when talking to his "old friend," and he keeps wanting to reminisce about the good old days. After learning that the doctor has refused to operate on the child, Gray insists that he change his mind—not out of benevolence, but only because MacFarlane does not want to do it. When the doctor decides to emphasise lecturing over dissection, in hopes of cutting himself off from Gray's trade, the cabman reassures him (on the usual two levels) that "I'll be stopping by once in a while to see you and Meg, for auld lang syne." Gray's treatment of Mac-Farlane is summed up in his lines to Fettes, after the latter has asked for a new specimen as soon as possible: "You may tell Toddy I'll do what I can, when I can, as he knows I will. But he must wait and see, like the children do."

Finally, the doctor cannot take the pressure any longer, and he visits Gray to confront him openly. At first Gray continues to play innocent, and he perceptively points out that the threat exists more in MacFarlane's own mind than in reality. Yet he also discusses, quite objectively and politely, the pleasure he gets from irritating MacFarlane, and the need he has for the doctor.

> *MacFarlane:* What do you want of me, Gray?
> *Gray:* Want of you? I want nothing of you, Toddy.
> *MacFarlane:* Gray—I must be rid of you. You've become a cancer—a malignant, evil cancer—rotting my mind.

Gray: You've made a disease of me, eh Toddy?
MacFarlane: There's only one cure! I must cut you out. I'll not leave here until I've finished with you, one way or another. I've got to be sure that I'm rid of you and if there's no *other* way—
Gray: Surely you're not threatening an old friend.
MacFarlane: We've never been friends.
Gray: Here, Toddy, have a drink of something good.

MacFarlane offers his nemesis a bribe, if only he will go away.

MacFarlane: I'll make you rich.
Gray: That wouldn't be half so much fun for me as to have you come here and beg.
MacFarlane: Beg! Beg of you, you crawling graveyard rat?
Gray: Aye, that is my pleasure.
MacFarlane: Very well then, I beg of you, I beseech you.
Gray: I would lose the fun of having you come back and beg again.
MacFarlane: But why, Gray, why?
Gray: It'll be a hurt to me to see you no more, Toddy. You're a pleasure to me.
MacFarlane: A pleasure to torment me?
Gray: No. A pride to know I can force you to my will. I am a small man, a humble man, and being poor I have had to do much that I did not want to do. And so long as the great Dr. MacFarlane jumps to my whistle, that long am I a man. And if I have not that, I have nothing. Then I'm only a cabman and a grave-robber. You'll *never* get rid of me, Toddy.

In an earlier discussion, Fettes had joked that a doctor could get rid of an enemy by dissecting him, and Gray declared: "You'll never get rid of me that way, Toddy. You and I have two bodies— aye, very different sorts of bodies—but we're closer than if we were in the same skin. For I saved that skin of yours once, and you'll not forget it." This conscience-like determination to be remembered leads to the film's climax. MacFarlane has killed Gray, but this does not eliminate that part of Gray's threat which exists in the doctor's mind. When MacFarlane himself digs up the body of an old woman, he places it next to himself on the driver's seat of a carriage; as he rides he hears Gray's voice echoing in the repetitious sound of hoof-beats and wheels: "Never get rid of me, never get rid of me." The horses stampede, causing the body to keep falling over Mac-Farlane, and its glowing face becomes that of the dead cabman. When the wagon crashes, MacFarlane dies—having destroyed himself by means of Gray. The doctor could not destroy his own past shame and the present degradation of having to rob graves.

One scene in particular illustrates how the script of *The Body*

Snatcher combines plot exposition with revelation of character, and also creates exciting opportunities for actors. MacFarlane needs to tell someone about his unsuccessful operation on the child, and Fettes is busy with his widow friend, so for a change the doctor accepts Gray's presence. The dialogue here contains necessary facts about the operation, while the cabman's interjections maintain his antagonism. Actually, Gray's criticism of MacFarlane is accurate, as shown by the doctor's failure to react to Gray's sarcasm or to understand his criticism.

> *MacFarlane:* Gray! You know something about the human body.
> *Gray:* I've had *some* experience.
> *MacFarlane:* Then you can understand this: the backbone is a lot of little blocks, and those blocks are all held together so that it works, works like that whip of yours. You know that, don't you?
> *Gray:* Never had it all explained by so learned a man.
> *MacFarlane:* I set those blocks together, patched the muscles, put the nerves where they should be. I did it and I did it right. [*pause*] She won't walk—
> *Gray:* You can't build life the way you put blocks together, Toddy.
> *MacFarlane:* What the devil are you talking about? I'm an anatomist; I know the body, I know how it works.
> *Gray:* You're a fool, Toddy, and no doctor. It's only the dead ones you know.
> *MacFarlane:* I am a doctor, I teach medicine.
> *Gray:* Like Knox taught you? Like I taught you? In cellars, in graveyards? Did Knox teach you what makes the blood flow?
> *MacFarlane:* The heart pumps it.
> *Gray:* Did he tell you how thoughts come and how they go and why things are remembered—and forgot?
> *MacFarlane:* The nerve centres of the brain.
> *Gray:* What makes a thought start?
> *MacFarlane:* The brain, I tell you. I know!
> *Gray:* You don't know, you'll never know or understand, Toddy. Not from Knox or me would you learn those things. Look, look at yourself. Could you be a doctor, a healing man, with the things those eyes have seen? There's a lot of knowledge in those eyes—but no understanding. [*pause*] You'll not get that from me.

Gray's murder of Joseph (Bela Lugosi), the doctor's servant who tries his inexperienced hand at blackmail, gives Karloff further opportunities for an acting *tour de force*. The two men sit by a fireplace, in Gray's darkened room. The kindly, smiling host periodically pets a cat which he holds on his lap, and he readily gives Joseph £16 and re-fills his brandy glass. Then he suggests that the two work together, like Burke and Hare. But Joseph is a foreigner who has not heard the story, so Gray sings part of a street song about the famous graverobbers:

> The ruffian dogs,
> The Hellish pair,
> The villain Burke,
> The meagre Hare . . .
> Nor did they handle axe or knife
> To take away their victim's life.
> No sooner done than in the chest
> They crammed their lately welcomed guest.

All Gray's good humour masks a growing tension that builds considerably until the slow-thinking Joseph asks exactly how the killings were done, and Gray gives him a personal demonstration. Even at the last minute, Gray maintains the pose of kindliness: "I'll show you how they did it, Joseph. I'll show you how they Burked them. No, put your hand down—how can I show you, man? *This* is how they did it, Joseph."

Though the acting and writing are responsible for much of *The Body Snatcher*'s quality, the direction (and photography) reinforce the dialogue, and create a strongly visual atmosphere of evil. Throughout, there is controlled and often chilling use of chiaroscuro lighting (as in the fireside murder of Joseph), and the choice of what to show is made with care. The film's finest example of how to tell a story and create chills visually, while avoiding cinematic tricks that call attention to themselves, is the episode that follows Fettes's visit to Gray and his request for a new "subject." The blind street singer had been introduced a short time before, and now as the youth leaves we hear her voice. Gray looks out the door after Fettes, and in an over-the-shoulder shot we are given his field of vision: the student walks directly away, and then the girl enters and crosses his path from right to left. There is a cut to Gray's face, as it dawns on him where to get the needed specimen —Karloff's expression, while not extreme, makes the decision frighteningly apparent. This is followed by a view down a dark, deserted side street. The girl, still singing, turns a corner and enters the street, walking away from the camera until she disappears in the shadows. Then Gray's cab appears and slowly moves after her. The girl's singing can still be heard, as the cab too blends into the darkness. Suddenly, her voice stops in mid-verse. The view of the dark, apparently deserted street is held for a few seconds more—just long enough for the event to strike home and for the viewer to start feeling uncomfortable. Then it fades out. This portion of the sequence uses only one camera position and no cutting, and it deserves a place in any textbook of film direction. Of course, the picture as a whole need not be so honoured, but it does have such a high level of writing, direction, and acting that it could hardly fail as a thriller of more than usual substance.

Isle of the Dead was Karloff's second Lewton film, and like other horror movies of the Forties it does not offer a supernatural explanation of events. In *Isle*, General Pherides (Karloff) is a skeptic who grows to believe in the existence of a *vorvolaka* (a spirit in human form that drains people of their vitality), and he even causes the girl under suspicion to doubt her own innocence. This situation resembles that in *Day of Wrath* (1943), but that classic by Carl Dreyer remains ambiguous and is therefore more disturbing than *Isle*. Lewton's picture inspires no such uncertainty; it occasionally makes us shiver with fear, but because we know the Truth, we feel superior to the General, who is in error.

The film takes place in 1912 on an island off the coast of Greece. An unidentified war is going on, and we first meet General Pherides amid the aftermath of a battle. This solid and reliable man is nicknamed "The Watchdog" because of a compelling desire to protect his country. Harsh and stern, he acts without hesitation when he feels he is right, ordering an officer executed because his troops had lagged behind. Still, he is not devoid of humanity, since he goes to the island to visit his wife's tomb. While there, he gets involved with psychological forces that cause his destruction. Disease, superstition, and to a lesser extent war are all related in this intelligently conceived script. The connections between the first two are especially important, since a contagious fear of the *vorvolaka* moves from an old peasant lady, Kyra, to the General, and then infects the girl, just as the physical plague spreads from person to person. A physician demands that there be no physical contact between individuals, and the parallel is explicit when the General orders that the suspected girl be kept away from everyone else.

The General's almost tragic downfall is caused by his inner conflict between science and superstition. At the start of the film he is efficient and practical, having outgrown the beliefs of his peasant background. As he tells one of the foreigners, "When I was a boy I was taught by the village priest and old women like Kyra. My belief had many sides—good sides and bad sides. As a man, I put all that away from me. I put my faith in what I can feel and see and know about." When the plague strikes, the General rejects Kyra's explanation of it as punishment for harbouring a *vorvolaka*; instead, he tries to save the inhabitants by demanding that they put their faith in medicine. "The doctor will tell you what to do, and I will see that you do it. We will *fight* the plague." He calls Kyra's ideas "nonsense," adding, "These are new days for

Greece. We don't believe in the old, foolish tales any more." But the General is not as free of his heritage as he thinks, and Kyra more and more inspires him with doubt. At first, he ignores her insinuations, but as Mrs. St. Aubyn becomes weaker and Thea seems in better and better health, the General becomes uncertain. The dormant fears begin to stir, and when his faith in science is shaken by the doctor's death, he becomes especially vulnerable. At this point, Kyra argues, "I'm trying to save you. I don't ask you to believe me. I ask you to think on the hours when one sleeps. Do you know what happens then? The body may lie still, in bed, but what happens to the thought, the spirit? With what ancient demons does it spend its time? And in what deeds? And Thea—does *she* know?" This suggestion lets the General accept Kyra's beliefs without rejecting his own, and as doubt grows within him, he passes it on to Thea.

> *General:* I'm just as unsure as you are. I don't *know* that this is a contagion of the soul that you carry, contagion bred of evil—nameless, unearthly. But until I do know, I must keep you away from the others, and if necessary—I will make an end in the only way that we know that a *vorvolaka* can be killed.
> *Thea:* Impossible! I'm flesh and blood, I remember my mother and father.
> *General:* Yes, but when you awaken in the morning what do you remember of the night before, of your visits to the English-woman?
> *Thea:* Sometimes at night I tend her, I help her when she feels ill, I loosen the nightgown at her throat—
> *General:* At her thoat! That you remember. Can you remember dreams? Can a *vorvolaka* in her human form remember the evil that she did at night? How can you be so sure? This much we know: You walk at night, your eyes in the morning refreshed and filled with life, and your friend—every day she grows paler, listless, weaker. It is best that you stay away from the others. [*pause*] I hope that I'm wrong, I hope that everything that Kyra said is untrue. But until I know, I *must watch you.*

The death of the other woman seems proof of the girl's guilt, but at this point a plot contrivance saves the General from having to do anything about Thea, and wraps up the situation somewhat too efficiently: Mrs. St. Aubyn, a cataleptic, turns out to have been buried alive, and when she escapes she insanely kills Kyra. The General finds Kyra's body and blames the innocent Thea, but Mrs. St. Aubyn again appears and, after stabbing him with a trident, falls off a cliff to her death. The General dies thinking that he had been right and had seen the *vorvolaka:* "grave clothes, wings, face—eyes of death and evil."

Though General Pherides is a fascinating individual, *Isle of the Dead* is not as tense or psychologically complex as *The Body Snatcher*. It has the textured photography and more than adequate direction associated with Val Lewton films, but most of the characters are uninteresting, especially a whining Englishman who says, "I'll give you all the bloomin' statues in Greece for one whiff of fish'n' chips, for one peek at Whitechapel." The only frightening part is the sequence inside Mrs. St. Aubyn's crypt, as water drips from the ceiling on to the coffin, and screams and clangings reverberate within the sealed and otherwise empty room. Contemporary critics and exhibitors were basically in agreement about the film. James Agee said that it was "tedious, overloaded, diffuse, and at moments arty, yet in many ways to be respected, up to its last half-hour or so; then it becomes as brutally frightening and gratifying a horror film as I can remember."[3] The same viewpoint was expressed by a West Virginia exhibitor: "The first part of the picture is boring, but the last part had my patrons screaming and shouting their heads off."[91] Ironically, it is this portion that contrivedly concludes the story, and even the shock effects seem dated because they are based entirely on situation, rather than characterisation.

Karloff portrays the General as less a fallen or falling giant than an ordinary person helplessly caught up in something he can not understand. Well-meaning, he wants to protect the people around him but finds he cannot stop the plague, and when he tries to save everyone from the *vorvolaka* he causes more trouble than he prevents. The superstitious past is too strong for him, and the watchdog becomes a destroyer. This is the character's irony and pathos; his aims are high but he is ineffectual, a simple man out of his depth. He dies believing that he had acted heroically, but everyone else knows that he was a failure who lost control of events.

Karloff's final effort for Lewton was *Bedlam* (1946). Like the others, it combines horror with history, emphasising realistic situations over supernatural ones. Vaguely inspired by one of William Hogarth's engravings (in the series, "The Rake's Progress") that depicted an asylum for pauper madmen, *Bedlam* re-created Eighteenth-century London's Bethlehem Hospital and depicted conditions that led to reforms in the treatment of mental illness. Somehow a "horror" movie set in the past was allowed to depict insanity and sadism with greater frankness than were other kinds of pictures. One reviewer found it hard to categorise the film, "since nothing quite like it has been seen . . . [It is] a powerful use of the camera to tell a story of importance."[141]

In retrospect, *Bedlam* seems divided in its desire to exploit

Karloff with Ian Wolfe in BEDLAM

insanity for thrills, while also treating the subject factually. After
all, the cruel, sadistic Master Sims (Karloff) who runs the asylum is
really just as sick as his put-upon patients. Yet here, he is presented
as a traditional villain, obsequious to his superiors and cruel to his
charges; when a young girl tries to expose him and effect some
reforms, he even has her committed. While interred, she works
with patients to improve conditions, and here the script resists
exploiting the basic fear that normal people have of being trapped
among the abnormal and unstable. However, at the end Sims is
captured by his victims, given a "trial," and killed—he is punished
for his villainy, not treated and understood for his illness, and the
patients, have become stereotyped menaces. *Bedlam* also includes a
romance between the unjustly committed girl and a stonemason
working at the institution, and he helps her to escape and bring

official intervention. Though not overstressed, this situation does give the narrative a feeling of contrivance. But despite its weaknesses, *Bedlam* is intelligent, worthwhile, and typical of the films produced by Lewton.

Karloff was divorced from his second wife near the end of 1945, and on April 11, 1946, he married Evelyn Helmore, an English-woman who had been in America for seven years. After *Bedlam*, horror films grew scarce, so Karloff accepted roles as ordinary criminals. From April 1946 until the end of that year, he worked almost continuously, performing in three separate films (none of which was released until late summer, 1947). First came Samuel Goldwyn's *The Secret Life of Walter Mitty*, a loose adaptation of James Thurber's story about a henpecked husband who imagines himself in several Heroic roles. In this version, Mitty also becomes involved in a real-life murder committed by a gang of jewel thieves led by Karloff, and he proves that this is not just another daydream by capturing the criminals himself. Karloff next worked in Cecil B. DeMille's *Unconquered*, a romance-adventure set in frontier Pennsylvania. His role was that of Guyasutra, a Seneca chief who leads his tribe in the climactic assault and siege at Fort Pitt. A recent spinal operation required Karloff to wear a brace hidden under a loin cloth and some fur, and an Indian on the set as an

Karloff with Thurston Hall and Danny Kaye in THE SECRET LIFE OF WALTER MITTY

advisor supposedly remarked, "This man is as patient as a horse."[23] *Personal Column* began shooting before *Unconquered* was finished, but since Karloff played secondary roles in both, there was no conflict in his schedule. This time he was a red herring murder suspect, a mad dress designer who lives in the past and conducts fashion shows before imaginary audiences; he even talks to his invisible, socially-prominent guests. The role is too contrived to mislead the audience and heroine into assuming his guilt, and it is also too obviously planned as an acting *tour de force* for Karloff. Just before release, the film was re-titled *Lured*.

After an employment pause of nearly three months, Karloff spent part of April 1947 filming *Dick Tracy Meets Gruesome*. This was the fourth Dick Tracy film, and despite a tiny budget it is a moderately successful melodrama that amusingly kids its own excesses. The tone is set right away, with a close-up of a hangman's noose in shadow; the camera pans to the noose itself as ominous piano chords enter the soundtrack; after another pan, the camera stops at the lettering on a bar window, "Hangman's Knot," and the music shifts into bouncy jazz. Karloff then enters the bar. He is Gruesome, a callous and unrepentant murderer. Tough and quiet, with his tie loosened and a toothpick constantly in his mouth, Karloff plays the role as the intended one-note cartoon figure, but because he does not overact, he makes Gruesome both amusing and suggestive of real violence. At one point, Tracy's sidekick Pat declares, "If I didn't know better, I'd swear we were doing business with Boris Karloff"; as *Arsenic and Old Lace* had shown, Karloff was now doomed to be haunted by his own image.

Gruesome was followed by another Indian character, this time a friendly one, in *Tap Roots*. As Tishomingo, a seventy-year-old Choctaw sage, he was again of minor importance to the story, which involved a Mississippi town that tried to remain neutral during the Civil War. The picture was filmed in the summer of 1947, but Universal-International did not release it until a full year later. Perhaps this was to avoid competition with DeMille's *Unconquered*, which appeared in August 1947. In fact, *Walter Mitty, Lured, Unconquered*, and *Gruesome* were all released within just a few months of each other. After finishing *Tap Roots*, Karloff experienced a long cinematic drought, and did not come before the cameras again until February 1949, when he began *Abbott and Costello Meet the Killer*. After that, he didn't appear in another film until 1951.

The fact that *Lured* and *Dick Tracy Meets Gruesome* calculatedly employed the audience's knowledge of him presented Karloff with a problem when the chance to be in a new play appeared. "The Linden Tree," by J. B. Priestley (author of the novel "The Old Dark

TAP ROOTS: (left to right) Richard Long, player, Susan Hayward, Ward Bond, player, and Karloff

Karloff with Marc Lawrence (at right) in UNCONQUERED

Karloff with Lou Costello in ABBOTT AND COSTELLO MEET THE KILLER

House"), was to be produced early in 1948 by Maurice Evans, who offered Karloff the lead. "I was delighted—but the playwright, J. B. Priestley, was not. 'Good Lord, not Karloff!' he told producer Maurice Evans. 'Put his name up on the marquee and people will think my play is about an axe murder.' I cabled Priestley in London: 'I promise you I would not have eaten the baby in the last act.' Upon that solemn assurance, he withdrew his objections. The part was mine."[61]

"The Linden Tree" opened in New York on March 2, 1948, at the Music Box Theatre, staged by George Schaefer and with Una O'Connor in the cast. Karloff portrayed Robert Linden, an elderly professor of history at a small English college who refuses to retire because he feels that too many people are retiring from the real world, in one way or another. The play is constructed with self-conscious efficiency—each character represents a different attitude toward contemporary England—and it unfashionably comes to clear and confident conclusions about life. But its points are well taken and the conclusion does not tie everything into a happy intellectual and emotional bundle. In fact, by the end of the play Linden has been left by his wife and children, has been forced to accept a demeaning compromise in order to stay on at the college, and has learned that he as an individual would not be missed if he did retire. His only solace is that "there might be something I could help to do here, before the light goes. A touch of colour. A hint of wonder. An occasional new glance at old stuff. A bit of insight."[102]

Even though "The Linden Tree" was then enjoying its sixth successful month in London, the American production closed after only seven performances. Years later, Karloff recalled the playwright's uncertainty about giving him the role and said, "I've always been haunted by the thought that possibly Priestley was right after all."[61] However, critical displeasure with the play did not extend to its star, and the influential Brooks Atkinson cited Karloff's acting as the evening's virtue. "It proves that Boris Karloff, made up to look like a human being, is an extraordinarily winning actor. He plays the venerable academician with attractive, humorsome conviction. Shaggy, tweedy, gray-haired, he has warmth and magnetism; and those beetling brows, which can scare you in his shiver-plays, can soothe you with wisdom when he is in a benevolent mood."[10]

Undaunted by the felling of "The Linden Tree," Karloff tried again with "The Shop at Sly Corner," a melodrama by Edward Percy that entered rehearsal in November 1948, and opened at the Booth Theatre on January 18, 1949; it was staged by Margaret Perry, and Una O'Connor was again in the cast. Although it had run for two years in London, on Broadway it lasted four days. But if Karloff was tempted to see himself as a jinx, the praise he received should have dissuaded him. The author was raked over the coals, not the actor. Karloff portrayed a former Devil's Island convict whose antique shop is a blind for criminal activities. When an assistant in the store finds out the truth and tries blackmail, Karloff strangles the unscrupulous young man. Later, a policeman arrives and Karloff poisons himself to avoid prison—then dies laughing when he learns that the Inspector had only wanted to buy a suit of armour.

While this story was closer to what was expected of Karloff, and his character is interestingly typical of other Karloff roles in his average-man qualities, the play itself lacked excitement. Brooks Atkinson's comments illustrate the general reaction: "Mr. Karloff is too good a man to waste on so much domestic banality . . . An extraordinarily gifted assassin, he deserves steady employment with plenty of work. But 'The Shop at Sly Corner' wastes most of the evening depicting his bourgeois devotion to his family and generosity as a parent. Mr. Karloff is good at this, too. His voice booms with loving tenderness. His manners are considerate. He is a connoisseur of good music and the drama. And he wears his tweeds like a self-respecting burgher. Probably he could push a baby carriage gently. These are modest virtues, common to a great many citizens. But no one else can do such a pretty job of garroting."[13]

"Sly Corner" closed on January 22, 1949, and the filming of

U-I's *Abbott and Costello Meet the Killer, Boris Karloff* began in February, so Karloff's participation could only have been a last minute decision. In fact, the picture was originally scheduled as *Abbott and Costello Meet the Killers,* and it was not until just before release in August that the title was changed to include, and flaunt, the famous actor's name. Bud Abbott and Lou Costello, as a detective and bellhop at the Lost Cavern Resort Hotel, become involved with murder, disappearing bodies, and attempts by the killers to blame the bumbling Lou. Karloff's role was the brief and unimportant one of Swami Talpur, a fake fortune-teller from Brooklyn.

Several months later, in January 1950, Karloff returned to the stage, this time in Atlanta, as Gramps in an arena theatre revival of "On Borrowed Time." Then came still another Broadway role, a revival of "Peter Pan" that opened on April 24, 1950, and for a change the production was a hit—Karloff's first since "Arsenic." According to Brooks Atkinson: "This is Mr. Karloff's day of triumph. As the father of the Darling children and the pirate King, he is at the top of his bent. Although he is best known for the monsters he has played on stage and screen, Mr. Karloff is an actor of tenderness and humor, with an instinct for the exact inflection. His Captain Hook is a horrible cutthroat of the sea; and Mr. Karloff does not shirk the villainies. But they are founded on an excellent actor's enjoyment of an excellent part, and a relish of Barrie's inscrutable humors. There is something of the grand manner in the latitude of his style and the roll of his declamation; and there is withal an abundance of warmth and gentleness in his attitude toward the audience."[11] "Peter Pan" ran for 321 performances and did not close until the end of January 1951; then the production went on a tour that included Boston, Philadelphia, and Chicago.

Karloff's fondness for children became more and more a part of his life as he attained a grandfatherly age and appearance. He often claimed that because children sensed the humanity beneath his character's ugliness, they were not hurt by horror stories, and he tested this theory while in "Peter Pan." "After the show I'd corral as many [children] as my dressing room would hold and ask, 'Would you like to try on my hook?' Even little blond angels would reply, 'Yes, sir.' They'd turn to the mirror, put on the most terrible face they could make and, without fail, take a terrific swipe at themselves in the glass. Far from being frightened by the villainous Captain Hook, they had caught on to his fun and pomposity."[61] Also in 1951, Karloff narrated a feature-length puppet film, made in Czechoslovakia a few years earlier by Jiří Trnka; called *The Emperor's Nightingale*, it was based on a Hans Christian Andersen story.

Separately, the 1951 success of *The Thing* inspired a rebirth

Karloff in THE STRANGE DOOR

of horror movies, but with new overtones and implications. The films of the Forties had been more mundane than those of the Thirties, but they still retained the old myths and legends. In the Fifties, science fiction provided different themes and another approach. Monsters were now invaders from Outer Space, atomic mutations of earthly insects, or dinosaurs awakened and irritated by A-bomb explosions. Rarely did these creatures possess individuality or arouse sympathy; they were simply malevolent Things that must be wiped out before they destroy the world. Science was generally blamed for causing these catastrophes, but scientists were also the heroes who figure out how the creatures could be killed. The scientists in these films are workaday types who have practical motives and are often employed by the government, in contrast to Karloff's scientist of the Columbia films, who would have been too much of an individual, idealist, and rebel for the Fifties.

Universal-International made two pictures with Karloff at this time, possibly hoping to revive its old style of horror film, but neither was good or financially successful. *The Strange Door,* made in the spring of 1951 just after *Peter Pan* ended its tour, was based on Robert Louis Stevenson's "The Sire de Maletroit's Door." Charles Laughton starred as a mad nobleman of Seventeenth-century France whose resentment at having the woman he loved marry his brother prompted him to keep them both imprisoned in his cellar dungeon for twenty years. Karloff's role was minor: a faithful servant of the brother, he functioned as his jailer for all those years. The picture's climax must have reminded Karloff of *The Raven,* because he again saves a pair of lovers from a room in which the walls come together. *The Strange Door* was released in December 1951.

Part of March-April 1952 was then devoted to *The Black Castle,* another period story about a mad nobleman, with an added man-hunt aspect that distantly evoked *The Most Dangerous Game.* Richard Greene, as an Eighteenth-century British adventurer, travels to the Black Forest castle of Count von Bruno (Stephen McNally), intending to find out what happened to some friends who had disappeared nearby. Stopping at an inn on the way, he indulges in some swordplay with a few of the Count's friends, which sets the film's tone as an uneven mixture of horror and action-adventure. Karloff appears as an old doctor, a role that requires very little of him. The hero spends a lot of time snooping around the castle with his host's beautiful and innocent young wife, and Karloff eventually gives these two a drug that simulates death, expecting this to help them escape. However, Von Bruno gets the old doctor to blurt out the truth, and it is only luck that saves the couple from being buried alive. Karloff's statement of regret at having revealed the secret, spoken over their immobile bodies, provides his only substantial scene and he handles it effectively, just before the Count stabs him in the back.

After *The Black Castle,* U-I limited its horror output to the popular Big Bug pictures, such as *Tarantula* (1955) and *The Deadly Mantis* (1957); these apocalyptic threats appealed more to the mood of the times than did any danger affecting only a few people. Meanwhile, Karloff was cast in *Abbott and Costello Meet Dr. Jekyll and Mr. Hyde,* which went before the cameras early in 1953 and was released that summer. The result is not as bad as it could have been: unexpected attention is paid to lighting and other technical aspects, and complete mockery of the *genre* is avoided. In fact, the Jekyll-Hyde scenes are played quite straight, even when the comics are around. The humour stems not from any irreverent treatment of Hyde, but from the frightened reactions of everyone else, so the integrity of the menace is preserved. As Jekyll, Karloff is adequate in a role without substance, but the monster make-up is just a mask and a stunt man was probably used for most of Hyde's appearances.

Significantly, Karloff now had to leave America, the country of his great success, and for the first time accept a role in a quickie foreign-language production. In 1953, he appeared in a dull Italian film called *Il monstro dell' isola* (*The Monster of the Island*), which has only recently become available in America. He played a minor role, the head of a gang of dope smugglers. The actor himself, when asked about the picture, seemed never to have seen it: "Oh, God. I haven't the least idea what it was like. Incredible! Dreadful! No one in the outfit spoke English. I don't speak Italian. Just hopeless. I had a very good time, but that's beside the point." He also spent part of 1953/54 filming the *Colonel March of Scotland Yard* TV series in London.

Television, in fact, was a major source of work for Karloff during the Fifties, and it happily gave him the chance to appear in different contexts. He turned up on game shows like "I've Got a Secret," and answered questions about children's stories on "The $64,000 Question." There also was room for him in variety shows, such as one hosted by Donald O'Connor in which Karloff played a wallflower at a lonely hearts club. "Even though he had only a few fleeting moments in the spotlight," said critic Jack Gould, "his delicate pantomime had the stamp of artistry and easily could have been developed into a hilarious interlude by itself."[46] On the Frankie Laine Show, Karloff recited "The September Song" and, according to Harriet Van Horne, "it was a clear case of technique triumphing over the too, too familiar."[134]

Karloff was always welcome for dramatic roles in "Suspense," "Climax," or "U. S. Steel Hour." He repeated his performance as Jonathan Brewster in "Arsenic and Old Lace" in January 1955, and the next month he was Mr. Mycroft (a character modeled after Sherlock Holmes) on "Elgin Hour." He starred in a "Playhouse 90" adaptation of Cornell Woolrich's "Rendezvous in Black" as a mentally deranged man whose *fiancée* is accidentally killed by a whiskey bottle thrown from a plane; in revenge, he murders the women most dear to the passengers on that flight. He also played the Judge in James Yaffee's version of Friedrich Duerrenmatt's "The Deadly Game." In March 1955, he was King Arthur in *A Connecticut Yankee in King Arthur's Court.* During the third act, he sang a duet with star Eddie Albert. "In a way, it's terrifying. It's a new wicket for me. I did two songs when I was with Jean Arthur in *Peter Pan,* but this will be much more elaborate." *A Connecticut Yankee* prompted Karloff to comment on this new medium: "I'm all for live television. It's much more exciting from the actor's point of view. In films you get a chance to rectify mistakes. On the stage you can look forward to an improvement the next night. But on live TV you are on, and if you make a muck of it, you just make a muck of it. There's a great challenge in it."[113]

During this period, Karloff's major triumph was his role in "The Lark," "the first solid, successful, serious acting part I've had on Broadway."[32] Rehearsals for this adaptation by Lillian Hellman of Jean Anouilh's "L'alouette" began in October 1955; the production was staged by Joseph Anthony, with Julie Harris, Christopher Plummer, Joseph Wiseman, and Theodore Bikel in the cast. Karloff played Cauchon, Bishop of Beauvais who was judge and moderator during the trial of Joan of Arc. Concerned mainly with saving the girl, Cauchon antagonises the British officer who wants a guilty verdict and a quick burning. Even though convinced that Joan must submit to the Church's beliefs, Cauchon is determined to be fair and to hear her story. This world-weary man is a fine, haunting role for Karloff. His attempt near the end to get Joan to recant is a moving revelation of his character: "Look at me, Joan, keep your mind here. I am an old man. I have killed people in defence of my beliefs. I am so close to death myself that I do not wish to kill again. I do not wish to kill a little girl. Be kind. [*Cries out*] Help me to save you."[6]

"The Lark" opened on November 17, 1955 at the Longacre Theatre, and in a cover story on Julie Harris, "Time" reported that "every member of the excellent cast, except Boris Karloff as the judge, was jittered off top form on opening night."[122] Over the next few months, Karloff received the respectful praise that he had long deserved. The critics emphasised Miss Harris, the play itself, and the direction, but most found space to call Karloff's role "admirably played."[39] Ironically, the world-famous bogeyman was the evening's most compassionate figure and "brings the play most of its humanity."[9] When "The Lark" closed in June 1956 it had completed 229 per-

Karloff on stage with Julie Harris in THE LARK

formances. The following February, a shortened version was revived for TV's *Hallmark Hall of Fame,* with Karloff and Miss Harris repeating their roles.

February 1955 saw the release of *Sabaka,* an insignificant work produced, directed, and written by Frank Ferrin. Though an English-language film, it was made in India. Reginald Denny and Victor Jory also starred, but the main character was an elephant boy played by Nino Marcel. The Maharajah (Denny) is a benevolent ruler misled by his military chief, General Pollegar (Karloff), into an antagonism toward the boy and a failure to capture the leader of a phoney religion worshiping Sabaka, a fire demon. Actually, the General is not really a villain; he is merely a self-important soldier who cares less about the death of a peasant than about his own uniform and braid. Mostly seen on parade and in a few conversations with the Maharajah, he is only part of the background for the boy's none-too-interesting story.

Voodoo Island marked a return to American films for Karloff, but not a particularly auspicious one. This production was shot in about two weeks in November 1956, and the result, released the following February, shows this lack of time and effort. Karloff portrays a sceptical author and investigator who is hired by a hotel builder to prove that tales about a certain island are untrue. The film bypasses shocks and thrills for their own sake in order to stress the characters of the expedition members: one man is greedy, the boat captain is arrogant and goading, another person is bitter and self-pitying, Karloff's secretary is preoccupied with her work, and a second woman seems attracted to the secretary ("I could make you become alive, dear"). This approach sounds promising, with the doubter being converted to a belief in "magic," and the dialogue drawing parallels between the voodoo "walking dead" and certain characters who are only alive physically. But the zombie theme is not developed and the characters are completely uninteresting, so the viewer is left with very little, not even shocks and thrills; it is almost one hour before anything potentially exciting happens and even then the man-eating plants are absurd.

In 1957, after recording the narration for a short, animated version of *The Juggler of Our Lady,* Karloff again returned to England, where he made two features for Amalgamated Productions. While *The Haunted Strangler* (called *Grip of the Strangler* in Britain) showed up right away in the States, it took *Corridors of Blood* (*Doctor of the 7 Dials* in Britain) until 1963 to cross the Atlantic. *The Haunted Strangler* was Karloff's first worthwhile horror film since the Forties, and its period setting, moderate intelligence, and awareness of social conditions place it insecurely in the Val Lewton tradition. Director Robert Day's main advantage lies in creating a natural domestic atmosphere among the main characters, who act and react in believable ways.

The story is set in 1880, with novelist and social reformer James Rankin (Karloff) suspecting that an executed sailor had been innocent and that the missing autopsy surgeon, Dr. Tenant, was in fact the guilty one. His investigation takes Rankin to Scotland Yard, Newgate Prison, and a music-hall named the Judas Hole. A guard is bribed into letting him dig up the sailor's coffin, in which he finds a scalpel missing from Tenant's surgical case. The blade's presence in Rankin's hand prompts his arm to become paralysed and his face to grow distorted; returning to the Judas Hole, he kills one of the performers. Later, Rankin realises that he himself is Tenant and that his wife, a nurse, had helped him escape from the hospital. Again he spies the scalpel and changes identity, this time killing the wife. Sent to an asylum because he *claims* to be a murderer, he escapes and is about to kill his stepdaughter when he sees the faces of his victims superimposed over her and changes back to his normal self. Confronted by the now-believing police, he flees to the cemetery, where he claws at the earth, apparently determined to return his scalpel to the coffin. When Rankin stands up, he is shot by the prison guard he had once bribed. This whole climax is weak and arbitrary, as if a final bit of action and violence had to be added at any cost.

Though self-consciously similar to *Dr. Jekyll and Mr. Hyde,* this story is an adequate look at Victorian schizophrenia, with the upright existence of Rankin's world contrasted with the bawdyness of the Judas Hole and the cruelty of the prisons and asylums. This is best seen in Rankin's embarrassment at the music-hall, where the freedom and exuberance are out of keeping with the controlled, proper society in which he lives, and which forces his baser impulses into extreme, sudden outbursts. Karloff handles this aspect of his role well, as when he is both attracted and repelled by a partially clothed dancer glimpsed though an open dressing room door. It is apt, in a Freudian sense, that she becomes his first knife victim!

In the latter portion of the film, Rankin is more victim than villain. Disbelieved by Scotland Yard, he becomes more and more harried, which in turn leads people to think him crazy. Committed to a public asylum, he is placed in a padded cell, strait-jacketed, and force-fed. Here his valid pleas and shouts only sound insane, and increased frustration drives him to further anger and futile struggle. In the light of scenes and situations like these, it is hard to understand how one reviewer could praise the actor by saying, "Karloff is indeed the villain we can unashamedly hiss and hate."[34]

If *The Haunted Strangler* parallels Lewton's *Bedlam,* then *Corridors of Blood* is akin to *The Body Snatcher.* In it, Karloff plays Dr. Thomas Bolton, one of England's best surgeons in 1840, who seeks an anaesthetic that will prevent pain during operations. Inevitably disdained by his reactionary colleagues, he is compelled to work outside acceptable society, and his dealings with Resurrection Joe (Christopher Lee) end in blackmail and violence; he also becomes addicted to the drugs he tests on himself. A lesser work than *The Haunted Strangler,* the film is still well-intentioned and above-average.

In 1957, the public's interest in monsters was revived when

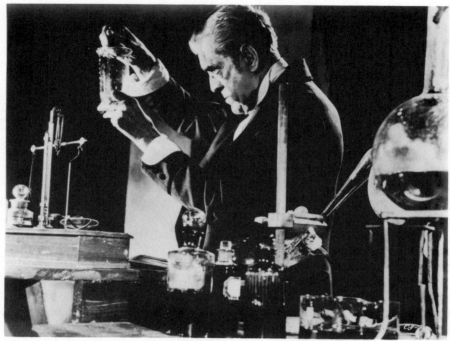

Karloff in CORRIDORS OF BLOOD

Universal released some of its old thrillers to TV in a package called "Shock Theater." Before long, stations all over the country were showing *Frankenstein* and *Dracula,* and a whole new generation discovered the pleasures lurking in the shadowy corridors of Gothic melodrama. Conveniently, the small British company Hammer Films was just then making *The Curse of Frankenstein* (1957), a new version of Mary Shelley's novel. The picture was a hit, and Gothic horror was now big business. 1958 saw the arrival of a monster fan magazine, as well as popular songs like "Dinner with Drac" and "Monster Rock and Roll".

Films, too, tried for up-to-date variations on the old standards, including *I Was a Teenage Frankenstein* and *The Return of Dracula.* Among these pictures was *Frankenstein 1970* (originally planned as *Frankenstein 1960*), an Allied Artists quickie that starred Karloff as a grandson of the original scientist. Released in the summer of 1958, the film is an interesting failure that tries to be an affectionate salute to the old style, but instead hovers too close to imitation and *cliché.* The only times when it succeeds at old-time Gothic horror are, significantly, both "phoney." One scene is the film's opening, in which a monster relentlessly chases a girl through darkness, past barren tree limbs, and into a river; finally, this is revealed as a sequence being shot for a TV show "honouring" the Monster's 140th anniversary. Another scene is a monologue "improvised" by Karloff, as his introduction to the show; in it, he explains the final fate of the Monster. "In this stone sarcophagus, deep in the bowels of the earth, he interred his creation. In a passage of the ancient family tomb he sealed it away to the end of time without vital organs or soul, so that nevermore would it bring terror to mortal man or challenge God, the true creator—whose merciful forgiveness he prayed!"

Baron Frankenstein, the last of the family and himself disfigured by Nazi tortures, wants to create a being in his own image as an heir or child-surrogate. This character is interesting only because of Karloff, who gives a richly articulated performance. There is his Byronic way of playing the organ, his sarcasm about his own deformity, and his irritation at the brash TV director who keeps clapping an arm over his shoulder. There is also his quiet, menacingly polite manner when a servant accidentally enters the secret laboratory, as well as his ominous references to "the story of the inquisitive commandant" at a Nazi prison camp. But the film rapidly loses what momentum it has: the laboratory is modern and dull-looking, the monster is so swathed in bandages that it resembles nothing worse than a huggable teddy bear, and during the operation the director resorts to close-ups of hands massaging a living heart and of a jar containing eyes.

Eventually, the monster's face is revealed as modelled on the Baron's predisfigurement visage, which in turn belongs to a twenty-years younger Karloff. This might inspire intriguingly Pirandellian thoughts about Frankenstein's "creating" Karloff, or Karloff's "creating" the monster, or even Karloff's "creating" Karloff, but unfortunately they would be pointless, because the fact that the Baron made the monster in his own image is included only as a gimmick, with no effect on the plot or situations.

TV work helped occupy Karloff until 1963, when he signed a contract with American-International. In 1958 he appeared in the "Playhouse 90" production of *Heart of Darkness*, from the novel by one of Karloff's favourite authors, Joseph Conrad. He played Kurtz, a character who resembles, on a higher plane, some of the grand but misguided heroes he had portrayed in the Thirties. An idealistic, talented man who had hoped to be a force for good, Kurtz entered uncivilised Africa and discovered there, and within himself, the primitive instincts of which most people are unaware. Superficially, he was evil, but his struggle had given him stature; he became a law unto himself, independent of everything and everyone else. Karloff also appeared on "Studio One" (as a prize-winning scientist who had "borrowed" the accomplishments of an associate), "Shirley Temple Storybook" (as Father Knickerbocker in "The

Legend of Sleepy Hollow"), and on "DuPont Show of the Month" (as Captain Billy Bones in "Treasure Island").

In 1960 Karloff hosted "Thriller," a series in the same vein as "Alfred Hitchcock Presents," and while not a tremendous successs, it lasted through a second season. The episodes were sometimes obvious and heavy-handed, but Karloff was an urbane host, and he himself occasionally starred. Since 1959, Karloff had lived in England. "Many things brought me back. An urge to return to my roots, homesickness, the countryside, the food, and the way of life. The pace is easier, more comfortable. More human. Britain has contrived to make a society which is freer, gentler, and fairer."[48] But, at the age of seventy-one he had no intention of settling into a comfortable retirement there. "If I did, I'd be dead in three months. I'd rather die with my boots on and grease paint on my face."[142] For "Thriller," the actor made about four trips a year to Hollywood, during which he filmed several introductions and appeared in an episode or two. "Well, they've been so nice about it. When I return to London next week I shall have flown a total of 12,000 miles just to do one day's work—filming six of the lead-ins, you see—and they let my wife come with me. I shall come back to do some more of them, 26 in all, I believe it is. They do it quite simply. I sort of intrude into the first scene and explain, for example, that this nice-looking couple is really in for a quite terrifying day, as you shall see, and then I quietly slip out again."[19]

As its 1962 Halloween episode, "Route 66" brought together Karloff, Lorre, and Chaney Jr. in a story about horror actors. During this hour, Chaney was seen in Quasimodo, Wolfman, and Mummy make-up, and an attempt was made to re-create Karloff's original Frankenstein Monster. The show was far from the connoisseur's treat it might have been, since the story was weak and the make-up sloppy and mask-like. As Karloff subsequently remarked, "It was a quick job, with no time to do the thing properly. In that show the Monster was just a distant cousin to the original—which was a pity." But Karloff's TV appearances continued, and each time he managed to withstand the mediocrity of his surroundings. In 1963 he made a British series of science fiction stories called "Out of This World." An ABC rock 'n' roll series, "Shindig," offered Karloff as "special guest host" of its 1965 Halloween show, in which he, looking a bit amused at it all, recited verses of "The Monster Mash" and "The Peppermint Twist," while a gaggle of nymphets danced around him. On "The Wild, Wild West" (1966) he was Singh, a Maharajah in Oklahoma; "The Girl from UNCLE" (1966) featured him as Mother Muffin, the female proprietor of a school for killers. He also narrated a half-hour cartoon version of Dr. Seuss's "How the Grinch Stole Christmas," and was the voice of the villainous Grinch, too.

In September 1968 he and Vincent Price were guests on "The Red Skelton Show." The main skit featured Karloff as a scientist and Price, fittingly, as his subservient son; the two mistake Skelton for their newly-invented robot. Most of the time Karloff functioned as the straight man, and this was just as well, since the writing and performing were more silly than satiric, with Karloff the only one to avoid breaking up on-stage. Price, indulging a penchant for over-acting, kept calling Karloff "daddy" and "dadsy-poo." One month later, Karloff also appeared on "The Jonathan Winters Show," and while this show's skit was no gem either, the production had a more professional quality; "clowning around" was avoided. This time, Karloff had many of the laugh-lines, and their success required timing and inflection, not just demeaning self-indulgence.

On Winters's show, Karloff also read (with musical background) the lyrics of Frank Sinatra's then-current hit, "It Was a Very Good Year." The bit was done perfectly straight, and because of Karloff's age the stanza about being in the "autumn" of his years and looking back with satisfaction on his life was especially moving. The overall effect was only slightly marred by a "kidding" conclusion in which Karloff says to a beautiful young woman, "Come to think of it, my dear, it's *still* a very good year."

Karloff's last dramatic role on TV was in a segment of "The Name of the Game"; called "The White Birch," it was shown in November 1968. As a controversial Czech novelist, he has one scene with some reporters in which he pretends to be senile, and one with star Gene Barry in which he sheds this pose. The role was limited, with few character revelations, and whatever substance it had was due to Karloff's own personality.

During his last years, Karloff was far from well and rarely free of pain. Arthritis and a bad knee required a leg brace, a cane, and often a wheel chair; a case of emphysema left him with only part of a single lung, and required that he keep an oxygen cylinder nearby; in addition, he fought an attack of pneumonia, recovered from a back operation, and suffered other illnesses. Merely living meant pain, yet he continued to perform. "You see, I'm one of that small, lucky band of people who does what he loves. And, so long as people put up with me, I'll work. I used to garden but, because of my leg, I can't bend anymore. I used to play lots of games, but they've given me up. So, you see, if I didn't work, I'd just sit here and grunt."[101] According to Vincent Price, when Karloff appeared with Red Skelton, "the whole show was devised to allow Boris to play it in a wheelchair but on his first entrance dress rehearsal night he sensed a chill from the audience at seeing him to their mind completely crippled. He set his mind to playing it standing up and on that gruelling day of the show he went through every run-through on his feet."[2]

Karloff in THE RAVEN

In 1963 Karloff read "The Three Little Pigs and Other Fairy Stories" on a Caedmon album; his other recordings include "Just-So Stories" by Kipling, two sets of fairy tales by Hans Christian Andersen, Shakespeare's "Cymbeline," and "Tales of the Frightened" by Michael Avallone. By 1963, American-International had become successful enough to sign contracts with Vincent Price, Peter Lorre, and in March, Karloff. AIP was willing to put as much money as possible into its films, and most of it showed up on the screen. Credit for this must go to producer-director Roger Corman, photographer Floyd Crosby, and art director Daniel Haller. The studio's pre-preparation was complete enough that despite short shooting schedules, there was no rush. "If I've played a scene badly and want to do it again they say, 'Sure,' not 'Oh Christ we haven't got the time.' "[17]

The Raven (1963) was Karloff's first film for AIP and Corman; financially successful, it was a rather amusing spoof of the *genre*, but hardly the major creation that might be expected from the combined talents of Karloff, Price, Lorre, Corman, Crosby, Haller, and writer Richard Matheson. Dr. Erasmus Craven (Price) is visited by Dr. Bedlo (Lorre), who has been turned into a raven by Dr. Scarabus (Karloff), the Grand Master of the United Brotherhood of Sorcerers. Scarabus is trying to lure Craven to his castle, for the purpose of gaining his rival's powers. The climax is a special-effects duel between the two "giants," and Craven emerges victorious; Scarabus, atop a pile of rubble, tries to repair a woman's dress and concludes, "I guess I just don't have it any more." So good-humoured is this picture that no one dies—not even the villainous Scarabus or his mistress.

Much of *The Raven* was improvised, which creates a feeling of both spontaneity and aimlessness. Typical of the tone is the way Price, in his first scene, keeps bumping his head against a telescope in his study. "Well," commented Price in an interview, "the original script of *The Raven* was supposed to have comedy overtones; that is, it was a lot straighter than it finally finished up. And Boris, Peter, and I got together and read though it and decided that it didn't make any sense at all. So then we all sort of dreamed up the broader laughs."[14]

After finishing *The Raven*, Karloff worked for two days on another Corman film, and an additional day or two were spent filming exteriors on a California beach. Considering the rapidity with which this picture, *The Terror*, was made, the result has striking visuals, but a confusing narrative. Karloff plays Baron Von Leppe, the lord of a medieval castle on the Baltic coast. Army officer Jack Nicholson is aided by a beautiful woman, who then disappears. He searches for her at Von Leppe's castle, and there learns that the woman was the Baron's wife and has been dead for twenty years—the Baron had killed her for being unfaithful, and his servant had helped by murdering her lover. Also involved is an old witch who has hypnotised the woman into "being" the spirit of the Baron's late wife; the witch is the mother of the murdered lover, and for revenge she is trying to make the Baron feel so guilty that he will commit suicide. Eventually, Von Leppe's servant admits that the lover had in fact killed the Baron and, since then, has believed himself to be his victim. Thus the lover's mother is ironically trying to cause her own son's death. The climax occurs in a flooded crypt, with everyone trying to strangle or drown everyone else; Nicholson rescues the girl, kisses her, and then sees her rot away in his arms. Could she really have been the long-dead wife, after all?

This complicated plot is hard to follow and even harder to believe, so it is not surprising that Karloff tried to talk the director out of making it. "Corman had no story, he had the sketchiest outline of one. I read it and begged him not to do it. 'That's all right, I know what I'm going to do. I want you for two days on this.' I was in every shot of course, sometimes I was walking through and then I would change my jacket and walk back. He nearly killed me in it. The last day he had me in a tank of cold water for about two hours . . . What he really wanted was to shoot the sets of *The Raven* which were still standing and which were so magnificent—they were done by Danny Haller. As they were being pulled down around our ears so Roger was dashing around with me and a cameraman two steps ahead of the wreckers, practically. It was very funny."[17]

Corman's confidence was not exactly warranted, as he himself later explained. "When I started to assemble the footage, I realised the story didn't make sense. There was only one thing to do. I called in two of the subsidiary actors, put them in a closeup—the sets had already been struck—and had one say to the other: 'Now tell me what all this means.' And the second character in two quick minutes of exposition, unraveled the plot!"[25]

Karloff's best scene is one in which he tells the soldier about his past, and about seeing his wife's restless spirit. Though this monologue begins with a striking profile shot, most of it addressed to the camera. Karloff's facial expressions and intonations are surprisingly good, considering that the lines are of the "You think me mad!" and "You saw it too—perhaps we're both mad?" variety. Afterward, Karloff summarised his reaction to Corman by contrasting him with the director of *Frankenstein*. "Whale was more used to directing actors; Corman expects the actor to get on with it himself . . . Vincent Price and Peter Lorre and I had to find our own way because he had all he wanted. He said, 'You're experienced actors, get on with it. I've got the camera, my lighting, the angles . . . I know how I'm going to put this together.' If you asked him about advice on a scene he'd say that's your pigeon"[17]

In December 1963, Karloff, Lorre, and Price again worked together in AIP's *The Comedy of Terrors,* another spoof written by Richard Matheson. Directed with a heavy hand by Jacques Tourneur, the picture is generally a waste of good talent. Price and Lorre portray an undertaker and his assistant who try to drum up business; Karloff, as Price's senile father-in-law, has almost no opportunity to perform. It is Basil Rathbone who, as one of Price's victims, steals what there is of the show with a phenomenally prolonged death scene while reciting the "'tomorrow and tomorrow" soliloquy from "Macbeth." The photography and set design are, as usual, attractive, but the film lacks pace, imagination, and control.

Plans to have Karloff co-star with Price in *The City in the Sea* in 1964 failed to surface, but he did contribute a guest bit to *Bikini Beach*. Two years later, he had a bigger part in the no more meritorious *Ghost in the Invisible Bikini* (originally conceived as *Pajama Party in a Haunted House*). This is the familiar tale of a dead old man, the reading of his will, and the attempt of an evil lawyer to kill off all the heirs in his way, including a bunch of wholesome beach party-type kids. Karloff, the dead man who must do a good deed or be denied Heaven, has an opening scene in which he sends a ghost girl to earth as protection for the kids. Then he watches the proceedings over closed-circuit crystal ball, and the film occasionally cuts to him for comments on the main action. Karloff's bits were all-too-obviously shot separately from the rest of the film and awkwardly inserted.

Karloff spent part of 1964 in Italy, where he made *Black Sabbath* (*I tre volti della paura*) for AIP release. Director Mario Bava's success with *Black Sunday* was followed by this set of three short stories; Karloff was the narrator-host, and he starred in the third and longest episode. The first two are effective exercises in fear, but the third, "The Wurdalak," is the most ambitious. A wurdalak is a kind of vampire that lives on the blood of those it loves. Karloff portrays a father who, after killing a bandit thought to be a wurdalak, himself becomes one. The destruction of his family inevitably follows. As this elderly, wild-haired peasant, Karloff looks and sounds impressive, but the role requires little real acting. In fact, no plot or character in *Black Sabbath* is fully developed. Ex-cameraman Bava's direction is oriented toward striking visuals and surface tension, and it is in these areas that the film excells, especially with the misty landscapes and serpentine tracking shots of the wurdalak sequence. Karloff enjoyed working in Italy, "except that it was brutally cold, and the hotel was a sort of marble palace . . . it was there that I got quite ill."[54] He completed the film with difficulty, and on returning to England was stricken with pneumonia. That disease weakened his lungs and no doubt contributed to his later ill health and eventual death.

AIP next cast him in a distant adaptation of H. P. Lovecraft's "The Colour Out of Space." Made in England in 1965, it was originally to be called *The House at the End of the World* but eventually appeared as *Die, Monster, Die*. The studio's publicity made much of the fact that this was Karloff's "first monster role in thirty years," although that was not literally true. He played most of the picture from an antique wheelchair; "it's rather a sinister contraption, but somebody thoughtfully wrote it into my part so that I won't have to work my poor old legs too hard."[44] The story's locale was changed from America to England, and its plot updated to the present. The basic AIP situation of a young man arriving at a strange house to visit his girl friend, and discovering that something odd is going on was unfortunately brought into play. The revelation, when finally achieved, is that Nahum Witley (Karloff) has been using a radioactive meteorite to create plant and insect mutations. Light from the broken stone eventually contaminates the old man, who is disfigured and dies in the usual fiery climax. In an interview, Karloff related this to his scientist roles in the Columbia series. "It is, in effect, the same formula as I talked about before—the man who gets a good idea, becomes fanatical about it and when the idea goes wrong, being so fanatical he cannot let go, he gets carried over the edge."[92] *Die, Monster, Die* marked the directorial *début* of Daniel Haller, the AIP art director, who provided a sense of visual style but failed to give life to the familiar proceedings. "He was under great pressure. I enjoyed working with him. I think he's going to make a good director."[54] A few years later, Haller more

Karloff in DIE, MONSTER, DIE!

successfully handled *The Dunwich Horror,* a kind of sequel to this film.

In 1966 Karloff was involved with two productions of Video-craft International, which utilised "Animagic," a process for ani-mating puppets. *The Daydreamer,* about a young Hans Christian Andersen who visualises four of his later tales, combined live action with animation. Karloff's voice was lent to a rat who threatens Thumbelina. *Mad Monster Party* used the same process, with the puppets representing various wisecracking movie creatures, including Baron Frankenstein (Karloff's voice), the Monster, King Kong, and Phyllis Diller. Both films were clever, though child-oriented. Karloff also made a brief appearance in a routine spy melodrama, M-G-M's *The Venetian Affair* (1967), in the catalyst role of Dr. Pierre Vaugiroud, a political scientist possessing a sought-after report. This film was made in the spring of 1966; a few months later, AIP's plans for co-starring Karloff with Price in still another Richard Matheson comedy, *The Graveside Story,* fell through. Karloff also narrated *Mondo Balordo* (1967), one of those shock documentaries that followed in the wake of *Mondo Cane.*

In the same year, Karloff starred in a Spanish production, *El coleccionista de cadaveres* (*The Corpse Collector*), as a blind sculptor whose wife (Viveca Lindfors) provides him with real skeletons for use as foundations for his statues. A mediocre production, it did not appear in America until several years after Karloff's death, under the titles *Blind Man's Bluff* and *Cauldron of Blood.* Karloff was not impressed by the circumstances of making the film: the weather was so bad "that plate glass windows blew in and we got no soundtrack because the wind just went straight into the microphones. Not only that, there was no script girl either, to note down which lines had been said in which shot. So we virtually had to make up our own words all over again in the dubbing studio."[115]

In the final years of his long career, Karloff appeared in two significant productions. For Tigon Pictures in England he made *The Sorcerers,* playing an ex-stage hypnotist who has developed a way to gain long-distance control over the brain of a young subject. He can make his unknowing victim do whatever he wants, and can also share whatever feelings the youth experiences. But the kindly Karloff is in turn dominated by his wife, who becomes possessed by her first taste of power. She starts in small ways by having the youth crush an egg in his hand and then steal a fur coat, but her demands and passions escalate. She discovers, in the words of critic Robin Wood, "the delights of experiencing anything she wishes to experience, with no consequences: especially, the delights of danger and violence, which even her nice old husband can't deny that he

Karloff with Peter Bogdanovich during shooting of TARGETS

rather enjoyed."[143] Michael Reeves directed this small but trim and convincing melodrama; after making the even more skillful *The Conqueror Worm* (*Witchfinder General*), Reeves died at the distressingly unfulfilled age of twenty-five.

After *The Sorcerers,* Karloff appeared in a film that is both one of his best and one that is in a sense about him. This was *Targets,* the first attempt at direction by critic Peter Bogdanovich. Karloff owed Roger Corman two days of shooting, so Corman agreed to finance a film for Bogdanovich (who had assisted him on *The Wild Angels*) if the latter would use twenty minutes of *The Terror,* twenty of Karloff, and forty of other material. As it worked out, only four minutes of *The Terror* were employed. Karloff spent five days on the film, with the remainder shot in twenty-five more days. The picture was completed in December 1967, and Paramount acquired it for release in May 1968.

Keeping Corman's requirements in mind, Bogdanovich constructed a story contrasting the world of Hollywood horror—epitomised by Karloff, his director (played amateurishly by Bogdanovich) , and scenes from *The Terror*—with that of the modern, impersonal killing that can be done by a sniper whose rifle is equipped with a telescopic sight. The tragedy at the University of Texas a short time before, when Charles Whitman killed fourteen people from a tower, served as inspiration for part of the story. As Bogdanovich said, "In the past people were killed usually by strangulation or by a knife. Now a machine does it for you. The horror of modern killing is that you can kill somebody and not get blood on you—not be physically stained."[121] In the film, the Karloff character describes himself as "an antique, out of date, an anachronism," and the real-life Karloff also asked, "What film could match the headlines we read every day?"[115]

All this calculation resulted in a film of considerable visual control, substantial intelligence, and limited passion. Nothing is overstated, and never do the characters sit down and verbalise a moral for what we have seen. Everything we are shown of the youth's life and surroundings becomes the explanation of his frustration, alienation, and insanity, so that by the end we can partly understand that he kills people to assert himself, to break out of the artificial orderliness encasing him. Ironically, he uses an artificial and "distant" method to do so.

According to Bogdanovich, Karloff was suffering considerable discomfort from "a shattered knee that necessitated a leg brace at least and sometimes cane or crutches, together with a severe case of emphysema that badly constricted his breathing. It was extremely difficult for him to move about and speak both at once, but he never complained, was always prepared, and never held up shooting. One scene in *Targets* required him to tell a two-minute fable— a great many words to learn—and I wanted it done without cuts, which meant he would have to say it all straight through. Everybody was tired by the time we got to it—after midnight—but when the camera rolled, he did it in one take. Spontaneous applause broke

Karloff in TARGETS

out, which you could see moved him. I like to remember that moment." In addition to being a powerful, convincing social statement, *Targets* is also a tribute to Karloff the performer and a lament for the fading of his gentlemanly style. It is a fitting summation of an identity and a heritage.

While *Targets* represents the aesthetic climax of Karloff's career, the eighty-year-old actor continued to make films and appear on TV (in a commercial for A-1 sauce, his final line was "Experiment with it!"). Early in 1968, after an attack of bronchitis, he acted for AIP-Tigon in *The Crimson Altar*, a witchcraft story co-starring Christopher Lee and Barbara Steele. It was shot, according to Karloff, "in jig time, about eight days."[115] Again Karloff used a wheelchair to conserve energy. "I'm a bit of a red herring in the story, actually, and you don't know whether I'm doing the murders or it's Christopher. At the end, it turns out I'm sort of trapping him and using the young leading man as bait, much to his annoyance I may say. I don't know which was worse, the script the producer got first or the one I saw first. He had to rewrite it at least three times, poor fellow. My main contribution to scripts is to see how much of myself I can cut out, to bring a four line speech down to two."[115]

A visitor to the set confirmed these script difficulties, and emphasised Karloff's contribution to the overall film. "As alert, and as much of a perfectionist as ever, Boris questioned some lines in the script which he thought were illogical as far as his character saying them was concerned. The director examined them and found Boris was right. Other script alterations also had to be made on the spot that afternoon while Boris sat patiently sipping coffee, and the typewriter thundered away on the rewriting."[58] Finished in 1968, the picture was released in the U.S. in the summer of 1970, under the more exploitable title, *The Crimson Cult*.

Shortly after finishing *Cult*, Karloff fought an attack of pneumonia, which had its origin in some night scenes filmed during a freezing rain. Then he returned to Hollywood to spend three weeks appearing in a quartet of features for Filmica Azteca, a Mexican subsidiary of Columbia. A plan to shoot in Mexico was changed because of Karloff's health, so his scenes were filmed in Hollywood, with the unit then returning home to finish work. Jack Hill directed Karloff's footage. The titles originally announced were *Isle of the Snake People*, *The Incredible Invasion*, *The Fear Chamber* and *The House of Evil*. This job, concluded in May 1968, was Karloff's last movie-making. In the autumn he appeared on the Skelton and Winters TV shows, and then, while returning to England in November, caught a chill and entered the King Edward VII Hospital in Midhurst, near London. On Sunday, February 2, 1969, he died there, at the age of eighty-one of a respiratory disease. As his wife commented, "He always said he wanted to work until the end and this is what he did."[110]

★ ★ ★

Unlike Bela Lugosi, Karloff had the satisfaction of seeing himself and his films "justified" instead of derided. Having lived into a period when his services and persona were again in demand, he did not need to become a distant eminence dusted off for praise but never needed for active service. On a more personal level, he became an emotional focus for many youthful fans. Karloff was much more than a grandfather image for them, since grandfathers seem always to have been old, whereas they had in a sense grown up with Karloff. Thanks to film, they had shared a condensed version of his lifetime and he became simultaneously a contemporary as well as an elderly gentleman from another generation. They expressed this double affection as best they could. "When I was in the hospital recently," said Karloff in April 1968, "I got a stack of letters from youngsters from all over. And it's very rewarding."[115] One young fan visited Karloff on the set of *The Incredible Invasion*. "I saw him act. I also was able to say to him on my behalf and for all lovers of fantasy films everywhere: 'Mr. Karloff, I can't begin to tell you how much I think of you. I have loved you all my life. You are my favourite actor.' I literally found myself unable to say more. Karloff smiled and patted my hand resting on the arm of his chair. He was somewhat embarrassed as he spoke. 'Why, thank you, young man. I've done my best and it is good to know someone cares.' "[140]

Because of TV, film society, and theatrical revivals, anyone can share in the career of Boris Karloff. But the man himself is gone, and all that can be done to revive him is to seek out the rare fragments of description that exist. In 1933, "Photoplay" noted that Karloff's success had been achieved with difficulty and fairly late in life. "And with it all, his most astonishing personal characteristic is the fact that he is a man without a grievance . . . Karloff has learned that there is nothing in life worth growing bitter about."[104] From then on, Karloff projected this image of a man who had come to terms with life, who achieved that most fragile of states, contentment, and was able to sustain it for decades. In 1937, Dorothy Kilgallen provided a verbal picture of him sitting, with dogs at his feet and poems in his lap, stirring a dry Martini in front of a log fire. "This tall, gaunt actor with skin tanned to mahogany color"[29] of 1936 had become, by 1950, "a big kind man in tweedy brown with a dark sports shirt and no necktie, dark brown eyes and glasses, greying hair, mustache almost white, but eyebrows still dark."[99]

Karloff's gentle, friendly simplicity remained. While rehearsing in New York for "Peter Pan," he commented, "I like the country-side. I live in a hotel on Central Park South and look out over the park, watch it change with the seasons. It's wonderful."[99] A few years later, in California, he "gazed over the wet rooftops of Los Angeles from his penthouse balcony and murmured, 'I love the beauty of rain.' "[69] If secret doubts and frustrations lurked beneath this sensitive, calm surface, they were never shown, but the important thing is the possi-bility that here indeed was an intelligent, civilised man who did what he could and was content with that. He comprehended so fully the agonies and sufferings of his characters, that it is almost as though he had mastered himself by vicariously enduring the tragedies of others.

When in 1932 he was compared with Lon Chaney, Karloff de-clared, "There will only be one Chaney, because he understood so well the souls of afflicted people . . . None of us can do what Chaney did, because none of us feel it just as he did."[24] However, Karloff too was able to feel and project this suffering, and as early as January 1933 one writer made this judgement and prediction: "These 'mon-ster' parts, when backed by the right plot, the right settings and skill-ful direction, seem almost invariably to have met with popular success. But obviously to secure these effects is something far more than a trick. It is an art and true art is something that cannot be mechan-ically copied. The taste for the weird and the uncanny is perennial in the human soul. It is easy to conceive of Karloff ten years from now, when the names of other outstanding actors of the day shall have practically been forgotten, still holding an undisputed eminence. Chaney's and Karloff's names should go down, linked together, in motion picture history."[33]

Karloff himself said the following about author Joseph Conrad, but the words function equally well as a requiem for the man who wrote them. "All my reading life I have been devoted to this great master of English prose. He too had the power of creating suspense and terror through suggestion. But he added one ingredient which drives his stories home. Compassion. He knew that compassion is the touchstone of our common humanity, and he never fails to make us share and understand the sufferings of his characters persevering hopelessly but gallantly in an unequal struggle . . . [The story "Amy Foster"] has for its theme the essential loneliness of every human being, and is a masterpiece of understatement, and that's reason enough for me."[60]

Bibliography

1 Aaronson, "The Mask of Fu Manchu," *Motion Picture Herald* (December 10, 1932).
2 Ackerman, Forrest J. (ed.), *The Frankenscience Monster* (New York, 1969).
3 Agee, James, "Isle of the Dead," *The Nation* (September 29, 1945).
4 Allan, "Juggernaut," *Motion Picture Herald* (October 17, 1936).
5 —— "The Man Who Lived Again," *Motion Picture Herald* (October 10, 1936).
6 Anouilh, Jean, *The Lark* (New York, 1956). Translated and adapted by Lillian Hellman.
7 Arliss, George, *My Ten Years in the Studios* (Boston, 1940).
8 "Ask the Answer Man," *Photoplay* (February 1932).
9 Atkinson, Brooks, "The Lark," N.Y. *Times* (November 27, 1955).
10 —— "The Linden Tree," N.Y. *Times* (March 3, 1948).
11 —— "Peter Pan," N.Y. *Times* (April 25, 1950).
12 —— "Peter Pan," N.Y. *Times* (April 30, 1950).
13 —— "The Shop at Sly Corner," N.Y. *Times* (January 19, 1949).
14 Austin, David, "Black Cats and Cobwebs: Interview with Vincent Price," *Films and Filming* (August 1969).
15 Baehler, "The Walking Dead," *Motion Picture Herald* (March 7, 1936).
16 Beale, Ken, "Boris Karloff, Master of Horror," *Castle of Frankenstein 1967 Annual.*
17 Bean, Robin, "Boris is Back," *Films and Filming* (May 1965).
18 Beebe, Lucius, "Stage Asides," N.Y. *Herald Tribune* (July 27, 1941).
19 "Being a Monster is Really a Game," *TV Guide* (October 15, 1960).
20 Bigland, Eileen, *Mary Shelley* (New York, 1959).
21 Bogdanovich, Peter, "Boris Karloff 1887–1969," N.Y. *Times* (February 9, 1969).
22 "Boris Karloff," *Current Biography* (March 1941).
23 Brady, Thomas F., "Monster's Memories," N.Y. *Times* (July 25, 1948).
24 "Cal York Announcing——," *Photoplay* (May 1932).
25 Canby, Vincent, "Roger Corman: A Good Man Gone to Pot," N.Y. *Times* (September 18, 1966).
26 Charman, "The Ghoul," *Motion Picture Herald* (October 28, 1933).
27 "Clive of *Frankenstein*," N.Y. *Times* (November 15, 1931).
28 Coughlin, Joseph F., "British Intelligence," *Motion Picture Herald* (February 17, 1940).
29 Creelman, Eileen, "Picture Plays and Players," N.Y. *Sun* (February 12, 1936).
30 Crowther, Bosley, "The Invisible Menace," N.Y. *Times* (February 14, 1938).
31 —— "West of Shanghai," N.Y. *Times* (October 29, 1937).
32 *Daily News* (March 4, 1956).
33 Dougherty, Kathryn, "Close-ups and Long Shots," *Photoplay* (January 1933).
34 Dowling, Maxine, "The Haunted Strangler," N.Y. *Daily News* (July 4, 1958).
35 *Evening Post* (October 9, 1935).
36 Everson, William K., "The Ghoul," Programme Note for The Theodore Huff Memorial Film Society.
37 Farrell, Nancy, "Letter to the Editor," N.Y. *Times* (March 9, 1969).
38 *Film Daily* (February 4, 1932).

173

[39] Flavin, Martin, *The Criminal Code*. In Burns Mantle (ed.), *The Best Plays of 1929–30* (New York, 1930).

[40] Florey, Robert, *Hollywood: D'hier et D'aujourd'hui* (Paris, 1948).

[41] "*Frankenstein* Finished," N.Y. *Times* (October 11, 1931).

[42] "Frankenstein" (play), *The Stage* (February 13, 1930).

[43] —— London *Times* (February 11, 1930).

[44] Gilmore, Eddy, "Accent on Terror," Newark *Evening News* (April 11, 1965).

[45] "Glenn Strange," *Mad Monsters* (November 1962).

[46] Gould, Jack, N.Y. *Times* (February 21, 1955).

[47] "Great Horror Figure Dies," *Famous Monsters of Filmland* (December 1964).

[48] Green, James, "London's Pride," *Evening News* (February 12, 1968).

[49] Hall, Mordaunt, "Alias the Doctor," N.Y. *Times* (March 3, 1932).

[50] —— "Behind the Mask," N.Y. *Times* (May 2, 1932).

[51] "Her Honor the Governor," N.Y. *Times* (July 20, 1926).

[52] "Hollywood in Review," N.Y. *Times* (March 6, 1932).

[53] Hopkins, Captain E. M., "Letter to the Editor," N.Y. *Times* (April 8, 1934).

[54] "Interview with Boris Karloff," *Castle of Frankenstein* (November 1966).

[55] "Interview with Boris Karloff," *Radio Times* (November 27, 1953).

[56] "Interview with Jack Pierce," *Monster Mania* (October 1966).

[57] "James Whale and *Frankenstein*," N.Y. *Times* (December 20, 1931).

[58] Jarman, Peter J., "The Shape of Things to Come," *Famous Monsters of Filmland* (January 1969).

[59] Karloff, Boris, "Introduction," *And the Darkness Falls* (New York, 1946).

[60] —— "Introduction," *Tales of Terror* (New York, 1943).

[61] —— "Memoirs of a Monster," *Saturday Evening Post* (November 3, 1962).

[62] —— "My Life as a Monster," *Journal of Frankenstein* (1959).

[63] —— "Screen's Frightful Fiend Just a 'Darling' to his Charming Wife," N.Y. *Evening-Journal* (July 11, 1936).

[64] King-Hele, Desmond, *Erasmus Darwin* (New York, 1963).

[65] Krutch, Joseph Wood, "Arsenic and Old Lace," *The Nation* (January 25, 1941).

[66] Lanchester, Elsa, "Letter to the Editor," *Life* (April 5, 1968).

[67] Landry, Robert J., "The Black Cat," *Variety* (May 22, 1934).

[68] Linden, Paul, "Karloff in the Magic Castle," *Famous Monsters of Filmland* (November 1967).

[69] "Love That Monster," *TV Guide* (c. 1957).

[70] M., G., "Son of Frankenstein," *Motion Picture Herald* (January 21, 1939).

[71] "M.M. Interviews Edgar G. Ulmer," *Modern Monsters* (August 1966).

[72] Mackey, Joseph, "Karloff—Is He Man or Actor?" N.Y. *Sun* (January 17, 1941).

[73] Mannock, P. L., "Building Up the Bogey Man," *Picturegoer Weekly* (April 8, 1933).

[74] —— "On the British Sets," *Picturegoer Weekly* (April 22, 1933).

[75] Mantle, Burns (ed.), *The Best Plays of 1950–51* (New York, 1951).

[76] "Mask of Fu Manchu," *Photoplay* (January 1933).

[77] McCarthy, "Bride of Frankenstein," *Motion Picture Herald* (April 20, 1935).

[78] —— "The House of Rothschild," *Motion Picture Herald* (March 10, 1934).

[79] —— "The Lost Patrol," *Motion Picture Herald* (February 3, 1934).

[80] —— "The Mummy," *Motion Picture Herald* (December 3, 1932).

[81] McManus, Margaret, "Monstrously Lucky Fellow, Karloff Says," N.Y. *World Telegram and Sun* (March 10, 1962).

[82] Meehan, Leo, "Frankenstein," *Motion Picture Herald* (November 14, 1931).

[83] *Motion Picture Herald* (October 15, 1932).

[84] —— (October 14, 1933).

[85] —— (April 21, 1934).

[86] —— (December 15, 1934).

[87] —— (June 15, 1935).

[88] —— (January 4, 1936).

[89] —— (June 6, 1936).

[90] —— (June 30, 1936).

[91] —— (April 6, 1946).

92 "My Life of Terror," *Shriek* (October 1965).

93 *Newsweek* (November 27, 1955).

94 Nolan, William F., "Meal with a Monster," *Famous Monsters of Filmland* (April 1963).

95 "Ogre of the Make-Up Box," N.Y. *Times* (March 31, 1935).

96 "Oh, You Beautiful Monster," N.Y. *Times* (January 29, 1939).

97 "Parisian Nights," N.Y. *Times* (June 2, 1925).

98 *Photoplay* (December 1932).

99 Pollock, Arthur, "Theatre Time," *Daily Compass* (March 29, 1950).

100 *Post* (October 30, 1939).

101 Prelutsky, Burt, *Screen* (July 5, 1968).

102 Priestley, J. B., *The Linden Tree.* In *The Plays of J. B. Priestley* (London, 1948).

103 —— *The Old Dark House* (New York, 1928).

104 Rankin, Ruth, "Meet the Monster," *Photoplay* (January 1933).

105 Reed, Rex, "Myrna's Back—And Boyer's Got Her," N.Y. *Times* (April 13, 1969).

106 Ripperger, Walter, "The Old Dark House," *The Mystery Magazine* (December 1932). A fictionalisation of the script.

107 Roman, Robert C., "Boris Karloff," *Films in Review* (August–September 1964).

108 Ruddy, Jonah Maurice, "The Dulwich Horror," source uncredited (c. 1936). Reprinted in *The Frankenscience Monster.*

109 Rush, "The Mad Genius," *Variety* (October 27, 1931).

110 Santora, Phil, "Boris Karloff: The Mellow Monster," N.Y. *Daily News* (February 4, 1969).

111 Sennwald, A. D., "The Mask of Fu Manchu," N.Y. *Times* (December 3, 1932).

112 —— "Night World," N.Y. *Times* (May 28, 1932).

113 Shanley, J. P., "Nothing to be Scared About," N.Y. *Times* (March 6, 1955).

114 Shelley, Mary, "Introduction" to the 1831 edition of *Frankenstein.*

115 Shivas, Mark, "Karloff, Still Eager to Scare Us Witless," N.Y. *Times* (April 14, 1968).

116 Skinner, Richard Dana, "The House of Rothschild," *The Commonweal* (March 30, 1934).

117 Smith, H. Allen, "Karloff Frightened over Appearing on Broadway Stage," N.Y. *World Telegram* (December 18, 1940).

118 Sobol, Louis, "The Voice of Broadway: Down Memory Lane with Boris Karloff," N.Y. *Evening Journal* (June 5, 1937).

119 "Son of Frankenstein," *Variety* (January 18, 1939).

120 "Special Interview: Glenn Strange," *Modern Monsters* (October–November 1966).

121 Thomas, Kevin, "Continental Critic Writes, Directs Karloff Horror Tale," Philadelphia *Inquirer* (June 18, 1967).

122 *Time* (November 28, 1955).

123 *Times* (March 28, 1926).

124 —— (May 22, 1931).

125 —— (May 1, 1932).

126 —— (August 28, 1932).

127 —— (December 2, 1932).

128 —— (January 26, 1934).

129 —— (January 27, 1934).

130 —— (April 8, 1934).

131 —— (January 11, 1936).

132 —— (February 4, 1969).

133 Troy, William, "The House of Rothschild," *The Nation* (April 4, 1934).

134 Van Horne, Harriet, N.Y. *World-Telegram* (August 9, 1956).

135 *Variety* (September 8, 1931).

136 —— (December 8, 1931).

137 —— (January 5, 1932).

138 —— (June 6, 1933).

[139] —— (April 27, 1938).
[140] Warren, Bill, "The Last Act of Boris Karloff," *Famous Monsters of Filmland* (July 1969).
[141] Weaver, William A., "Bedlam," *Motion Picture Herald* (April 20, 1946).
[142] Williams, Bob, "On the Air," N.Y. *Post* (April 2, 1959).
[143] Wood, Robin, "In Memoriam Michael Reeves," *Movie* (Winter, 1969/70).
[144] *World-Telegram* (May 19, 1934).

Filmography of Boris Karloff

1919
His Majesty, the American. United Artists. Direction, Joseph Henabery. Script, Henabery and Elton Banks. Cast: Douglas Fairbanks, Marjorie Daw, Frank Campeau, Sam Southern.

1920
The Prince and Betty. Pathe. Direction, Robert Thornby. Original story, P. G. Wodehouse. Cast: William Desmond, Mary Thurman, Anita Kay, George Swann.
The Deadlier Sex. Pathe. Direction, Robert Thornby. Original story, Fred Myton. Cast: Blanche Sweet, Mahlon Hamilton.
The Courage of Marge O'Doone. Vitagraph. Direction, David Smith. Adaptation, Robert North Bradbury. Original story, James Oliver Curwood. Cast: Pauline Starke, Jack Curtis, Niles Welch, William Dyer.
The Last of the Mohicans. Associated Producers. Direction, Maurice Tourneur and Clarence Brown. Script, Robert Dillon. Original novel, James Fenimore Cooper. Cast: Wallace Beery, Barbara Bedford, Albert Roscoe, Lillian Hall.

1921
The Hope Diamond Mystery (serial). Kosmik. Direction, Stuart Payton. Adaptation, Charles Goddard and John B. Clymer. Original story, May Yohe. Cast: Grace Darmond, George Cheseboro, Harry Carter, Carmen Phillips.
Without Benefit of Clergy. Pathe. Direction, James Young. Original story, Rudyard Kipling. Cast: Virginia Brown Faire, Percy Marmont.
The Cave Girl. Inspiration. Direction, Joseph J. Franz. Script, William Parker. Original play, Guy Bolton and George Middleton. Cast: Teddie Gerard, Charles Meredith.

Cheated Hearts. Universal. Direction, Hobart Henley. Script, Wallace Clifton. Original story, William F. Payson. Cast: Herbert Rawlinson, Warner Baxter, Marjorie Daw.

1922
The Man from Downing Street. Vitagraph. Direction, Edward Jose. Script, Bradley J. Smollen. Original story, Clyde Westover, Lottie Horner, and Florine Williams. Cast: Earle Williams.
The Infidel. Preferred. Direction, James Young. Script, Young. Cast: Katherine MacDonald, Robert Ellis.
Omar the Tentmaker. Associated First National. Direction, James Young. Adaptation, Richard W. Tully. Original play, "Omar Khayyam, the Tentmaker," Tully. Cast: Guy Bates Post, Virginia Brown Faire, Patsy Ruth Miller.
The Altar Stairs. Universal. Direction, Lambert Hillyer. Script, Doris Schroeder and George Hively. Original story, G. B. Lancster. Cast: Frank Mayo.
The Woman Conquers. Preferred. Direction, Tom Forman. Original story, Violet Clark. Cast: Katherine MacDonald, Bryant Washburn.

1923
The Prisoner. Universal. Direction, Jack Conway. Script, Edward T. Lowe. Original story, "Castle Craneycrow," George Barr McCutcheon. Cast: Herbert Rawlinson.
The Gentleman from America. Universal. Direction, Edward Sedgwick. Script, George Hull. Cast: Hoot Gibson, Tom O'Brien, Louise Lorraine.

1924
Dynamite Dan. Sunset-States Rights. Direction, Bruce Mitchell. Cast: Kenneth McDonald.

Parisian Nights. R. C. Pictures. Direction, Alfred Santell. Script, Fred Myton and Doty Hobart. Original story, Emile Forst. Cast: Renee Adoree, Elaine Hammerstein, Lou Tellegen, William J. Kelly.

The Hellion. Sunset-States Rights. Direction: Bruce Mitchell. Cast: Alline Goodwin, William Lester.

1925

Forbidden Cargo. R. C. Pictures. Direction, Tom Buckingham. Script, Frederick Kennedy Myton. Original story, Myton. Cast: Evelyn Brent.

The Prairie Wife. Eastern. Direction, Hugo Ballin. Continuity, Ballin. Original story, Arthur Stringer. Cast: Dorothy Devore, Herbert Rawlinson, Gibson Gowland.

Lady Robinhood. R. C. Pictures. Direction, Ralph Ince. Script, Fred Myton. Original story, Clifford Howard and Burke Jenkins. Cast: Evelyn Brent, Robert Ellis.

Never the Twain Shall Meet. Cosmopolitan. Direction, Maurice Tourneur. Script, Eugene Mullin. Original story, Peter B. Kyne. Cast: Anita Stewart, Bert Lytell, Huntley Gordon, George Siegmann.

1926

The Greater Glory. First National. Direction, Curt Rehfeld. Script, June Mathis. Original novel, "Viennese Medley," Edith O'Shaughnessy. Cast: Anna Q. Nilsson, Conway Tearle, Jean Hersholt, Ian Keith.

Flames. Associated Exhibitors. Direction, Lewis H. Moomaw. Script, Alfred A. Cohn. Original story, Cohn. Cast: Eugene O'Brien, Virginia Valli, Jean Hersholt, Bryant Washburn.

The Bells. Chadwick. Direction, James Young. Script, Young. Original play, "The Polish Jew," Erckmann-Chatrian. Photography, L. William O'Connell. Lighting effects, Perry Harris. Cast: Lionel Barrymore (*Mathias*), Boris Karloff (*The Mesmerist*), Gustav von Seyffertitz (*Jerome Frantz*), E. Alyn Warren (*Baruch Koweski; Jethro Koweski*).

The Nickelhopper. Hal Roach. Direction, Hal Yates. Cast: Mabel Normand, Theodore van Eltz.

Valencia. M-G-M. Direction, Dimitri Buchowetzki. Script, Alice Miller. Cast: Mae Murray.

The Golden Web. Lumas. Direction, Walter Lang. Script, James Bell Smith. Original novel, E. Phillips Oppenheim. Cast: Lillian Rich, Huntley Gordon.

Her Honor, the Governor. R. C. Pictures. Direction, Chet Withey. Script, Doris Anderson. Original story, Hyatt Daab and Weed Dickinson. Cast: Pauline Frederick, Carrol Nye, Greta von Rue, Tom Santschi.

The Eagle of the Sea. Paramount. Direction, Frank Lloyd. Script, Julian Josephson. Original novel, "Captain Sazarac," Charles Tenney Jackson. Cast: Florence Vidor, Ricardo Cortez, Sam DeGrasse, Andre Beranger.

Flaming Fury. R. C. Pictures. Direction, James Hogan. Continuity, Ewart Adamson. Original story, Adamson. Cast: Ranger (*Dog*), Betty May.

1927

Tarzan and the Golden Lion. R. C. Pictures. Direction, J. P. MacGowan. Script, William E. Wing. Original story, Edgar Rice Burroughs. Cast: James H. Pierce, Edna Murphy, Dorothy Dunbar, D'Arcy Corrigan.

Let It Rain. Paramount. Direction, Edward Cline. Script, Wade Boteler, George J. Crone, and Earle Snell. Cast: Douglas MacLean, Shirley Mason, Wade Boteler, Frank Campeau.

The Meddlin' Stranger. Pathe. Direction, Richard Thorpe. Script, Christopher Booth. Cast: Wally Wales.

The Phantom Buster. Pathe. Direction, William Bertram. Script, Betty Burbridge. Cast: Buddy Roosevelt.

Soft Cushions. Paramount. Direction, Edward Cline. Script, Wade Boteler and Frederick Chapin. Original story, George Randolph Chester. Cast: Douglas MacLean, Sue Carol, Richard Carle, Russell Powell.

Two Arabian Knights. Caddo. Direction, Lewis Milestone. Script, James O'Donohue. Adaptation, Wallace Smith and Cyril Gardner. Original story, Donald McGibney. Cast: Louis Wolheim, William Boyd, Mary Astor, Michael Vavitch.

The Love Mart. First National. Direction, George Fitzmaurice. Script, Benjamin Glazer. Original novel, "The Code of Victor Jallot," Edward Childs Carpenter. Cast: Billie Dove, Gilbert Roland, Noah Beery, Armand Kaliz.

The Princess from Hoboken. Tiffany.

Direction, Allan Dale. Script, Sonya Levien. Cast: Blanche Mehaffey, Lou Tellegen.

1928

Old Ironsides. Paramount. Direction, James Cruze. Adaptation, Harry Carr and Walter Woods. Original story, Laurence Stallings. Cast: Esther Ralston, Charles Farrell, Wallace Beery, George Bancroft.

Vultures of the Sea (serial). Mascot. Direction, Richard Thorpe. Cast: Shirley Mason, Johnny Walker, Tom Santschi.

1929

The Fatal Warning (serial). Mascot. Direction, Richard Thorpe. Cast: Helene Costello, Ralph Graves, Sid Crossley, George Periolat.

Burning the Wind. Universal. Direction, Henry McRae and Herbert Blanche. Script, George Plympton and Raymond Schrock. Original novel, "A Daughter of the Dons," William McLeod Raine. Cast: Hoot Gibson, Virginia Brown Faire, Cesare Gravina.

Little Wild Girl. Trinity. Direction, Frank Mattison. Script, Cecil B. Hill. Original story, Putnam Hoover. Cast: Lila Lee, Cullen Landis, Frank Merrill, Sheldon Lewis.

Phantom of the North. Biltmore. Direction, Harry Webb. Script, George Hull and Carl Kursada. Original story, Flora E. Douglas. Cast: Edith Roberts, Donald Keith, Kathleen Key, Joe Bonomo.

The Devil's Chaplain. Rayart. Direction, Duke Worne. Script, Arthur Hoerl. Original story, George Bronson Howard. Cast: Cornelius Keefe, Virginia Brown Faire, Josef Swickard.

Two Sisters. Rayart. Direction, Scott Pembroke. Script, Arthur Hoerl. Original story, Virginia T. Vandewater. Cast: Viola Dana, Rex Lease, Claire DuBray, Tom Lingham.

Behind That Curtain. Fox. Direction, Irving Cummings. Script, Sonya Levien and Clarke Silvernail. Original novel, Earl Derr Biggers. Cast: Warner Baxter, Lois Moran, Claude King, Gilbert Emery.

The King of the Kongo (serial). Mascot, Direction, Richard Thorpe. Cast: Jacqueline Logan, Walter Miller, Richard Tucker.

The Unholy Night. M-G-M. Direction, Lionel Barrymore. Script, Edwin Justus Mayer. Original story, "The Doomed Regiment," Ben Hecht. Cast: Ernest Torrence, Roland Young, Dorothy Sebastian, Claude Fleming.

1930

The Bad One. UA. Direction, George Fitzmaurice. Script, Carey Wilson and Howard Emmett Rogers. Original story, John Farrow. Cast: Dolores Del Rio, Edmund Lowe, Don Alvarado, Blanche Friderici.

The Sea Bat. M-G-M. Direction, Wesley Ruggles. Script, Bess Meredyth and Howard Lawson. Original story, Dorothy Yost. Cast: Raquel Torres, Charles Bickford, Nils Asther, George F. Marion.

The Utah Kid. Tiffany. Direction, Richard Thorpe. Script, Frank Howard Clark. Original story, Clark. Cast: Rex Lease, Dorothy Sebastian, Tom Santschi, Mary Carr.

Mothers Cry. First National. Direction, Hobart Henley. Script, Lenore J. Coffee. Original novel, Helen Grace Carlisle. Cast: Dorothy Peterson, Helen Chandler, David Manners, Evalyn Knapp.

1931

The Criminal Code. Columbia. Direction, Howard Hawks. Adaptation and additional dialogue, Fred Niblo, Jr., and Seton I. Miller. Original play, Martin Flavin. Cast: Walter Huston, Phillips Holmes, Constance Cummings, Mary Doran, DeWitt Jennings, John Sheehan.

King of the Wild (serial). Mascot. Direction, Richard Thorpe. Original story, Wyndham Gittens and Ford Beebe. Cast: Walter Miller, Nora Lane, Tom Santschi, Victor Potel.

Cracked Nuts. RKO-Radio. Direction, Edward Cline. Script, Al Boasberg. Dialogue, Ralph Spence. Cast: Bert Wheeler, Robert Woolsey, Dorothy Lee, Edna May Oliver.

Young Donovan's Kid. RKO-Radio. Direction, Fred Niblo. Script, J. Walter Ruben. Original story, "Big Brother," Rex Beach. Cast: Richard Dix, Jackie Cooper, Marion Shilling, Frank Sheridan.

Smart Money. Warners. Direction, Alfred E. Green. Script and original story, Kubec Glasmon, John Bright, Lucien Hubbard, and Joseph Jackson. Cast:

Karloff with Regis Toomey in GRAFT

Edward G. Robinson, James Cagney, Evalyn Knapp, Ralf Harolde.
The Public Defender. RKO-Radio. Direction, J. Walter Ruben. Script, Bernard Schubert. Original novel, "The Splendid Crime," George Goodschild. Cast: Richard Dix, Shirley Grey, Edmund Breese, Paul Hurst.
Graft. Whirlwind. Direction, Christy Cabanne. Script, Barry Barringer. Original story, Barringer. Cast: Regis Toomey, Dorothy Revier, Sue Carol, Willard Robertson.
Five Star Final. First National. Direction, Mervyn LeRoy. Script, Byron Morgan. Adaptation, Robert Lord. Original play, Louis Weitzenkorn. Cast: Edward G. Robinson, H. B. Warner, Marian Marsh, Anthony Bushell, George E. Stone, Frances Starr, Ona Munson, Aline MacMahon.
I Like Your Nerve. First National. Direction, William McGann. Adaptation, Houston Branch. Dialogue, Roland Pertwee. Original story, Pertwee. Cast: Douglas Fairbanks, Jr., Loretta Young, Claude Allister.
The Yellow Ticket. Fox. Direction, Raoul Walsh. Script, Jules Furthman.

Dialogue, Furthman and Guy Bolton. Original play, Michael Morton. Cast: Elissa Landi, Lionel Barrymore, Laurence Olivier, Walter Byron.
The Mad Genius. Warners. Direction, Michael Curtiz. Script, J. Grubb Alexander and Harvey Thew. Original play, "The Idol," Martin Brown. Cast: John Barrymore, Marian Marsh, Donald Cook, Carmel Myers, Charles Butterworth, Luis Alberni.
Frankenstein. Universal. Production, Carl Laemmle Jr. Direction, James Whale. Script, Garrett Fort and Francis Edwards Faragoh. Adaptation, John L. Balderston. Original play, Peggy Webling. Original novel, Mary Shelley. Photography, Arthur Edeson. Electrical and photographic effects, John P. Fulton. Art Direction, Charles D. Hall. Set Design, Herman Rosse. Make-up, Jack Pierce. Editing supervision, Maurice Pivar. Editing, Clarence Kolster. 71 min. Cast: Colin Clive (*Dr. Henry Frankenstein*), Mae Clarke (*Elizabeth*), John Boles (*Victor Moritz*), Boris Karloff (*Monster*), Edward van Sloan (*Dr. Waldman*), Dwight Frye (*Fritz*), Frederick Kerr (*Baron Frankenstein*), Lio-

Karloff reacts to the drug in FRANKENSTEIN (frame enlargement)

nel Belmore (*Burgomaster*), Michael Mark (*Peasant Father*), Marilyn Harris (*Maria*), Arletta Duncan and Pauline Moore (*Bridesmaids*).

The Guilty Generation. Columbia. Direction, Rowland V. Lee. Script, Jack Cunningham. Original play, Jo Milward and J. Kirby Hawkes. Cast: Leo Carrillo (*Mike Palmero*), Constance Cummings (*Maria Palmero*), Robert Young (*Marco Ricca*), Boris Karloff (*Tony Ricca*).

Tonight or Never. Feature Productions. Direction, Mervyn LeRoy. Script, Ernest Vajda. Adaptation, Frederick Hatton and Fanny Hatton. Original play, Lily Hatvany. Cast: Gloria Swanson, Ferdinand Gottschalk, Robert Grieg, Melvyn Douglas.

1932

Business and Pleasure. Fox. Direction, David Butler. Script, William Counselman and Gene Towne. Original play, "The Plutocrat," Arthur Goodrich. Original novel, Booth Tarkington. Cast: Will Rogers, Jetta Goudal, Joel McCrea, Dorothy Peterson.

Alias the Doctor. First National. Direction, Michael Curtiz. Script, Houston Branch and Charles Kenyon. Original play, Emric Foeldes. Cast: Richard Bar-thelmess, Marian Marsh, Norman Foster, Lucille La Verne.

The Miracle Man. Paramount. Direction, Norman Z. McLeod. Adaptation, Waldemar Young. Dialogue, Young and Samuel Hoffenstein. Original story, Frank L. Packard and Robert H. Davis, and play, George M. Cohan. Cast: Sylvia Sidney, Chester Morris, Irving Pichel, John Wray.

Behind the Mask. Columbia. Direction, John Francis Dillon. Continuity, Dorothy Howell. Adaptation and dialogue, Jo Swerling. Original story, Swerling. Cast: Jack Holt (*Jack Hart*), Constance Cummings (*Julie Arnold*), Boris Karloff (*Jim Henderson*), Claude King (*Arnold*), Edward van Sloan (*Dr. August Steiner*).

Night World. Universal. Direction, Hobart Henley. Script, Richard Schayer. Original story, P. J. Wolfson and Allen Rivkin. Cast: Lew Ayres (*Michael Rand*), Mae Clarke (*Ruth Taylor*), Boris Karloff ("*Happy" MacDonald*), Dorothy Revier (*Mrs. MacDonald*), Hedda Hopper (*Mrs. Rand*).

The Cohens and Kellys in Hollywood. Universal. Direction, John Francis Dillon. Script, Howard J. Green. Comedy construction, James Mulhouser. Cast: George Sidney, Charlie Murray, June

Clyde, Norman Foster, Emma Dunn, Esther Howard, Luis Alberni. *As Themselves:* Tom Mix, Lew Ayres, Sydney Fox, Boris Karloff, Genevieve Tobin.

Scarface. Caddo. Direction, Howard Hawks. Continuity and dialogue, Seton I. Miller, John Lee Mahin, and W. R. Burnett. Story: Ben Hecht. Original novel, Armitage Trail. Cast: Paul Muni (*Tony Camonte*), Karen Morley (*Poppy*), Ann Dvorak (*Cesca Camonte*), Osgood Perkins (*Johnny Lovo*), Boris Karloff (*Gaffney*), George Raft (*Rinaldo*), Purnell Pratt (*Publisher*).

The Old Dark House. Universal. Direction, James Whale. Script and adaptation, Benn W. Levy. Additional dialogue, R. C. Sherriff. Original novel, "Benighted," J. B. Priestley. Photography, Arthur Edeson. Editing supervision, Maurice Pivar. Editing, Clarence Kolster. 74 mins. Cast: Boris Karloff (*Morgan*), Melvyn Douglas (*Roger Penderel*), Charles Laughton (*Sir William Porterhouse*), Gloria Stuart (*Margaret Waverton*), Lillian Bond (*Gladys DuCane*), Ernest Thesiger (*Horace Femm*), Eva Moore (*Rebecca Femm*), Raymond Massey (*Philip Waverton*), Brember Wills (*Saul Femm*), John Dudgeon (*Sir Roderick Femm*).

The Mask of Fu Manchu. M-G-M. Direction, Charles Brabin. Script, Irene Kuhn, Edgar Allan Woolf, and John Willard. Original novel, Sax Rohmer. Photography, Gaetano Gaudio. Editing, Ben Lewis. Art direction, Cedric Gibbons. Gowns, Adrian. 72 mins. Cast: Boris Karloff (*Fu Manchu*), Lewis Stone (*Sir Denis Nayland Smith*), Karen Morley (*Sheila Barton*), Charles Starrett (*Terrence Granville*), Myrna Loy (*Fah Lo See*), Jean Hersholt (*Prof. von Berg*), Lawrence Grant (*Sir Lionel Barton*), David Torrence (*McLeod*).

The Mummy. Universal. Direction, Karl Freund. Script, John L. Balderston. Original story, Nina Wilcox Putnam and Richard Schayer. Photography, Charles Stumar. Editing, Milton Carruth. Art direction, Willy Pogany. Make-up, Jack Pierce. 78 or 72 mins. Cast: Boris Karloff (*Imhotep/Ardath Bey*), Zita Johann (*Helen Grosvenor*), David Manners (*Frank Whemple*), Edward van Sloan (*Dr. Muller*), Arthur Byron (*Sir Joseph Whemple*), Bramwell Fletcher (*Norton*), Noble Johnson (*The Nubian*), Leonard Mudie (*Prof.*

Pearson), Katheryn Byron (*Frau Muller*), Eddie Kane (*Doctor*), Tony Marlow (*Inspector*), James Crane (*Pharaoh*), Arnold Gray (*Knight*), Henry Victor (*Warrior*).

1933

The Ghoul. Gaumont-British. Direction, T. Hayes Hunter. Script, Robert Downing. Original play and novel, Frank King and Leonard Hines. Photography, Günther Krampf. Editing, Ian Dalrymple. Art direction, Alfred Junge. Make-up, Heinrich Heitfeld. 73 or 85 mins. Cast: Boris Karloff (*Prof. Morlant*), Cedric Hardwicke (*Broughton*), Ernest Thesiger (*Laing*), Dorothy Hyson (*Betty Harlow*), Anthony Bushell (*Ralph Morland*), Kathleen Harrison (*Kaney*), Harold Huth (*Aga Ben Dragore*), D. A. Clarke-Smith (*Mahmoud*), Ralph Richardson (*Nigel Hartley*).

1934

The Lost Patrol. RKO. Direction, John Ford. Script, Dudley Nichols. Adaptation, Garrett Fort. Original story, "Patrol," Philip MacDonald. Photography, Harold Wenstrom. Editing, Paul Weatherwax. Art direction, Van Nest Polglase and Sidney Uliman. Music, Max Steiner. 75 mins. Cast: Victor McLaglen (*Sergeant*), Boris Karloff (*Sanders*), Wallace Ford (*Morelli*), Reginald Denny (*Brown*), J. M. Kerrigan (*Quincannon*), Billy Bevan (*Hale*).

The House of Rothschild. 20th Century. Direction, Alfred Werker. Script, Nunnally Johnson. Original play, George Hembert Westley. Photography, Peverell Marley. Technicolor photography, Ray Rennahan. Editing, Alan McNeil and Barbara McLean. Music, Alfred Newman. 86 mins. Cast: George Arliss (*Mayer Rothschild/Nathan Rothschild*), Boris Karloff (*Baron Ledrantz*), Loretta Young (*Julie Rothschild*), Robert Young (*Captain Fitzroy*), C. Aubrey Smith (*Duke of Wellington*), Arthur Byron (*Baring*), Reginald Owen (*Herries*).

The Black Cat. Universal. Direction, Edgar G. Ulmer. Script, Peter Ruric. Original story, Ruric and Ulmer. Suggested by the Poe story. Photography, John Mescall. Editing, Ray Curtis. Art direction, Charles D. Hall. 65 mins. Cast: Boris Karloff (*Hjalmar Poelzig*), Bela

Lugosi (*Dr Vitus Werdegast*), David Manners (*Peter Alison*), Jacqueline Wells (*Joan Alison*), Luis Alberni (*Train Steward*), Egon Brecher (*Majordomo*), Harry Cording, (*Thamal*), Lucille Lund (*Karen Poelzig*), Anna Duncan (*Maid*), Herman Bing (*Car Steward*), Andre Cheron (*Train Conductor*), George Davis (*Bus Driver*), Alphonse Martell (*Porter*), Tony Marlow (*Border Patrolman*), **Paul Weigel** (*Station Master*), Albert Polet (*Waiter*), Rodney Hildebrant (*Brakeman*).
Gift of Gab. Universal. Direction, Karl Freund. Script, Rian James. Adaptation, Lou Breslow. Original story, Jerry Wald and Philip G. Epstein. Photography, Harold Wenstrom and George Robinson. Editing, Raymond Curtis. 70 mins. Cast: Edmund Lowe, Gloria Stuart, Alice White, Victor Moore, Ethel Waters, Guest Stars: Paul Lukas, Boris Karloff, Bela Lugosi, Chester Morris, **Ruth Etting.**

1935
Bride of Frankenstein. Universal. Direction, James Whale. Script, William Hurlbut. Adaptation, Hurlbut and John L. Balderston. Suggested by the Mary Shelley novel. Photography, John Mescall. Special photographic effects, John P. Fulton. Editing supervision, Maurice Pivar. Editing, Ted Kent. Art direction, Charles D. Hall. Music, Franz Waxman. 80 mins. Cast: Boris Karloff (*The Monster*), Colin Clive (*Henry Frankenstein*), Valerie Hobson (*Elizabeth*), Elsa Lanchester (*Monster's Mate/Mary Shelley*), Ernest Thesiger (*Dr. Pretorius*), **O. P. Heggie** (*Blind Hermit*), **Dwight Frye** (*Karl*), **E. E. Clive** (*Burgomaster*), Una O'Connor (*Minnie*), Anne Darling (*Shepherdess*), Douglas Walton (*Percy Shelley*), Gavin Gordon (*Lord Byron*), Neil Fitzgerald (*Rudy*), Reginald Barlow (*Hans*), Mary Gordon (*His Wife*), Gunnis Davis (*Uncle Glutz*), Tempe Piggott (*Auntie Glutz*), Ted Billings (*Ludwig*), Lucien Prival (*Butler*), John Carradine (*Hunter*).
The Raven. Universal. Direction, Louis Friedlander. Script, David Boehm. Suggested by the Poe poem. Photography, Charles Stumar. Editing supervision, Maurice Pivar. Editing, Alfred Akst. Art direction, Albert S. D'Agostino. Music supervision, Gilbert Kurland. Dance arrangements, Theodore Kosloff. 60 mins.

Cast: Boris Karloff (*Edmond Bateman*), Bela Lugosi (*Dr. Richard Vollin*), Lester Matthews (*Dr. Jerry Halden*), Irene Ware (*Jean Thatcher*), Samuel S. Hinds (*Judge Thatcher*), Spencer Charters (*Colonel Grant*), Inez Courtney (*Mary Burns*), Ian Wolfe (*Geoffrey*), Maidel Turner (*Harriet*), Arthur Hoyt (*Chapman*).
The Black Room. Columbia. Direction, Roy William Neill. Script, Henry Meyers and Arthur Strawn. Original story, Strawn. Photography, Al Siegler. Editing, Richard Cahoon. Art direction, Stephen Goosson. 67 or 75 mins. Cast: Boris Karloff (*Gregor/Anton*), Marian Marsh (*Thea*), Katherine de Mille (*Mashka*), Robert Allen (*Lt. Lussan*), John Buckler (*Beran*), Thurston Hall (*Colonel Hassel*), Henry Kolker (*De Berghman*).

1936
The Invisible Ray. Universal. Direction, Lambert Hillyer. Script, John Colton. Original story, Howard Higgin and Douglas Hodges. Photography, George Robinson. Special photography, John P. Fulton. Editing, Bernard Burton. Art direction, Albert S. D'Agostino. Music, Franz Waxman. 75 or 81 mins. Cast: Boris Karloff (*Dr. Janos Rukh*), Bela Lugosi (*Dr. Felix Benet*), Beulah Bondi (*Lady Arabella Stevens*), Frances Drake (*Diane Rukh*), Frank Lawton (*Ronald Drake*), Violet Kemble Cooper (*Mother Rukh*), Walter Kingsford (*Sir Francis Stevens*), Frank Reicher (*Prof. Meiklejohn*), Paul Weigel (*M. Noyer*), Georges Renevant (*Chief of the Sûreté*), Nydia Westman (*Briggs*), Daniel Haines (*Headman*), Adele St. Maur (*Mme Noyer*), Lawrence Stewart (*Number One Boy*), Etta McDaniels (**Zulu Woman**), Inez Seabury (*Celeste*), Winter Hall (*Minister*).
The Walking Dead. Warners. Direction, Michael Curtiz. Script, Ewart Adamson. Original story, Adamson and Joseph Fields. Photography, Hal Mohr. Editing, Thomas Pratt. Art direction, Hugh Reticker. 65 mins. Cast: Boris Karloff (*John Ellman*), Marguerite Churchill (*Nancy*), Ricardo Cortez (*Nolan*), Edmund Gwenn (*Dr. Beaumont*), Barton MacLane (*Loder*), Warren Hull (*Jimmy*), Joe Sawyer (*Trigger*), Henry O'Neill (*Werner*), Robert Strange

Karloff with Marguerite Churchill and Warren Hull in THE WALK-
ING DEAD

(*Merritt*), Joseph King (*Judge Shaw*), Paul Harvey (*Blackstone*).

The Man Who Changed His Mind (*The Man Who Lived Again*). Gainsborough. Gaumont release. Direction, Robert Stevenson. Script, L. du Garde Peach, Sidney Gilliat, and John L. Balderston. Photography, Jack Cox. Editing, R. E. Dearing and Alfred Roome. Art direction, Vetchinsky. Dresses, Molyneux. 64 mins. Cast: Boris Karloff (*Dr. Laurience*), Anna Lee (*Dr. Claire Wyatt*), John Loder (*Dick Haslewood*), Frank Cellier (*Lord Haslewood*), Lynn Harding (*Prof. Holloway*), Cecil Parker (*Dr. Gratton*), Donald Calthrop (*Clayton*).

Juggernaut. Twickenham. Grand National release. Direction, Henry Edwards. Script, Cyril Campion, H. Fowler Mear, and H. Fraenkel. Original novel, Alice Campbell. Photography, Sidney Blythe and William Luff. Editing, Michael Chorlton. Art direction, James Carter. 64 or 70 mins. Cast: Boris Karloff (*Dr. Sartorius*), Joan Wyndham (*Eve Rowe*), Arthur Margetson (*Roger Clifford*), Anthony Ireland (*Capt. Arthur* *Halliday*), Morton Selten (*Sir Charles Clifford*), Nina Boucicault (*Mary Clifford*).

Charlie Chan at the Opera. Fox. Direction, H. Bruce Humberstone. Script, Scott Darling and Charles S. Belden. Original story, Bess Meredyth. Based on the character created by Earl Derr Biggers. Photography, Lucien Andriot. Editing, Alex Troffey. 66 mins. Cast: Warner Oland (*Charlie Chan*), Boris Karloff (*Gravelle*), Keye Luke (*Lee Chan*), Charlotte Henry (*Mlle Kitty*).

1937

Night Key. Universal. Direction, Lloyd Corrigan. Script, Tristram Tupper and John C. Moffitt. Original story, William Pierce. Photography, George Robinson. Editing, Otis Garrett. Art direction, Jack Otterson. 65 mins. Cast: Boris Karloff (*Dave Mallory*), Warren Hull (*Travers*), Jean Rogers (*Joan Mallory*), Hobart Cavanaugh (*Petty Louie*), Samuel S. Hinds (*Ranger*), Alan **Baxter** (*Kid*).

West of Shanghai. Warners. Direction, John Farrow. Script, Crane Wilbur.

Original play, "The Bad Man," Porter Emerson Browne. Photography, L. W. O'Connell. Editing, Frank Dewar. 65 mins. Cast: Boris Karloff (*Gen. Wu Yen Fang*), Gordon Oliver (*James Hallet*), Beverly Roberts (*Jane Creed*), Sheila Bromley (*Lola Galt*), Ricardo Cortez (*Gordon Creed*), Vladimir Sokoloff (*Fu Shan*).

1938

The Invisible Menace. Warners. Direction, John Farrow. Script, Crane Wilbur. Original play, Ralph Spencer Zink. Photography, L. W. O'Connell. Editing, Harold McLernon. 55 mins. Cast: Boris Karloff (*Jevries*), Marie Wilson (*Sally*), Eddie Craven (*Eddie Pratt*), Eddie Acuff (*Corporal Sanger*), Regis Toomey (*Lt. Matthews*), Henry Kolker (*Col. Hackett*).

Mr. Wong, Detective. Monogram. Direction, William Nigh. Script, Houston Branch. Original story, Branch. Based on a magazine series by Hugh Wiley. Photography, Harry Neuman. Editing, Russell Schoengarth. 67 mins. Cast: Boris Karloff (*James Lee Wong*), Grant Withers (*Captain Street*), Maxine Jennings (*Myra*), Evelyn Brent (*Olga*), George Lloyd (*Devlin*).

Devil's Island. Warners. Direction, William Clemens. Script, Don Ryan and Kenneth Gamet. Original story, Anthony Coldeway and Raymond L. Schrock. Photography, George Barnes. Editing, Frank Magee. Art direction, Max Parker. 60 or 62 mins. Cast: Boris Karloff (*Dr. Charles Gaudet*), James Stephenson (*Col. Armand Lucien*), Nedda Harrigan (*Mme Lucien*), Adia Kuznetzoff (*Pierre*), Rolla Gourvitch (*Collette*), Will Stanton (*Bobo*), Edward Keane (*Dr. Duval*), Robert Warwick (*Demontre*), Leonard Mudie (*Advocate General*), Egon Brecher (*Debriac*).

Son of Frankenstein. Universal. Direction, Rowland V. Lee. Script, Willis Cooper. Photography, George Robinson. Editing, Ted Kent. Art Direction, Jack Otterson. Make-up, Jack Pierce. Musical direction, Charles Previn. Music, Frank Skinner. 95 mins. Cast: Basil Rathbone (*Baron Wolf von Frankenstein*), Boris Karloff (*The Monster*), Bela Lugosi (*Ygor*), Lionel Atwill (*Inspector Krogh*), Josephine Hutchinson (*Elsa von Frankenstein*), Donnie Duna-

gan (*Peter von Frankenstein*), Emma Dunn (*Amelia*), Edgar Norton (*Benson*), Perry Ivins (*Fritz*), Lawrence Grant (*Burgomaster*), Lionel Belmore (*Lang*), Michael Mark (*Ewald Neumuller*), Caroline Cook (*Mrs. Neumuller*), Gustav von Seyffertitz, Lorimer Johnson, Tom Rickets (*Burghers*).

The Mystery of Mr. Wong. Monogram. Direction, William Nigh. Script, Scott Darling. Based on a magazine series by Hugh Wiley. Photography, Harry Neumann. Editing, Russell Schoengarth. 67 mins. Cast: Boris Karloff (*James Lee Wong*), Dorothy Tree (*Valerie*), Grant Withers (*Sergeant Street*), Lotus Long (*Drina*), Morgan Wallace (*Edwards*).

Mr. Wong in Chinatown. Monogram. Direction, William Nigh. Script, Scott Darling. Based on a magazine series by Hugh Wiley. Photography, Harry Neumann. Editing, Russell Schoengarth. 68 mins. Cast: Boris Karloff (*James Lee Wong*), Grant Withers (*Captain Street*), Marjorie Reynolds (*Bobby Logan*), William Royle (*Captain Jaime*).

The Man They Could Not Hang. Columbia. Direction, Nick Grinde. Script, Karl Brown. Original story, Leslie T. White and George W. Sayre. Photography, Benjamin Kline. Editing, William Lyon. 65 mins. Cast: Boris Karloff (*Dr. Henryk Savaard*), Lorna Gray (*Janet Savaard*), Robert Wilcox ("*Scoop*" *Foley*), Roger Pryor (*District Attorney Drake*), Don Beddoe (*Lt. Shane*), Ann Doran (*Betty Crawford*), Joseph De Stefani (*Dr. Stoddard*), Charles Trowbridge (*Judge Bowman*), Byron Foulger (*Lang*), Dick Curtis (*Kearney*), James Craig (*Watkins*), John Tyrrell (*Sutton*).

Tower of London. Universal. Direction, Rowland V. Lee. Script, Robert N. Lee. Photography, George Robinson. Editing, Ed Curtiss. Art direction, Jack Otterson. Musical direction, Charles Previn. Orchestrations, Frank Skinner. Technical advisors, Maj. G. O. T. Bagley and Sir Gerald Grove. 92 mins. Cast: Basil Rathbone (*Richard, Duke of Gloucester*), Boris Karloff (*Mord*), Barbara O'Neil (*Queen Elizabeth*), Ian Hunter (*King Edward IV*), Vincent Price (*Duke of Clarence*), Leo G. Carroll (*Lord Hastings*), Miles Mander (*King Henry VI*), Nan Grey (*Lady Alice Barton*), John Sutton (*John Wyatt*), Lionel Belmore (*Beacon*), Rose Hobart (*Anne*

Neville), Donnie Dunagan (*Baby Prince*).

1940

The Fatal Hour. Monogram. Direction, William Nigh. Script, Scott Darling. Adaptation and story, Joseph West. Based on a magazine series by Hugh Wiley. Photography, Harry Neumann. Editing, Russell Schoengarth. 68 mins. Cast: Boris Karloff (*James Lee Wong*), Grant Withers (*Captain Street*), Marjorie Reynolds (*Bobbie Logan*), Charles Trowbridge (*Forbes*), John Hamilton (*Belden, Sr.*), Craig Reynolds (*Belden. Jr.*), Jack Kennedy (*Mike*), Frank Puglia (*Hardway*), Jason Robards (*Griswold*).
British Intelligence. Warners. Direction, Terry Morse. Script, Lee Katz. Original play, "Three Faces East," Anthony Paul Kelly. Photography, Sid Hickox. Editing, Thomas Pratt. 62 mins. Cast: Boris Karloff (*Valdar*), Margaret Lindsay (*Helen von Lorbeer*), Maris Wrixon (*Dorothy*), Holmes Herbert (*Arthur Bennett*), Leonard Mudie (*James Yeats*), Bruce Lester (*Frank Bennett*), Winifred Harris (*Mrs. Bennett*), Lester Matthews (*Thompson*).
The Devil Commands. Columbia. Direction, Edward Dmytryk. Script, Robert D. Andrews and Milton Gunzburg. Original novel, "The Edge of Running Water," William Sloane. Photography, Allen G. Siegler. Editing, Al Clark. Art direction, Lionel Banks. Musical direction, M. W. Stoloff. 65 mins. Cast: Boris Karloff (*Dr. Julian Blair*), Richard Fiske (*Dr. Richard Sayles*), Amanda Duff (*Anne Blair*), Anne Revere (*Mrs. Walters*), Ralph Penney (*Karl*), Dorothy Adams (*Mrs. Marcy*), Walter Baldwin (*Seth Marcy*), Kenneth MacDonald (*Sheriff Willis*).
Black Friday. Universal. Direction, Arthur Lubin. Script, Kurt Siodmak and Eric Taylor. Photography, Elwood Bredell. Editing, Philip Cahn. Musical direction, Hans J. Salter. 70 mins. Cast: Boris Karloff (*Dr. Ernest Sovac*), Bela Lugosi (*Eric Marnay*), Stanley Ridges (*Prof. George Kingsley*), Anne Nagel (*Sunny*), Anne Gwynne (*Jean Sovac*), Virginia Brissac (*Mrs. Margaret Kingsley*), Edmund MacDonald (*Frank Miller*), Paul Fix (*Kane*).
The Man With Nine Lives. Columbia. Direction, Nick Grinde. Script, Karl

Brown. Original story, Harold Shumate. Photography, Benjamin Kline. Editing, Al Clark. Art direction, Lionel Banks. 73 mins. Cast: Boris Karloff (*Dr. Leon Kravaal*), Roger Pryor (*Dr. Tim Mason*), Byron Foulger (*Dr. Bassett*), Stanley Brown (*Bob Adams*), Jo Ann Sayers (*Judith Blair*), Hal Taliaferro (*Sheriff Stanton*).
Doomed to Die. Monogram. Direction, William Nigh. Script, Ralph Bettinson. Adaptation, Michael Jacoby. Based on a magazine series by Hugh Wiley. Photography, Harry Neumann. Editing, Robert Golden. 67 mins. Cast: Boris Karloff (*James Lee Wong*), Grant Withers (*Captain Street*), Marjorie Reynolds (*Bobbie Logan*), William Stelling (*Dick*), Catherine Craig (*Cynthia*), Guy Usher (*Fleming*), Henry Brandon (*Martin*).
Before I Hang. Columbia. Direction, Nick Grinde. Script, Robert D. Andrews. Original story, Karl Brown and Andrews. Photography, Benjamin Kline. Editing, Charles Nelson. Art direction, Lionel Banks. Musical direction, M. W. Stoloff. 62 mins. Cast: Boris Karloff (*Dr. John Garth*), Evelyn Keyes (*Martha Garth*), Bruce Bennett (*Dr. Paul Ames*), Edward van Sloan (*Dr. Ralph Howard*), Ben Taggart (*Warden Thompson*), Pedro de Cordoba (*Victor Sondini*).
The Ape. Monogram. Direction, William Nigh. Script, Kurt Siodmak and Richard Carroll. Original play, Adam Hull Shirk. Photography, Harry Neumann. Editing, Russell Schoengarth. 61 mins. Cast: Boris Karloff (*Dr. Bernard Adrian*), Maris Wrixon (*Frances*), Gertrude Hoffmann (*Housekeeper*), Henry Hall (*Sheriff*), Gene O'Donnell (*Danny*), Jack Kennedy (*Tomlin*), Jessie Arnold (*Mrs. Brill*).
You'll Find Out. RKO. Direction, David Butler. Script, Butler and James V. Kern. Music and lyrics, James McHugh and John Mercer. Special material, Monte Brice, Andrew Bennison, R. T. M. Scott. Photography, Frank Redmond. Special effects, Vernon Walker. Editing, Irene Morra. Art direction, Van Nest Polglase. Musical direction, Roy Webb. Special sound and musical effects, Sonovox. 97 mins. Cast: Kay Kyser (*Kay*), Peter Lorre (*Fenninger*), Boris Karloff (*Judge Mainwaring*), Bela Lugosi (*Prince Saliano*), Helen Parrish (*Janis*),

Dennis O'Keefe (*Chuck Deems*), Alma Kruger (*Aunt Margo*), Joseph Eggenton (*Jurgen*), and Kay Kyser's Band.

1942
The Boogie Man Will Get You. Columbia. Direction, Lew Landers. Script, Edwin Blum. Original story, Hal Fimberg and Robert B. Hunt. Photography, Henry Freulich. Editing, Richard Fantl. Musical direction, M. W. Stoloff. 66 mins. Cast: Boris Karloff (*Prof. Nathaniel Billings*), Peter Lorre (*Dr. Lorentz*), Maxie Rosenbloom (*Maxie*), Larry Parks (*Bill Layden*), Jeff Donnell (*Winnie Layden*), Don Beddoe (*J. Gilbert Brompton*), George McKay (*Ebenezer*), Maude Eburne (*Amelia Jones*), Frank Puglia (*Silvio Bacigalupi*).

1944
The Climax. Universal. Direction, George Waggner. Script, Curt Siodmak and Lynn Starling. Adaptation, Siodmak. Original play, Edward Locke. Photography (Technicolor), Hal Mohr and W. Howard Greene. Editing, Russell Schoengarth. Art direction, John B. Goodman and Alexander Golitzen. Musical score, Edward Ward. Musical direction, Don George. 86 mins. Cast: Boris Karloff (*Dr. Hohner*), Susanna Foster (*Angela*), Turhan Bey (*Franz*), Gale Sondergaard (*Luise*), Thomas Gomez (*Count Seebruck*), June Vincent (*Marcellina*), George Dolenz (*Amato*), Ludwig Stossel (*Carl Bauman*).
House of Frankenstein. Universal. Direction, Erle C. Kenton. Script, Edward T. Lowe. Original story, Curt Siodmak. Photography, George Robinson. Special effects photography, John P. Fulton. Editing, Philip Cahn. Art direction, John B. Goodman and Martin Obzina. Music, H. J. Salter. Make-up, Jack Pierce. 70 mins. Cast: Boris Karloff (*Dr. Gustav Niemann*), Lon Chaney (*Larry Talbot*), J. Carrol Naish (*Daniel*), John Carradine (*Count Dracula*), Anne Gwynne (*Rita Hussman*), Peter Coe (*Carl Hussman*), Lionel Atwill (*Inspector Arnz*), George Zucco (*Prof. Lampini*), Elena Verdugo (*Ilonka*), Glenn Strange (*The Monster*), Sig Ruman (*Russman*), Frank Reicher (*Ullman*), Brandon Hurst (*Dr. Geissler*).

1945
The Body Snatcher. RKO. Direction, Robert Wise. Script, Philip MacDonald and Carlos Keith. Original story, Robert

Louis Stevenson. Photography, Robert De Grasse. Editing, J. R. Whittredge. Art direction, Albert S. D'Agostino and Walter E. Keller. Music, Roy Webb. Musical direction, C. Bakaleinikoff. 78 mins. Cast: Boris Karloff (*John Gray*), Bela Lugosi (*Joseph*), Henry Daniell (*Dr. MacFarlane*), Edith Atwater (*Meg*), Russell Wade (*Fettes*), Rita Corday (*Mrs. Marsh*), Sharyn Moffett (*Georgina*), Donna Lee (*Street Singer*).
Isle of the Dead. RKO. Direction, Mark Robson. Script, Ardel Wray and Josef Mischel. Photography, Jack Mackenzie. Editing, Lyle Boyer. Art direction, Albert S. D'Agostino. Music, Leigh Harline. Musical direction, C. Bakaleinikoff. 72 mins. Cast: Boris Karloff (*Gen. Pherides*), Ellen Drew (*Thea*), Marc Cramer (*Oliver*), Katherine Emery (*Mrs. St. Aubyn*), Helene Thimig (*Kyra*), Alan Napier (*St. Aubyn*), Jason Robards (*Albrecht*), Ernst Dorian (*Dr. Drossos*), Skelton Knaggs (*Robbins*), Sherry Hall (*Greek Colonel*).

1946
Bedlam. RKO. Direction, Mark Robson. Script, Carlos Keith and Robson. Suggested by an engraving by William Hogarth. Photography, Nicholas Musuraca. Editing, Lyle Boyer. Art direction, Albert S. D'Agostino and Walter E. Keller. Music, Roy Webb. Musical direction, C. Bakaleinikoff. 79 mins. Cast: Boris Karloff (*Master Sims*), Anna Lee (*Nell Bowen*), Billy House (*Lord Mortimer*), Richard Fraser (*Hannay*), Glenn Vernon (*Gilded Boy*), Ian Wolfe (*Sidney Long*), Jason Robards (*Oliver Todd*), Leland Hodgson (*John Wilkes*), Joan Newton (*Dorothea the Dove*), Elizabeth Russell (*Mistress Sims*).

1947
The Secret Life of Walter Mitty. Samuel Goldwyn. Direction, Norman Z. McLeod. Script, Ken Englund and Everett Freeman. Original story, James Thurber. Photography (Technicolor), Lee Garmes. Editing, Monica Collingwood. Art direction, George Jenkins and Perry Ferguson. Music, David Raskin. Musical direction, Emil Newman. 105 mins. Cast: Danny Kaye (*Walter Mitty*), Virginia Mayo (*Rosalind van Hoorn*), Boris Karloff (*Dr. Hollingshead*), Fay Bainter (*Mrs. Mitty*), Ann Rutherford (*Gertrude Griswold*), Thurston Hall (*Bruce Pierce*), Gordon Jones (*Tubby Wadsworth*), Reginald Denny (*Col-

onel), Frank Reicher (*Maasdam*).
Unconquered. Paramount. Direction, Cecil B. DeMille. Script, Charles Bennett, Fredric M. Frank, and Jesse Lasky Jr. Original novel, Neil H. Swanson. Photography (Technicolor), Ray Rennahan. Editing, Anne Bauchens. Art direction, Hans Dreier and Walter Tyler. Music, Victor Young. 135 mins. Cast: Gary Cooper (*Capt. Christopher Holden*), Paulette Goddard (*Abby Hale*), Howard Da Silva (*Martin Garth*), Boris Karloff (*Gayasuta*), Cecil Kellaway (*Jeremy Love*), Ward Bond (*John Fraser*), Katherine de Mille (*Hannah*), Henry Wilcoxon (*Captain Steele*), C. Aubrey Smith (*Lord Chief Justice*).
Lured. Oakmont. Direction, Douglas Sirk. Script, Leo Rosten. Original story, Jacques Companeez, Ernest Neuville, and Simon Gantillon. Photography, William Daniels. Editing, John M. Foley. Art direction, Nicolai Remisoff. Music, Michel Michelet. 102 mins. Cast: George Sanders (*Robert Fleming*), Lucille Ball (*Sandra Carpenter*), Charles Coburn (*Inspector Temple*), Cedric Hardwicke (*Julian Wilde*), Boris Karloff (*Charles van Druten*).
Dick Tracy Meets Gruesome. RKO. Direction, John Rawlins. Script, Robertson White, and Eric Taylor. Original story, William H. Graffis and Robert E. Kent. Based on the cartoon strip by Chester Gould. Photography, Frank Redman. Editing, Elmo Williams. Art direction, Albert S. D'Agostino and Walter E. Keller. Music, Paul Sawtell. Musical direction, C. Bakaleinikoff. 65 mins. Cast: Boris Karloff (*Gruesome*), Ralph Byrd (*Dick Tracy*), Anne Gwynne (*Tess Truehart*), Edward Ashley (*L. E. Thal*), June Clayworth (*I. M. Learned*), Lyle Latell (*Pat Patton*), Tony Barrett (*Melody*), Skelton Knaggs (*X-ray*), Jim Nolan (*Dan Sterne*), Joseph Crehan (*Chief Brandon*), Milton Parsons (*Dr. A. Tomic*).

1948
Tap Roots. Walter Wanger. Direction, George Marshall. Script, Alan LeMay. Original novel, James Street. Photography (Technicolor), Lionel Lindon and Winton C. Hoch. Editing, Milton Carruth. Art direction supervision, Bernard Herzbrun. Art direction, Alex Golitzen and Frank Richards. Music, Frank Skinner. 108 mins. Cast: Van Heflin (*Keith Alexander*), Susan Hayward (*Morna Dabney*), Boris Karloff (*Tishomingo*),

Ward Bond (*Hoab Dabney*), Whitfield Connor (*Clay MacIvor*), Richard Long (*Bruce Dabney*), Julie London (*Aven Dabney*), Arthur Shields (*Rev. Kirkland*).

1949
Abbott and Costello Meet the Killer, Boris Karloff. Universal-International. Direction, Charles T. Barton. Script, Hugh Wedlock Jr., Howard Snyder, and John Grant. Original story, Wedlock and Snyder. Photography, Charles van Enger. Editing, Edward Curtiss. Art direction, Bernard Herzbrun and Richard H. Riedel. Music, Milton Schwartzwald. 84 mins. Cast: Bud Abbott (*Casey Edwards*), Lou Costello (*Freddie Phillips*), Boris Karloff (*Swami Talpur*), Lenore Aubert (*Angela Gordon*), Gar Moore (*Jeff Wilson*), Donna Martell (*Betty Crandall*), Alan Mowbray (*Melton*), Roland Winters (*T. Hanley Brooks*).

1951
The Emperor's Nightingale. Rembrandt Films release. Direction, Jiri Trnka. Script, Jiri Brdecka and Trnka. Original story, Hans Christian Andersen. Photography (Agfa Color), Ferdinand Pecenka. Music, Vaclav Trojan. Narration written by Phillis McGinley and spoken by Boris Karloff. 70 mins.
The Strange Door. U-I. Direction, Joseph Pevney. Script, Jerry Sackheim. Original story, "The Sire de Maletroit's Door," Robert Louis Stevenson. Photography, Irving Glassbery. Editing, Edward Curtiss. Art direction, Bernard Herzbrun and Eric Orbom. Music, Joseph Gershenson. 81 mins. Cast: Charles Laughton (*Alain de Maletroit*), Boris Karloff (*Voltan*), Sally Forrest (*Blanche de Maletroit*), Richard Stapley (*Denis de Beaulieu*), Michael Pate (*Talon*), Alan Napier (*Count Grassin*), William Cottrell (*Corbeau*).
1952

The Black Castle. U-I. Direction, Nathan Juran. Script and story, Jerry Sackheim. Photography, Irving Glassberg. Editing, Russell Schoengarth. Art direction, Bernard Herzbrun and Alfred Sweeney. Musical direction, Joseph Gershenson. 81 mins. Cast: Richard Greene (*Richard Beckett*), Boris Karloff (*Dr. Meissen*), Stephen McNally (*Count von Bruno*), Paula Corday (*Elga*), Lon Chaney (*Gargon*), Michael Pate (*Von Melcher*),

Tudor Owen (*Romley*), John Hoyt (*Stieken*).

1953
Abbott and Costello Meet Dr. Jekyll and Mr. Hyde. U-I. Direction, Charles Lamont. Script, Leo Loeb and John Grant. Original story, Sidney Fields and Grant Garrett. Photography, George Robinson. Editing, Russell Schoengarth. Art direction, Bernard Herzbrun and Eric Orbum. 76 mins. Cast: Bud Abbott (*Slim*), Lou Costello (*Tubby*), Boris Karloff (*Dr. Jekyll/Mr. Hyde*), Helen Westcott (*Vicky Edwards*), Craig Stevens (*Bruce Adams*), Reginald Denny (*Inspector*), John Dierkes (*Batley*).
Il monstro dell' isola (*The Island Monster*). Romana-Misiano. Direction, Roberts Montero. Script, Montero and Alberto Vecchietto. Photography, Augusto Tiezzo. Music, Mo. Carlo Innocenzi. 87 mins. Cast: Boris Karloff, Renato Vicario, Frana Marzi, Patricia Remiddi, Carlo Duse.

1955
The Hindu (*Sabaka*). Frank Ferrin. Direction, Frank Ferrin. Script, Ferrin. Photography (colour), Allen Svensvold and Jack McCoskey. Editing, Jack Foley. 81 mins. Cast: Nino Marcel (*Gunga Ram*), Boris Karloff (*Gen. Pollegar*), Reginald Denny (*Maharajah*), Victor Jory (*Ashok*), Jay Novello (*Damji*).

1957
Voodoo Island. Oak Pictures/Bel-Air Production. Direction, Reginald LeBorg. Script, Richard Landau. Photography, William Margulies. Editing, John F. Schreyer. Art direction, Jack T. Collis. Music, Les Baxter. 78 mins. Cast: Boris Karloff (*Philip Knight*), Beverly Tyler (*Sara Adams*), Murvyn Vye (*Barney Finch*), Elisha Cook (*Schuyler*).
The Juggler of Our Lady. 20th Century Fox. Direction, Robert Blechman. CinemaScope and colour. Animation, Gene Deitch and Al Kousel. Narrated by Boris Karloff. 1 reel.
The Haunted Strangler (*The Grip of the Strangler*). Amalgamated Productions. MGM release. Direction, Robert Day. Script, Jan Read and John Cooper. Original story, Read. Photography, Lionel Banes. Special effects, Les Bowie. Editing, Peter Mayhew. Art direction, John Elphick. Music, Buxton Orr. 79 mins. Cast: Boris Karloff (*James Rankin*), Anthony Dawson (*Supt. Burk*),

Derek Birch (*Hospital Supt.*), Dorothy Gordon (*Hannah*), Elizabeth Allan (*Mrs. Rankin*), Diane Aubrey (*Lily*), Jean Kent (*Cora*).

1958
Corridors of Blood (*Doctor of the 7 Dials*). Amalgamated Productions. Altura release. Direction, Robert Day. Script, Jean Scott Rogers. Photography, Geoffrey Faithfull. Editing, Peter Mayhew. Art direction, Anthony Masters. Music, Buxton Orr. 85 mins. Cast: Boris Karloff (*Dr. Thomas Bolton*), Betta St. John (*Susan*), Francis Matthews (*Jonathan Bolton*), Andrienne Corri (*Rachel*), Finlay Currie (*Spt. Matheson*), Christopher Lee (*Resurrection Joe*), Francis De Wolff (*Black Ben*).
Frankenstein 1970. Aubrey Schenck. Allied Artists release. Direction, Howard W. Koch. Script, Richard Landau and George Worthington Yates. Original story, Schenck and Charles A. Moses. Photography (CinemaScope), Carl E. Guthrie. Editing, John A. Bushelman. Art direction, Jack Collins. Music, Paul A. Dunlap. 83 mins. Cast: Boris Karloff (*Baron Frankenstein*), Tom Duggan (*Mike Shaw*), Jana Lund (*Carolyn Hayes*), Donald Barry (*Douglas Row*), Charlotte Austin (*Judy Stevens*), Irwin Berk (*Insp. Raab*), Rudolph Anders (*Wilhelm Gotfried*), John Dennis (*Morgan Haley*), Norbert Schiller (*Shuter*), Mike Lane (*Hans*).

1963
The Raven. American-International. Direction, Roger Corman. Script, Richard Matheson. Photography (Panavision, colour), Floyd Crosby. Editing, Ronald Sinclair. Art direction, Daniel Haller. Music, Les Baxter. 85 mins. Cast: Vincent Price (*Dr. Erasmus Craven*), Boris Karloff (*Dr. Scarabus*), Peter Lorre (*Dr. Bedlo*), Hazel Court (*Lenore Craven*), Olive Sturgess (*Estelle Craven*), Jack Nicholson (*Rexford Bedlo*), Connie Wallace (*Maidservant*), William Baskin (*Grimes*), Aaron Saxon (*Gort*).
The Terror. Corman-Filmgroup. A-I release. Direction, Roger Corman. Script, Leo Gordon and Jack Hill. Photography (Vitascope, colour), John Nicholaus. Editing, Stuart O'Brien. Art direction, Daniel Haller. Music, Arnold Stein. 81 mins. Cast: Boris Karloff (*Baron von Leppe*), Sandra Knight (*Hélène*), Jack Nicholson (*André Duvalier*), Richard

Miller (*Stefan*), Dorothy Neumann (*Old Woman*), Jonathan Haze (*Gustaf*).

The Comedy of Terrors. A-I. Direction, Jacques Tourneur. Script, Richard Matheson. Photography (Panavision, colour), Floyd Crosby. Editing, Anthony Carras. Art direction, Daniel Haller. Music, Les Baxter. 86 mins. Cast: Vincent Price (*Mr. Trumbull*), Peter Lorre (*Felix Gillie*), Boris Karloff (*Amos Hinchley*), Basil Rathbone (*John F. Black*), Joe E. Brown (*Cemetery Keeper*), Joyce Jameson (*Amaryllis Trumbull*), Beverly Hills (*Mrs. Phipps*).

1964

Bikini Beach. A-I. Direction, William Asher. Script, Asher, Leo Townsend, and Robert Dillon. Photography (Panavision, colour), Floyd Crosby. Editing, Fred Feitshans. Art direction, Daniel Haller. Music, Les Baxter. 100 mins. Cast: Frankie Avalon (*Frankie/Potato Bug*), Annette Funicello (*Dee Dee*), Martha Hyer (*Vivien Clements*), Keenan Wynn (*Harvey Huntington Honeywagon*). Karloff had an unbilled walk-on.

Black Sabbath (*I tre volti della paura*). Emmepi Cinematografica, Lyre Cinematografica, Galatea. A-I release. Direction, Mario Bava. Script, Marcello Fondato, Alberto Bevilacqua, and Mario Bava. Original stories, "The Wurdalak," Tolstoi; "The Drop of Water," Chekhov, "The Telephone," F. G. Snyder. Photography (colour), Ubaldo Terzano. Editing, Mario Serandrei. Art direction, Giorgio Giovannini. Music, Les Baxter. 95 mins. Cast: Boris Karloff (*Gorca*), Mark Damon (*Vladimir*), Susy Andersen (*Sdenka*).

1965

Die, Monster, Die. Alta Vista. A-I release. Direction, Daniel Haller. Script, Jerry Sohl. Original story, "The Colour Out of Space," H. P. Lovecraft. Photography (colour), Paul Beeson. Editing, Alfred Cox. Art direction, Colin Southcott. Music, Don Banks. 78 mins. Cast: Boris Karloff (*Nahum Witley*), Nick Adams (*Stephen Reinhart*), Freda Jackson (*Letitia Witley*), Suzan Farmer (*Susan Witley*), Terence De Marney (*Merwyn*), Patrick Magee (*Dr. Henderson*).

1966

Ghost in the Invisible Bikini. American-International. Director, Don Weis.

Script, Louis M. Heyward, Elwood Ullman. Original Story, Heyward. Photography (Panavision, Pathecolor), Stanley Cortez. Editing, Fred Feitshans, Eve Newman. Music, Les Baxter. Songs, Guy Hemric, Jerry Styner. 82 mins. Cast: Tommy Kirk (*Chuck Phillips*), Deborah Walley (*Lilli Morton*), Aron Kincaid (*Bobby*), Quinn O'Hara (*Sinistra*), Jesse White (*J. Sinister Hulk*), Harvey Lembeck (*Eric von Zipper*), Nancy Sinatra (*Vicki*), Claudia Martin (*Lulu*), Francis X. Bushman (*Malcolm*), Benny Rubin (*Chicken Feather*), Bobbi Shaw (*Princess Yolanda*), George Barrows (*Monstro*), Basil Rathbone (*Reginald Ripper*), Patsy Kelly (*Myrtle Forbush*), Boris Karloff (*Hiram Stokeley*), Susan Hart (*Ghost*).

The Daydreamer. Videocraft International. Embassy release. Direction, Jules Bass. Script, Arthur Rankin Jr. Original stories, Hans Christian Andersen. 101 mins. Cast: Paul O'Keefe (*Hans Christian Andersen*), Jack Gilford (*Papa Andersen*), Ray Bolger (*Pieman*), Margaret Hamilton (*Mrs. Klopplebobbler*). Voices: Hayley Mills (*Little Mermaid*), Burl Ives (*Father Neptune*), Tallulah Bankhead (*Sea Witch*), Terry-Thomas (*1st Tailor*), Victor Borge (*2nd Tailor*), Ed Wynn (*Emperor*), Patty Duke (*Thumbelina*), Boris Karloff (*Rat*), Sessue Hayakawa (*Mole*).

Mad Monster Party. Videocraft International. Embassy release. Direction, Jules Bass. Script, Harvey Kurtzman and Leo Korobkin. Original story, Arthur Rankin Jr. 93 mins. Cast: Voices of Boris Karloff, Phyllis Diller, Alan Swift, Gale Garnet.

1967

The Venetian Affair. M-G-M. Direction, Jerry Thorpe. Script, E. Jack Neuman. Original novel, Helen MacInnes. Photography (colour), Milton Krasner. Editing, Henry Berman. Music, Lalo Schifrin. 92 mins. Cast: Robert Vaughn (*Bill Fenner*), Elke Sommer (*Sandra Fane*), Karl Boehm (*Robert Wahl*), Luciana Paluzzi (*Giulia Almeranti*), Felicia Farr (*Claire Connor*), Boris Karloff (*Dr. Pierre Vaugiroud*), Joe de Santis (*Jan Aarvan*), Roger C. Carmel (*Mike Ballard*).

Mondo Balordo. Cine Produzioni. Crown International release. Direction, Roberto Bianchi Montero. Script, Castalda and Tori. Photography (colour),

Giuseppe La Torre. Editing, Enzo Alfonsi. Music, Lallo Gori. English version, Ted Weiss; editing, Fred von Bernewitz. 87 mins. Narration spoken by Boris Karloff.
The Sorcerers. Tigon. Direction, Michael Reeves. Script, Reeves and Tom Baker. Original idea, John Burke. Photography (colour), Stanley Long. Editing, Ralph Sheldon. Art direction, Tony Curtis. Music, Paul Ferris. 86 mins. Cast: Boris Karloff (*Prof. Monseratt*), Catherine Lacey (*Estelle*), Ian Ogilvy (*Mike*), Elizabeth Ercy (*Nicole*), Victor Henry (*Alan*), Susan George (*Audrey*).

1968
Targets. Saticoy. Paramount release. Direction, Peter Bogdanovich. Script, Bogdanovich. Original story, Polly Platt and Bogdanovich. Photography (colour), Laszlo Kovacs. Production design, Platt. 90 mins. Cast: Boris Karloff (*Byron Orlock*), Tim O'Kelly (*Bobby Thompson*), Nancy Hsueh (*Jenny*), Peter Bogdanovich (*Sammy*), James Brown (*Mr. Thompson*), Sandy Baron (*Kip Larkin*), Tanya Morgan (*Ilene Thompson*), Mary Jackson (*Mrs.*

Thompson), Arthur Peterson (*Ed Loughlin*).

1969
The Crimson Cult. Tigon. A-I release. Direction, Vernon Sewell. Script, Mervyn Haisman and Henry Lincoln. Photography (colour), Johnny Coquillon. Editing, Howard Lanning. Art direction, Derke Barrington. Music, Peter Knight. 87 mins. Cast: Boris Karloff (*Prof. Marshe*), Christopher Lee (*Morley*), Mark Eden (*Robert Manning*), Barbara Steele (*Lavinia*), Michael Gough (*Elder*), Rupert Davies (*Dr. Radford*).
El coleccionista de cadaveres (*The Corpse of Blood*). Hispamer-Weinbach. Cauldron of Blood). Hispamer-Weinbach. Direction, Edward Mann (Santos Alcocer). Script, Alcocer and John Melson and J. L. Bayonas. Photography (Colour), Francisco Sempere. Editing, Parrando. Music, José Luis Navarro. 97 or 101 mins. Cast: Boris Karloff (*Charles Badulescu*), Viveca Lindfors (*Tania Badulescu*), Jean-Pierre Aumont (*Claude Marchand*), Rosenda Monteros (*Valerie*), Ruben Rojo (*Lover*), Dianik Zurakowska (*Helga*).

Karloff with Peter Bogdanovich and Nancy Hsueh in TARGETS

Index to Names

Index to Films

(*excluding Filmography*)